BLOODY FLAG OF
ANARCHY

CONFLICTING WORLDS

New Dimensions of the American Civil War

T. Michael Parrish, *Series Editor*

BLOODY FLAG OF
ANARCHY

Unionism in
South Carolina
during the
Nullification
Crisis

BRIAN C. NEUMANN

LOUISIANA STATE UNIVERSITY PRESS

BATON ROUGE

Published by Louisiana State University Press
lsupress.org

Manufactured in the United States of America
First printing

Designer: Mandy McDonald Scallan
Typeface: Sentinel

Maps created by Mary Lee Eggart

Cover illustration: *Nullification and Despotism,* 1833, detail from a lithograph by Endicott and Swett, New York

Library of Congress Cataloging-in-Publication Data
Names: Neumann, Brian, author.
Title: Bloody flag of anarchy : Unionism in South Carolina during the
    Nullification Crisis / Brian C. Neumann.
Other titles: Unionism in South Carolina during the Nullification Crisis
Description: Baton Rouge : Louisiana State University, 2022. | Series:
    Conflicting worlds: new dimensions of the American Civil War | Includes
    bibliographical references and index.
Identifiers: LCCN 2021044216 (print) | LCCN 2021044217 (ebook) | ISBN
    978-0-8071-7690-0 (cloth) | ISBN 978-0-8071-7755-6 (pdf) | ISBN 978-0-8071-7756-3
    (epub)
Subjects: LCSH: Union Party (S.C.)—History. | United States—Politics and
    government—1829–1837. | Nullification (States' rights) | South
    Carolina—Politics and government—1775–1865.
Classification: LCC F273 .N48 2022 (print) | LCC F273 (ebook) | DDC
    975.7/03—dc23/eng/20211012
LC record available at https://lccn.loc.gov/2021044216
LC ebook record available at https://lccn.loc.gov/2021044217

. . . .

For My Mother

Whatever beauty or poetry is to be found in my little book is owing to
your . . . encouragement of all my efforts from the first to the last, and if
ever I do anything to be proud of, my greatest happiness will be that I can
thank you for that, as I may do for all the good there is in me.

—LOUISA MAY ALCOTT to her mother

And For Desiree

One corner of the earth with her
Is more to me than all the stars.

—HAFEZ

. . . .

Contents

Acknowledgments

I've looked forward to writing this section for the past six years. Only now do I realize that these are the hardest pages to write—because no words can convey how grateful I am for all the people in my life or express how much their friendship, encouragement, and mentorship have meant to me.

At the University of Virginia, I had the privilege of learning from three of the best Civil War scholars in the country. Elizabeth R. Varon, my academic advisor, is brilliant, efficient, and endlessly supportive, and she represents academia at its very best. Gary W. Gallagher's books inspired me to attend graduate school, and I felt blessed (and a little star-struck) each time I entered his classroom. I greatly appreciate his kindness, his thoughtful feedback, and his wonderfully wry sense of humor. Finally, Caroline Janney is a generous and incredibly insightful scholar, and I owe my career in large part to her support.

The John L. Nau III Center for Civil War History provides a wonderful academic community. I'm especially grateful for William B. Kurtz for allowing me to take part in the Nau Center's digital projects. It is truly an honor to succeed him as the Center's managing director. I owe a tremendous debt of gratitude to the Nau Center and the Bradley Foundation, whose generous funding enabled me to finish this book. Additional fellowships from the Andrew W. Mellon Foundation, the Jefferson Scholars Foundation, the South Caroliniana Library, the Pearlstine/Lipov Center for Southern Jewish Culture, and the Virginia Museum of History & Culture also proved crucial to my research.

At Louisiana State University Press, my superb editors, T. Michael Parrish and Rand Dotson believed in my project and helped shepherd it toward publication.

Growing up, I was blessed to have many phenomenal teachers and professors. In eighth grade, Joe Greene taught me that "attention to detail is the key to success," and Diana Wright helped me discover my voice as a writer.

At Chesnee High School, Eric Luedeman challenged me to think critically about the past, while Kim Willard taught me to trust my instincts and believe in myself.

At Furman University, Lloyd Benson encouraged me to pursue my passion for history, and his eloquence and enthusiasm continue to inspire me. Steve O'Neill has been an incredible mentor and friend, and I wouldn't be where I am today if not for the opportunities that he made possible. Diane Vecchio is a brilliant and generous scholar whose "Women in European History" course remains the most powerful class I've ever taken. Tim Fehler and David Spear are two of the kindest and most thoughtful people I know, and their classes pushed me to become a stronger writer and historian.

At the University of Virginia, my history cohort (Chris Halsted, Monica Blair, Allison Kelley, Hannah Tucker, Abeer Saha, Adele McInerney, and Nicole Schroeder) has been an invaluable source of friendship, support, and solidarity. Chris, in particular, has become one of my closest friends, and I will always cherish his openhearted exuberance. My Civil War Seminar colleagues provided insightful discussion and animated baseball banter time after time, and I'm especially grateful to Clayton Butler, Lauren Haumesser, Ian Iverson, Jack Furniss, Brianna Kirk, Daniel Sunshine, and Jake Calhoun. Clayton is a brilliant historian and a dear friend whom I've looked up to for the past six years. Lauren, too, is a gifted and insightful scholar and a kindred spirit, who shares my joy for cycling, great food, and good dogs. My time at the University of Virginia wouldn't have been the same without their friendship or the friendship of Shira Lurie, Alice King, and Cecily Zander.

UVA Club Running forged some of my most meaningful friendships, and the four years I spent as club secretary rank among the highlights of my graduate school career. I am grateful for every single one of my teammates, especially Brandon von Kannewurff, Ryan Torbic, Skyler Moon, Jeremy Levine, May Robison, Nate Bolon, Jack Wren, Logan Burns, Jacob Bushey, Trevor Marchhart, and Adam Lenox. Brandon, in particular, is one of the best people I've ever known—a joyful, sincere, compassionate soul who makes everyone around him feel welcome.

I am forever grateful for family members all over the country who have loved and supported me unconditionally. My mother Marisa Neumann is the strongest, kindest, and most selfless person I know. She taught me to love history, reading, travel, and nature, and she is the person I aspire to be.

And, finally, Desiree embodies radiance and joy. She fills the world around her with light and makes every day immeasurably better. I'm so incredibly grateful for the life we've built together.

Introduction

General Winfield Scott arrived in Charleston, South Carolina, in November 1832, hoping desperately to avert secession and civil war. After years of protest, South Carolinians had declared two federal tariffs null and void and threatened to dissolve the Union if the president tried to enforce them. In the weeks that followed, they began mobilizing for war: building factories and supply depots, stockpiling weapons, and raising an army of 25,000 men. President Andrew Jackson, in turn, offered Scott *"carte blanche* in respect to troops" and ordered revenue cutters and warships to patrol Charleston Harbor. He reinforced the city's federal garrison and vowed to send 150,000 volunteers to crush the incipient rebellion. A civil war appeared imminent, and many feared—and a few hoped—that the Union would not survive the crisis.[1]

As Scott strategized, his mind drifted to the War of 1812, when South Carolinians had united across party lines and rallied to their country's defense. Those "days of general harmony," he mourned, "may never return." South Carolinians had forsaken "patriotism and glory" and imagined themselves as a "foreign nation." If the Palmetto State seceded, Scott observed, the "whole arch of the Union would tumble in," leaving either "broken fragments" or new northern, southern, and western confederacies. Violence would erupt almost inevitably, and armies would drench the fractured Union in blood. He prayed that moderation would prevail—that neither side would "take a rash step." As a staunch Unionist, however, he vowed that the "forts in [Charleston] harbor shall not be wrested from the United States."[2]

The 600 soldiers under Scott's command crowded into Fort Moultrie and Fort Johnson, and as days stretched into weeks the uncertainty grew almost

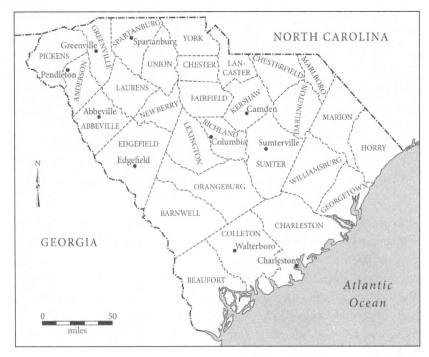

South Carolina in 1830

unbearable. As New Englander Jacob Bailey reported, the men "live[d] in a queer way," unsure if "war or peace" lay ahead. They slept with muskets loaded and cannons ready, always "prepared for the worst." If a war erupted, Bailey observed, its first battle would take place at Fort Moultrie, which lay at the mouth of Charleston Harbor and "completely locks up nullification." He assured his family that the fort "will not be taken in the hurry," and he echoed President Andrew Jackson's promise that the "Union *must* and *shall* be preserved."[3]

In Charleston, thousands of men trained and braced for battle. Over the past four years, the state's radical Nullifiers had stitched together a powerful political movement—a network of local State Rights Associations, party newspapers, and partisan militia companies. They had organized hundreds of banquets, rallies, and parades and steadily won control of the state. They captured the South Carolina General Assembly in 1830, and two years later they held a commanding three-fourths majority. Those lawmakers, in turn, selected governors, senators, and militia officers all fiercely loyal to their cause. Most hoped nullification would peacefully preserve states' rights within the Union, restoring the "proper" balance of state and federal power. Still, a small but growing number had begun openly calling for disunion, and countless more were prepared to defend their families and their freedom with "fixed bayonets."[4]

These Nullifiers, however, faced fierce resistance from within their own state. During the winter of 1832–33, more than 9,000 South Carolinians joined paramilitary Union Societies, vowing to hold the country together or "perish in the attempt." They declared that they had drawn their swords and "flung away the scabbards," and they would march at a moment's warning to defend the American flag. In Charleston alone, nearly 1,500 Union men drilled and prepared for war, and diplomat Joel R. Poinsett assured Jackson that they would "remain firm at our posts." The storm of civil war, Poinsett wrote, "may yet pass off and not burst upon us," but if it came, they would "resist it like men."[5]

The American public has largely forgotten the nullification crisis, and recent scholars have devoted relatively little attention to the topic. At the time, however, many Americans feared the conflict would destroy the fragile young republic. Andrew Jackson warned that nullification "strikes at the very existence of society," and James Madison agreed that it would "speedily put an end to the Union itself." The crisis inspired some of Daniel Webster's most stirring rhetoric, and his "second reply to Hayne" became a touchstone of American patriotism. In that speech, memorized by statesmen and students for the next hundred years, he declared the United States the "people's government, made for the people, made by the people, and answerable to the people." Webster gave voice to the "sentiment dear to every true American heart—Liberty *and* Union, now and forever, one and inseparable!"[6]

As contemporaries understood, the country came perilously close to civil war in the winter of 1832–33. After a decade of slave conspiracies and thwarted rebellions, South Carolinians feared they could no longer trust the federal government to safeguard slavery. Northern reformers were ridding their states of slavery, and nine state legislatures had called for a federal plan of gradual emancipation. More urgently, the movement's vocal vanguard had begun demanding an immediate end to slavery. In this atmosphere of anxiety, South Carolinians viewed the high protective tariff of 1828 as a northern plot to devastate southern agriculture and weaken slavery from within. With their society apparently under siege, radical leaders pushed the Palmetto State to defy the law and perhaps dissolve the Union altogether.[7]

The country survived, in part, because of the resolve and restraint of national statesmen. Senator Henry Clay helped forge a compromise, gradually lowering the tariff while empowering the president to use military force to carry out the laws. Crucially, however, the country also survived because of the depth and resilience of southern proslavery Unionism. South Carolina's Nullifiers hoped to unify their state and convert the rest of the South to their cause. As they faced down the federal government, they convinced themselves that "thousands of volunteers from these [southern] States will come to our aid." Ultimately, though, the other states rejected nullification, and public meetings across the South urged Jackson to "execute the laws and preserve the Union." Even in South Carolina, 40 percent of voters staunchly opposed nullification, and 9,000 men vowed to fight against their own brothers and neighbors to preserve the Union.[8]

Previous scholars, searching for the "origins of southern radicalism," have insightfully analyzed the state's Nullifiers and the struggle between South Carolina and the federal government. *Bloody Flag of Anarchy,* however, reframes the crisis, emphasizing the partisan conflict *within* South Carolina. It restores the state's Union Party to the center of the story, providing insight into the hopes, anxieties, and convictions of Jacksonian-era southern Unionists. It argues that they viewed the Union as a fragile experiment in self-government—the last hope of liberty in a world dominated by despotism. The Constitution was barely forty years old, and no one knew if it would survive. Crises like the Whiskey Rebellion of 1791–94, the War of 1812, and the Missouri statehood debate of 1819–21 had already shaken the country's foundations, and Union men feared that nullification would seal its destruction. Nullification, they imagined, would unfurl the "bloody flag of Anarchy"—shattering the Union, tearing the social order apart, and inspiring slave rebellions across the South. Galvanized by these fears, Union men rallied to save their country from chaos.[9]

These Union men were often reluctant partisans. Many still clung to the political theories of the early republic, which decried partisanship as a danger to national stability. As one scholar explains, antebellum South Carolinians viewed opposition parties as "constitutional challenge[s]" rather than political alternatives. During the nullification crisis, Union men equated Nullifiers' local State Rights Associations with the Jacobin Clubs of the French Revolution—clubs that "deluged in blood, so many nations of the world." As Nullifiers stormed to power, however, some Union men realized that they could only save their state by "fight[ing] the Nullifiers with their own weapons." By creating a party of their own, they hoped to "preserve the Union," "sustain the Government of our fathers," and "defend ourselves when danger comes."[10]

In general, districts with higher concentrations of slaves embraced nullification, while those with lower concentrations opposed it (Table 1). Nullifiers framed the tariff as a threat to slavery and white supremacy, and their message resonated powerfully in the slave-dense parishes of the South Carolina lowcountry. The Union Party, however, was a broad coalition with support throughout the state. It drew its greatest strength from swampbound Horry District, from Charleston, and from the upcountry districts along the North Carolina border. In Charleston, the city's economic elite flocked to the Union Party, along with many federal employees, urban professionals, mariners, and storekeepers. Outside the city, one-third of the lowcountry's slaveholders rejected radicalism, fearing nullification would destabilize society and endanger their "domestic institutions."[11]

In the state's hilly upcountry, small farmers formed the backbone of the Union Party, and in some districts, they fielded commanding majorities. In Greenville and Spartanburg Districts, for example, Union men made up 70 percent of the population. On average, upcountry Union men were older and owned fewer slaves than their opponents. Some had lived through the American Revolution and hoped to preserve the country they had helped to create. The largest group, however, was born in the 1780s and 1790s. They were the children of the founding generation, and many had come of age in the nationalist fervor of the 1810s. They had watched the country expand and prosper, doubling in size and quadrupling in population, stretching across the continent and trading around the world. Now, tasked with safeguarding their parents' legacy, they refused to allow the Union to perish.[12]

In addition to reinterpreting the nullification crisis, *Bloody Flag of Anarchy* builds upon and contributes to four fields of scholarship. First, it helps

TABLE 1. Slavery in South Carolina, 1830

District	African Americans in Population (%)	Slaveholding Households (%)	Planter Households (%)	Support for Nullification in 1832 (%)
Abbeville	47	58	6	64
Anderson	26	32	2	75
Barnwell	46	45	6	65
Beaufort	85	68	32	86
Charleston	74	91	14	55
Chester	42	50	4	59
Chesterfield	37	34	4	38
Colleton	80	59	22	67
Darlington	51	46	7	42
Edgefield	51	55	8	72
Fairfield	55	58	10	94
Georgetown	90	71	32	61
Greenville	30	36	3	28
Horry	33	36	3	14
Kershaw	63	50	10	37
Lancaster	41	47	4	41
Laurens	35	52	3	60
Lexington	42	49	3	100
Marion	35	42	3	61
Marlboro	51	45	9	100
Newberry	49	61	6	89
Orangeburg	59	65	12	86
Pickens	20	22	2	60
Richland	65	59	10	75
Spartanburg	23	29	1	31
Sumter	68	58	15	56
Union	41	45	5	71
Williamsburg	69	56	19	50
York	37	51	2	51

Note: "Planter Household" is defined here as a household with twenty or more slaves.

Sources: Percentage of African Americans drawn from William W. Freehling, *Prelude to Civil War: The Nullification Controversy in South Carolina, 1816–1836* (New York: Oxford University Press, 1965), 365–67. Percentage of slaveholding and planter households drawn from 1830 United States Census. Author's calculations.

reframe the discussion over the coming of the Civil War. Generations of scholars have debated why the Union fell apart in 1860–61. As Cynthia Nicoletti contends, however, historians must also ask how "this Union actually held together for as long as it did." Elizabeth R. Varon agrees, encouraging scholars to grapple with the "tricky question of timing." Although slavery was the "fundamental cause" of secession and Civil War, she observes, that issue had divided the states as far back as the Constitutional Convention of 1787. Nonetheless, it "took another seventy-five years for the war to come." This book engages with these questions by examining the hopes and fears that inspired South Carolina's beleaguered Union Party to resist the tide of radicalism in their state.[13]

Second, building on the work of Gary W. Gallagher and others, this book demonstrates the ideological power of antebellum Unionism. The Union, Gallagher explains, "represented the cherished legacy of the founding generation": a republican government that enshrined political liberty and economic opportunity for all white men. While most of the literature on Unionism focuses on the Civil War era, the nullification crisis also provides a rich avenue for research. By the 1830s, the generation that fought the Revolution and founded the country was rapidly passing away, fueling intense anxieties among younger Americans. Union men clung to the symbols of that struggle, hoping to keep the memory of the Revolution—and the promise of the Union—alive. Crucially, the nullification crisis also provided a lexicon of Unionism for all future crises. When Abraham Lincoln drafted his First Inaugural Address, for example, he reportedly drew upon only four sources, including Jackson's Nullification Proclamation and Webster's "second reply to Hayne."[14]

Third, *Bloody Flag of Anarchy* contributes to the literature on antebellum southern manhood. As Stephanie McCurry and James Brewer Stewart have shown, Nullifiers invoked a martial conception of manhood, rallying men to defend their homes and defy the federal government. At militia musters and partisan rallies, Nullifiers urged listeners to "obey the maternal call of South Carolina" and protect their "firesides from pollution." They depicted Union men as timid "submission men" who were "degraded as men and freemen." As this book reveals, Union men responded by reaffirming their manhood— but they did so in conflicting ways. Some embraced martial manhood and violently defended their honor. They battled Nullifiers on dueling grounds and village streets, unleashing a wave of small-scale violence with each new election cycle. Others embraced an ideal of moderate manhood, insisting that "true men" would preserve law and order and protect their families from the "horrors of civil war." These moderate Union men warned that nullification would destroy the social order and incite disunion, gender radicalism, and racial warfare.[15]

Finally, this book adds to a growing conversation about the transnational context of antebellum American history. In recent years, scholars have perceptively explored the relationship between Atlantic World events and American political development. They have traced the hopes and horrors released by the Haitian Revolution, the British abolition movement, and the failed European upheavals of 1848. These scholars, however, have largely ignored the impact of Europe's 1830 revolutions, despite these having coincided with a moment of profound political crisis in the United States.[16]

From the beginning, Union men viewed the nullification crisis against the backdrop of global history. They feared nullification would unleash the social chaos of the French and Haitian Revolutions, in which men, women, and children had been "swept away in one vast overwhelming tide of blood." Then, in 1830, a wave of liberal revolutions crashed across Europe as protestors in France, Belgium, Italy, Switzerland, and Poland demanded independence or constitutional reform. These revolutions raised the stakes of the nullification crisis. Union men viewed America as a "bright example to suffering humanity"—a beacon of hope in a world ravaged by war and despotism. Nullification now tested the Union's providential purpose. By 1832, with the European revolutions faltering, Union men feared that America might fail at the very moment the world needed its example the most. In their minds, the crisis in South Carolina assumed global significance, and its outcome could determine the fate of human liberty for all time.[17]

1.

Containing Chaos

Slavery, Tariffs, and the Rise of Radicalism, 1822–28

In September 1828, four thousand people gathered at Abbeville Court House in northwestern South Carolina to denounce the "tariff of abominations." For more than a year, lowcountry radicals had been calling for "open resistance" to the country's rising tariffs, and their ideas were slowly taking root across the state. Earlier that summer, Abbeville residents had resolved to "draw a wall" around South Carolina and oppose oppression by "every means in our power." If Congress demanded tribute, they had warned, they would rise in rebellion and pay the "price in steel." As the crowd again gathered that September, radicals hoped for more militant resolutions, while moderates prayed that cooler heads would prevail. For many South Carolinians, this "Great Anti-Tariff Meeting" would serve as a bellwether of the state's political future, and they awaited its outcome with anxious uncertainty.[1]

Witnesses marveled at the "grand and imposing" spectacle, declaring it the "largest [meeting] ever held in this State." The massive crowd came from across South Carolina and Georgia and included Senator Robert Y. Hayne and Congressmen James Hamilton and George McDuffie—former nationalists who had turned decisively toward radicalism. The Reverend William Barr opened the meeting with a fervent prayer, speaking with a "deep-toned piety" that sounded almost "unearthly." While other ministers denounced him for "preaching political sermons," Barr viewed his presence there as a sacred defense of freedom. He declared the tariff unjust and unconstitutional and invoked the Bible to legitimize resistance. McDuffie followed with a powerful three-hour address, and a local leader offered a series of unyielding resolutions. As the crowd approved them one-by-one, an artillery company added a "cannon's roar" to the "loud bursts of applause."[2]

With these resolutions, the men and women in the crowd reaffirmed their devotion to the Union. For fifty years, they declared, they had rejoiced in its triumphs and shared in its struggles, and they still viewed it as the "lasting security of our liberties." Nonetheless, they understood the Constitution as a narrowly defined compact among sovereign states, and they argued that the Union could only survive if it maintained this "original purity." By enacting the high protective tariff of 1828, they insisted, the US Congress had gone "beyond the limits of its delegated powers" and violated the "fundamental principles of our government." In response, these South Carolinians turned to "our State sovereignty for relief." They argued that states had formed the Constitution and therefore held the power to declare federal laws null and void. If the rest of the Union upheld an unconstitutional law, then a state could "renounce [its] obedience to the Constitution" and proclaim its independence. These resolutions marked a turning point in the state's political history. For the first time, a large group of South Carolinians had publicly endorsed nullification—a principle that would divide the state for the next seven years and bring the country to the brink of civil war.[3]

By the fall of 1828, a small but growing number of South Carolinians believed their state was under attack—that northerners had subverted the Constitution and turned the federal government against them. In the past decade, these radicals observed, Congress had restricted the westward expansion of slavery, expanded its program of internal improvements, and passed an escalating series of tariff laws. These acts of federal "oppression" had coincided with a wave of insurrectionary panics, most notably the Denmark Vesey conspiracy of 1822. The anxieties these events unleashed helped reshape the state's political culture. As news of the tariff of 1828 reached South Carolina, political leaders sought to direct and harness the "political excitement" that consumed the state. Moderates counseled patience, trusting the democratic process to resolve the crisis. Conjuring the chaos of the French and Haitian Revolutions, they warned that political unrest could provoke racial warfare and a new "Reign of Terror." These moderates planned to petition Congress for relief, boycott northern manufactured goods, and wear homespun clothing as peaceful acts of protest.

Radicals, meanwhile, called for "prompt and firm resistance." They cast the tariff as a federal plot to impoverish the South and destroy the Constitution, and they accused moderates of betraying South Carolina. Compromise, they claimed, would only empower the federal government and ensure the state's destruction. Ultimately, in December 1828, moderate lawmakers thwarted plans to nullify the tariff and worked diligently to calm the unrest and stem the tide of radicalism. Most South Carolinians maintained hope that Congress would rescind the tariff and restore the balance of state and federal power. Radicals' ideas, however, had seeped into the state's political consciousness, overshadowing other solutions and setting the terms of political debate for the next seven years.

In the 1810s, with the Federalist Party essentially dead, the state's Democratic-Republicans fragmented and struggled for power. After the War of 1812, Congressman John C. Calhoun and his allies embraced a "qualified nationalism," supporting federally funded infrastructure projects ("internal improvements"), a national bank, and a mildly protective tariff. These measures, they hoped, would help weave the states' economies together and ensure the Union's strength and stability. Calhoun, James Hamilton, Robert Hayne, George McDuffie, and others opposed the rising tariffs of the early 1820s but continued to champion "truly national" legislation. Senator William Smith, however, rejected this expansive vision of federal power, insisting Calhoun's policies would erode state sovereignty and devastate the South's agricultural economy. The two men remained in Washington, DC, for most of the 1820s, with Smith serving as a congressman and senator and Calhoun as secretary of war and vice president. Their allies in South Carolina, however, vied for control of the state legislature throughout the decade.[4]

Their ideological dispute centered on conflicting interpretations of the Constitution. Strict constructionists—including Smith and state legislators Stephen D. Miller and David R. Williams—believed the federal government only possessed the powers specifically outlined in the Constitution. Broad constructionists like Calhoun countered that the Constitution implied a larger role for the federal government. It empowered Congress to enact all "necessary and proper" laws and to levy taxes to "provide for the common defense and general Welfare." Calhounites envisioned a dynamic yet limited federal government that could creatively respond to problems while still respecting states' rights.[5]

Calhounites controlled the state legislature from 1816 until 1824. In 1820, when upcountry lawyer Pleasant May pronounced a new tariff bill unconstitutional, lawmakers overwhelmingly opposed him. They observed that the Constitution sanctioned "enlarged and uniform principles" and granted Congress the power to enact "all laws relating to commerce." They warned that May's principles would imperil the Union, and they vowed to uphold the "general welfare of the republic." The following year, lawmakers confirmed that the state faced "no danger" from Congress, and in 1822, they elected nationalist Robert Y. Hayne to the United States Senate over William Smith.[6]

By the mid-1820s, however, many South Carolinians began reevaluating this optimistic nationalism. An economic downturn hit the state early in the decade, and cotton planters blamed protective tariffs for their declining fortunes. Roughly 56,000 white South Carolinians left the state in the 1820s seeking economic opportunity in the cotton fields of Georgia, Alabama, and Mississippi. While northern cities expanded and flourished, Charleston's population stagnated. In 1790, it had been the country's fourth largest city; by 1820, it was only the sixth largest, and by midcentury it would fall to fifteenth. As one scholar explains, the state's political leaders sought to reverse this decline and recapture the "economic miracle of colonial South Carolina." As Congress debated raising tariff duties in 1820 and 1824, South Carolinians began viewing the tariff as a plot to impoverish the agricultural South and enrich the industrializing North.[7]

The Denmark Vesey conspiracy hastened the state's turn toward sectionalism, fusing economic tensions with anxieties over slavery's survival. In May 1822, several enslaved men warned their owners of an impending rebellion in Charleston. Intendant (Mayor) James Hamilton summoned the militia to patrol the streets, and the city council convened a Court of Magistrates and Freeholders to try the suspects. They accused Denmark Vesey, a free Black carpenter, of orchestrating a rebellion and recruiting hundreds or even thousands of followers. South Carolinians understood these local events as part of a broader revolutionary world: Vesey allegedly planned his rebellion for Bastille Day and modeled it on the Haitian Revolution. According to rumor, he planned to capture the city arsenal, burn Charleston to the ground, raid the surrounding countryside, and escape to the safety of Haiti. As the court convened, Vesey and his followers went into hiding. By August, however, officials had arrested 135 people for conspiracy and sentenced thirty-five—including Vesey—to death.[8]

Scholars have fiercely debated the nature and extent of the conspiracy, working to untangle historical fact from the fears and fantasies that engulfed the city. Historian Michael P. Johnson argues that the "official record" reveals more about white anxiety than African American insurgency. White officials, he contends, "expanded the scope of the alleged conspiracy" by forcing slaves and free Blacks to make fraudulent confessions. While the truth remains unclear, most white South Carolinians accepted the rumors as facts, and the "evidence" that the court uncovered terrified them. Anna Johnson, the daughter of US Supreme Court Justice William Johnson, reported that "our city is now in the most fearful state." If the rebellion had succeeded, she wrote, "the [white] men and Black women were to have been indiscriminately murdered—& we poor devils were to have been reserved to fill their harams." Panic spread across the lowcountry and lingered for months. In November, residents on Johns Island still reported bands of "armed fugitive slaves ... infesting [the] Parish"—killing cattle, robbing houses, and threatening to murder "faithful domestics."[9]

Hamilton blamed the Denmark Vesey conspiracy on overly lenient masters and the subversive power of slave literacy and religion. As early as 1820, lowcountry residents had petitioned to close Charleston's Black schools and churches, restrict slave manumissions, and banish free African Americans from the state. One petitioner explained that African American literacy was "impolitick and at variance with slavery," while another denounced northern missionaries for "subverting the state" and preaching insurrection. The slave panics of 1822 seemed to confirm these fears, and lawmakers responded with sweeping new restrictions on the state's African American population. Lawmakers levied an annual $50 tax on newly arrived Black men, banned free African Americans who left the state from returning, and declared that all free African Americans had to procure white guardians or face expulsion. In 1823, Charleston's civic and economic leaders established the South Carolina Association, an extralegal organization dedicated to policing the city's Black population. Auxiliary societies soon formed across the lowcountry, organized by many of the same men who later championed nullification.[10]

The state assembly also passed the Negro Seaman's Act, which detained Black sailors while their ships were docked in Charleston Harbor. Lawmakers hoped this would insulate South Carolina's slaves from outside "agitators." Memories of the Haitian Revolution still haunted their imaginations, and they feared that West Indian sailors would "beguile our slaves into rebellion with false hopes." Ship captains protested the law, insisting it violated the Constitution and flouted America's foreign treaties. Unsurprisingly, however, the state's courts upheld the act. In August 1823, officials arrested Henry Elkison, a free Jamaican-born British subject, who immediately requested a writ of habeas corpus. Supreme Court Justice William Johnson—a Charleston planter—denied the request on the grounds that federal courts lacked the power to release state prisoners.[11]

In his ruling, however, Johnson pronounced South Carolina's law "irreconcilable" with the Constitution. He argued that the federal government had the "paramount and exclusive right" to regulate commerce and ratify treaties. He viewed the Negro Seaman's Act as a "direct attack upon the sovereignty of the United States," observing that it empowered state officials to "throw off the federal constitution" and tear the Union apart. For Johnson, the greatest threat to national harmony came not from northern reformers but rather from proslavery radicals. Across South Carolina, he reported, "Disunion appears to be losing its Terrors," and he feared these radical ideals would soon become "systematic Policy" in the state.[12]

Johnson's ruling enraged many South Carolinians and launched a long public debate about the balance of state and federal power. A Charleston radical accused Johnson of betraying the South by adopting the "Northern feeling on the slave system." If the Supreme Court upheld Johnson's ruling, he wrote, then the "Constitution of the United States must be altered, or it must be violated." Another writer warned that Johnson's ruling allowed "the brigands of St. Domingo to come here freely and securely." In 1824, when Attorney General William Wirt declared the Negro Seaman's Act unconstitutional, South Carolina lawmakers denounced the federal government. The house declared the Negro Seaman's Act essential to public safety, and the senate resolved that South Carolina's duty to defend itself superseded "all *laws*, all *treaties*, all *constitutions*." They refused to rescind the law, and it remained in place for decades in what one historian has called the state's "first nullification."[13]

With the political tide turning, William Smith and his lieutenants seized the initiative. In 1824, the state senate declared protective tariffs and federally funded internal improvements unconstitutional. Calhounites tabled the resolutions in the house, and Charleston planter Samuel Prioleau responded with a defiant declaration of nationalism. He insisted that South Carolinians owed a "double allegiance" to the state and the Union, which were "equally entitled to [their] love and reverence." The following year, however, the house overwhelmingly approved the Smithite resolutions. Voters elected Smithites Joseph Gist and John Wilson to Congress in 1824, and two years later, the lawmakers sent Smith to the US Senate.[14]

By the mid-1820s, many South Carolinians feared they could no longer trust the federal government to safeguard slavery. In 1824, nine states—including the slave state of Delaware—passed resolutions declaring slavery a national evil and calling for gradual emancipation. Enraged, South Carolina lawmakers declared slavery "inseparably connected with their social and political existence" and claimed that Congress had no power over the institution. The following year, New York Senator Rufus King proposed that Congress use the revenue from federal land sales to finance emancipation—a plan Robert Hayne believed would endanger the "safety of the States" and "disturb the peace and harmony of the Union." Soon after, President John Quincy Adams accepted an invitation for the United States to attend the Panama Congress, a meeting of American republics meant to foster unity and cooperation in the Western Hemisphere. The news horrified many southerners, who feared the meeting would promote emancipation and legitimize racially inclusive governments in Latin America.[15]

Then, in 1827, the American Colonization Society (ACS) petitioned Congress for funding to support its fledgling Liberian settlement. The ACS was an uneasy coalition between northern reformers (who hoped that sending freedmen to Africa would encourage voluntary emancipation) and southern slaveholders (who sought to shore up slavery by removing free African Americans from their states). Although supporters viewed colonization as a safe and conservative course, most South Carolinians saw it as a direct assault upon slavery. If Congress could "legislate in one way on the coloured population," state senators warned, "it may legislate in various other ways." Lawmakers argued that colonization would ignite "fires of intestine commotion on our borders" and ultimately "consume our country."[16]

By 1827, primed by these events, South Carolina's radicals began linking the tariff to their anxieties over slavery. That February, the US House of Representatives passed a bill raising duties on imported woolen goods. The Senate was evenly divided, and Vice President John C. Calhoun ultimately cast the tie-breaking vote against it. Across South Carolina, local leaders organized meetings and drafted petitions denouncing the woolens bill. An upcountry militia officer feared it would "destroy our republican institutions" and return the country to monarchy. If the bill became law, Congressman George McDuffie warned, the Union "cannot exist twenty years." Thomas Cooper, president of South Carolina College, went even further, insisting the state would secede within a year.[17]

In the antebellum era, many Americans invoked disunion as a prophecy or a threat, often hoping to preserve—rather than destroy—the Union. Their prophecies worked to inspire renewed devotion to the country, while their threats used "fear as a political weapon" to force opponents to back down. During the divisive Missouri statehouse debates of 1819–21, for example, South Carolina Congressman Charles Pinckney envisioned disunion and civil war in order to silence antislavery activism. By 1827, however, a few radical South Carolinians began questioning the Union's purpose and imagining disunion as a necessary alternative.[18]

At a meeting in Columbia that July, Thomas Cooper cast the tariff debate in stark terms. He claimed that northern congressmen were transforming the southern states into "colonies and tributaries." While southern moderates wasted time signing petitions and drafting resolutions, he observed, the chains of tyranny were tightening around them. Before long, he declared, the crisis would compel southerners to "calculate the value of our union"—to ask themselves if it was "worth our while to continue this union of states." Faced with the choice between submission and secession, Cooper urged South Carolinians to "hold fast to *principle*." If they placed their faith in Congress, then they "trust to a broken anchor, and all that is worth preserving will be irretrievably lost."[19]

State Senator Whitemarsh Seabrook used similar rhetoric at an Independence Day meeting on Johns Island. He blamed protective tariffs for the state's economic depression and warned that the new woolens bill would revolutionize the federal government. The bill, he claimed, would "array one branch of industry against another" and endanger the "domestic institutions of the Southern States." Seabrook attacked the American Colonization Society and cautioned northern congressmen that slavery was "not a legitimate topic of discussion." The American people, he warned, could only remain at peace as long as slavery remained secure. Like Cooper, he appealed to southern honor to galvanize resistance, asking planters if they were willing to "tamely submit" and "humbly kiss the rod which chastens [them]."[20]

That summer, Charleston lawyer Robert J. Turnbull published *The Crisis,* a series of essays that one Nullifier later called the "first bugle call of the South to rally." Turnbull occupied the vanguard of proslavery militancy. He served on the court that convicted the Denmark Vesey conspirators, cofounded the South Carolina Association, helped write the Negro Seaman's Act, and published articles denouncing Johnson's ruling in the *Elkison* case. Now, in *The Crisis,* he warned that tariffs, internal improvements, and colonization were part of a larger plot to "trample to dust the Federal Constitution, and with it the hopes and safety of the South." Like Cooper, Turnbull believed petitions and protests were not enough: lawmakers needed to "*embody* that [public] feeling—not simply by resolving, but BY ACTING." He saw "no hope for our domestic safety, or for our agricultural interests, but in RESISTANCE"—and if that resistance led to disunion, he raged, then "let Disunion come."[21]

Most South Carolinians rejected this radicalism. A writer calling himself *Senex* published essays pleading for unity and affirming a moderate ideal of manhood. He dismissed radicals as "passionate young men," "rash politicians," and "reckless zealots." He accused them of preying on voters' passions, "keeping up a constant excitement" in order to tear the Union apart. Faced with this crisis, he reminded all "men of family" that the "welfare of their children depends on the success of our happy Federal Constitution." He hoped that moderate, rational men would help "calm the agitations" and restore peace to the state. If the Union fractured, *Senex* warned, the states would become "tributar[ies] to foreign countries," and British abolitionists would erode the bonds of slavery.[22]

A writer who called himself *Prudence* offered a similar, gendered plea for peace. He condemned radical "enthusiasts," whose passionate "ravings" threatened to sever the "sacred compact of National union." He placed his faith in the country's "discreet men, whose homes and fortunes, and offspring, demand their serious care." These men, he prayed, would demonstrate the patience and patriotism that had held the country together for more than a generation. Like *Senex,* he argued that the Union safeguarded slavery. If South Carolina seceded, he observed, it would have to bear the cost of its own national defense or seek "protection" from the abolitionists in Great Britain.[23]

The essayist *Mediator* urged South Carolinians to "listen to the voice of reason" and let "angry passions cease." True independence, he observed, came not from riotous partisanship but rather from "firmness and mutual forbearance," and he trusted the country's rational men to weigh the disastrous consequences of disunion. Editor Aaron S. Willington agreed, accusing "enthusiasts" of corrupting the "passions of the people." He insisted that radicals were turning democracy against itself, using the constitutional freedoms of assembly, petition, and the press to undermine the Constitution. Men like Cooper and Turnbull had transformed local public meetings into sectional rallies and crowded newspaper columns with language that "strike[s] at the very foundations of our Republican Government." Willington believed that all "good men" had a duty to speak out against radicalism, and he declared unequivocally that disunion was treason.[24]

Radicals' tactics, however, proved highly effective in shaping public debate. Most South Carolinians still decried disunion and civil war, and they maintained their faith in the democratic process. They petitioned Congress, wrote letters to local representatives, and hoped the next election would bring political change. By 1828, however, many viewed the tariff as an unconstitutional attack on southern agriculture and feared that slavery itself might hang in the balance. At precisely this moment, Congress passed the "tariff of abominations," dramatically increasing the duties on imported manufactured goods. The news ignited a firestorm in South Carolina that proved almost impossible to contain.

Most observers expected the 1828 tariff bill to fail. As Massachusetts Congressman John Bailey explained, the bill "was framed precisely to defeat itself." With the election of 1828 approaching, Andrew Jackson's supporters hoped to discredit President John Quincy Adams by forcing his allies to cast unpopular votes. The bill, for example, contained high tariffs on molasses and raw wool imports. If Adams's allies approved these duties, they would draw the ire of politically powerful rum distillers and woolen manufacturers. If they rejected the bill, however, they would disappoint voters in critical battleground states like New York and Pennsylvania. Southern congressmen supported the ploy, repeatedly voting against amendments to lower tariff rates on raw materials. Their strategy, however, backfired spectacularly. Despite its flaws, western and border state lawmakers overwhelmingly supported the tariff, and the House narrowly passed the bill in April 1828. The Senate followed three weeks later, and Adams promptly signed it into law.[25]

The outcome stunned South Carolina's congressmen and helped erode the state's old political factions. Smithite and Calhounite congressmen met at Robert Hayne's Washington boarding house and discussed mounting a formal protest. At the meeting, Hamilton vented his rage, predicting the tariff would lead to secession and civil war. If South Carolina took the first step, he thundered, the other southern states would rally to their cause. Virginia and North Carolina, he observed, would never allow federal troops to march across their territory. Invoking a martial conception of manhood, Hamilton expected South Carolina's "gallant and free" citizens to "meet our invaders like men" and reenact the glorious victories of the American Revolution. William Drayton, however, sought to calm his colleagues' tempers. Although Drayton considered the tariff oppressive and unconstitutional, he viewed disunion as a "more serious calamity." He persuaded the men to return home and discourage radical action in their state.[26]

South Carolina, however, quickly erupted in protest. Ship captains in Charleston Harbor lowered their flags to half-mast, and a Columbia mob burned statesmen Henry Clay and Daniel Webster in effigy. In the village of Walterboro, state legislator Robert Barnwell Smith (later Rhett) called for "open resistance to the laws of the union." South Carolinians, he observed, had spent four years pleading and petitioning for relief. They had "done by words all that words can do," yet tariff duties had only increased. Smith thundered that liberty was more sacred than the Union, and he urged lawmakers to "follow up your principles wherever they may lead, to their very last consequences." Thomas Cooper agreed, hoping that southern congressmen would resign en masse and organize a "government for themselves." Another radical declared that this "Tariff and this Union cannot exist together" and spurred South Carolinians to resist "now—OPENLY—unto BLOOD if necessary."[27]

Once again, these radicals framed the tariff as a threat to slavery and public safety. If Congress could impose a protective tariff, one writer warned, it could bring the "the territory of all the states under federal jurisdiction" and force them to emancipate their slaves. Henry Pinckney, editor of *The Charleston Mercury*, raged that northerners were waging war against slavery, and Cooper claimed that "Tariff-men rely on exciting a revolt among our slaves." They also appealed to southern honor and manhood to forge a political consensus. A Columbia writer insisted that anyone who opposed secession was a "base coward" and a "traitor to the SOUTH." A Georgetown editor agreed, writing that moderates had "no claim to the name of Republican, still less to that of MAN." Edgefield radicals confronted moderate editor Abner Landrum, with one man shaking a finger in Landrum's face and warning him to "speak the language of the South." They later assaulted a visiting Georgia editor and threatened to destroy his printing press unless he embraced their principles.[28]

Moderates denounced this violence and worked to calm the political excitement. A northern-born doctor, comparing the crisis to the French Revolution, dismissed his neighbors as "hotheaded Jacksonites and Jacobins . . . panting for a field [of battle]." He feared that South Carolinians, obsessed with honor, "would not hesitate to open the floodgates of civil war and plunge our land in blood." State Senator David R. Williams agreed, warning that young men would "risk their lives, if not their necks, in a military career, if only for the fun of it." Former Governor Richard Manning added that South Carolinians had "every thing to fear from rashness." If they took up arms against the federal government, he explained, the struggle would lead to chaos, destroying the Constitution and the balance of state and federal power. These men derided radicals' martial conception of manhood. They appealed to reason, wisdom, and common sense, arguing that "true men" would help preserve the social order. Manning, for example, trusted the "good sense of the people" and prayed that all "discreet, sober minded, or aged [men]" would work toward compromise.[29]

A few moderates—mostly concentrated in Charleston—continued to champion protective tariffs. An essayist calling himself *Hamilton* insisted that Congress had the power to regulate foreign trade, and he denounced the state's radicals for "rush[ing] into mortal strife." Another writer claimed the new tariff would strengthen the country's economy, enriching northern manufacturers and expanding the market for southern cotton. These economic ties, he declared, would solidify the Union, as "fair and honorable commerce" promoted "candor and justice" between the North and South.[30]

Most moderates, however, adamantly opposed the "tariff of abominations." Local leaders drafted petitions, published articles, and hosted anti-tariff meetings. They organized boycotts of northern goods and encouraged South Carolinians to build their own factories. Nonetheless, they worked to calm the state's political excitement, assuring voters that Congress would lower the tariff during its next session. Quoting the Declaration of Independence, Greenville editor Obadiah Wells urged readers to "suffer while evils are sufferable" rather than rush into civil war. If the state tried to secede, he warned, the upcountry districts would "separate from South Carolina" and resume their place in the Union. A lowcountry meeting declared the Union the "best safe-guard of our liberties," and another celebrated the country's "Great Experiment in Government." Moderates denounced "all hasty measures of violence" and pleaded with voters to pursue every peaceable avenue of redress.[31]

As the election of 1828 approached, the new tariff began to realign the state's political factions. Many Calhounites, who had once supported economic nationalism, now sought to out-flank their opponents as the true defenders of states' rights. In September 1828, a friend warned Smithite Senator Stephen D. Miller that Calhounites were trying to "fight you with your own weapons" by "bring[ing] your attachment to State Rights into dispute." Calhounites, he explained, hoped to present themselves as the "only true Radicals in South Carolina." This political climate encouraged radicalism, and the writer warned Miller that a "fit of extreme moderation . . . would probably prove fatal" in the upcoming election.[32]

Ironically, although Smithies had championed strict construction for more than a decade, some now condemned the state's radical course. State Senator David R. Williams thought the tariff was unconstitutional, but he believed the "majority ought to rule" and "the minority [ought] to obey." If South Carolinians defied the tariff, he warned, they would provoke a war they could never win. They were desperately outnumbered, and each of their soldiers would have to "shoot down twenty-three Kentuckians and Yankees" just to even the balance. When a former Smithite ally accused him of betraying his principles, Williams appealed to moderate manhood. All "influential" men, he insisted, had a duty to calm political passions and save the state from ruin.[33]

Undaunted, radicals began publicly endorsing nullification in September 1828. Abbeville's "Great Anti-Tariff Meeting" declared that states could refuse to obey unconstitutional laws. In Walterboro that October, James

Hamilton reaffirmed these principles and looked to history to legitimize their struggle. Thirty years earlier, he observed, Federalists had passed the Alien and Sedition Acts, restricting freedom of the press and empowering the president to imprison foreign residents. In response, Thomas Jefferson and James Madison had drafted the Kentucky and Virginia Resolutions, which argued that states held the power to judge federal laws unconstitutional. In an early draft, Jefferson had described this process as *nullification,* and by reviving the word, Hamilton helped give a name to radicals' emerging political movement.[34]

One observer claimed that the tariff issue dominated the state election of 1828, pitting the "moderate men against the *hot* men." In most districts, however, the breakdown of old political factions prevented a clear referendum. In Charleston, for example, voters selected from among the People's Union ticket, the Jackson ticket, the Anti-Tariff and Union ticket, and the Andrew Jackson and State Rights ticket. Several candidates appeared on multiple tickets, blurring the distinctions between them. Moderate Congressman William Drayton, meanwhile, ran unopposed in his bid for reelection.[35]

The tariff crisis, furthermore, failed to increase voter turnout in the state's largest and most politically vibrant city. Since 1820, elections in Charleston had drawn about 2,072 voters each year. In 1828, amid the "greatest struggle we have had in this State for many years," that number actually dropped slightly to 2,067—roughly 66 percent of the city's eligible voters. Election results throughout the state confirmed these trends, showing a lack of clear partisan alignment or mobilization. Job Johnston, clerk of the state senate, observed that "there is no mind for party divisions in the state," and moderate lawyer Thomas Grimké declared himself "opposed to the principle of a caucus in every shape." In most districts, political leaders were reluctant to embrace open partisanship, and elections still hinged on candidates' personalities and networks of local influence.[36]

The state's election results were therefore ambiguous. When the state legislature convened in November 1828, editor Henry L. Pinckney confessed that he could only "conjecture the course" it would pursue, and Beaufort legislator William Elliott agreed that "everything is in uncertainty." Most lawmakers opposed the tariff, but they disagreed over how best to respond. Moderates planned to draft resolutions and petition Congress for relief, while radicals hoped to nullify the tariff altogether. Even men who supported nullification, however, disagreed over its meaning and purpose. Some saw it as a revolutionary defense of states' rights; others, saw it as a conservative means of preserving their freedom within the Union.[37]

Calhoun, still serving as vice president, drafted an anonymous essay declaring nullification a peaceful and constitutional remedy. This *Exposition* sought to temper the state's extremists while providing a clear legal mechanism for resistance. South Carolina's most radical leaders believed the legislature should immediately nullify the tariff. Calhoun countered that since nullification was an act of state sovereignty, only a state constitutional convention possessed that power. He urged lawmakers to give newly elected president Andrew Jackson time to lower the tariff, trusting the president to restore the "pure principles of our government." Nonetheless, Calhoun remained resolute, imbuing the crisis with global significance. If the federal government refused to back down, he wrote, the state had a "sacred duty" to "herself—to the Union—to the present, and to future generations—and to the cause of liberty over the world" to call a convention and nullify the tariff.[38]

The South Carolina General Assembly published five thousand copies of the *Exposition* to distribute throughout the state. As a compromise measure, Edgefield legislator Andrew Butler called for a state convention to meet in December 1829, giving Congress time to rescind the tariff while holding out the threat of nullification. The house, however, rejected the resolution by a vote of 40 to 81. Lawmakers lodged another protest against the "oppressive" tariff, once again underscoring their defense of slavery. They declared that South Carolina depended on "agriculture and commerce, not only for her prosperity, but for her very existence as a state." Planters' cotton and rice crops, they claimed, were "among the very few that can be cultivated with any profit by slave labor." If the tariff remained in place, then, South Carolina's economy would collapse, slavery would become unprofitable, and white residents would abandon the state. In time, the "whole frame and constitution of her civil polity" could be "dissolved entirely."[39]

Lawmakers, however, took no further action against the tariff, and by mid-December, it was clear that "Nothing violent . . . will be done." As one writer observed, legislators evinced a "strong attachment" to the Union and an "unyielding resolution to protect, to the utmost, the constitution of the United States." Even so, the emerging nullification party was stronger than it appeared. William Elliott, a moderate, believed that caution rather than conviction had stayed the assembly's hand. If lawmakers were "sure of the cooperation of the Southern States," he wrote, they would "proceed to a direct defiance of the Genl Government" and perhaps even risk secession. Without that assurance, however, they "hesitate to go to extremes." Although the convention resolution failed 2-to-1, radicals elected many of their candidates to state office. As Elliott explained, a "private cabal" had "arranged before hand all the play of the machinery" of government. They elected William Harper as speaker of the house, Stephen D. Miller as governor, and Robert Y. Hayne as US Senator—all of whom were fiercely committed to nullification.[40]

This maneuvering underscored the state's emerging political realignment. In the early 1820s, Miller had been a Smithite radical, while Hayne had been a Calhounite nationalist; now, they stood united in their support for nullification. Earlier that year, when an antitariff meeting in Edgefield had nominated Hamilton for governor, the congressman had declined the call. In McDuffie's words, Hamilton refused to let his own "personal advancement" stand in the way of "cordial cooperation of the [Calhounite and Smithite] parties." Partisanship, he insisted, should not exist in "such a crisis . . . when every thing dear to the state is at hazard."[41]

A Columbia editor captured the state's mood as the assembly adjourned that December. He observed that lawmakers had worked to "vindicate [South Carolinians'] rights" without jeopardizing the Union's survival. They viewed the tariff as "unconstitutional, unequal, [and] oppressive" but maintained hope that the new administration would secure its repeal. The editor insisted that South Carolinians would "suffer somewhat longer, rather than interrupt the success of our grand political experiment." He warned, however, that their patience was wearing thin. If Congress failed to lower the tariff, they would take "more decisive" action to defend their trampled liberties.[42]

Moderate lawmakers had temporarily triumphed, committing the state to peaceful petition rather than nullification. The session's speeches and protests, however, revealed that the "tariff of abominations" had irrevocably shifted the political debate. In 1820, the assembly overwhelmingly refused to call a tariff bill unconstitutional, and it affirmed Congress's power to pass "all laws relating to commerce." Four years later, the state senate tabled resolutions declaring protective tariffs unconstitutional. By 1828, however, those sentiments had become widespread, even among moderate South Carolinians. Few accepted Thomas Cooper's call to "calculate the value of the Union," but radical conceptions of states' rights had pervaded political discourse. That year's assembly debate centered not on *whether* the tariff was unconstitutional but, rather, on *how* the state should resist it. That question, however, had already begun to divide South Carolinians in new and unexpected ways and was realigning the state's political factions. As radicals regrouped and looked ahead to 1830, they began piecing together a political organization that could carry them to power and perhaps unify the state behind their principles.

2.

Defining Convictions

The Process of Political Realignment, 1828–30

In July 1830, Charleston's civic leaders hosted a grand public dinner to honor Congressman William Drayton and Senator Robert Y. Hayne. At least 600 people attended, and Nullifiers carefully choreographed the event to demonstrate their party's power. On a pillar behind the speakers' table, they placed a large eagle with wings outspread and clutching a banner that read, "STATE RIGHTS." Portraits of national figures like George Washington and Andrew Jackson hung alongside those of the state's Revolutionary heroes. A ten-foot-tall transparency hovered above the crowd, depicting a woman—*Liberty*—surrounded by storm clouds and resting on the South Carolina state seal, the Latin motto of which read, *"Prepared in Mind and Resources."*[1]

The official toasts to George Washington, the Union, and the Constitution affirmed the crowd's national devotion. The volunteer toasts that followed, however, struck a more radical chord. One guest declared that the "crisis has arrived"—that South Carolina needed the "arms as well as [the] voices" of its citizens. A local doctor argued that disunion was *"our only preservation,"* and a city marshal proclaimed the day South Carolina's "second declaration of Independence." If the southern states could not secure their rights within the Union, one planter agreed, they should establish a "Republic South of the Potomac." The crowd greeted these toasts with "deafening" applause, cheering louder with each radical response.[2]

When Hayne finally rose to speak, he tied the state's political struggle to its Revolutionary past. He claimed that South Carolina was fighting for freedom—the same ideal "for which our fathers fought and bled, and conquered." He argued that the Constitution was a compact among independent states, held together by mutual interest and affection. The states, he said, maintained their sovereignty and held the power to "interpose" to protect their citizens from federal tyranny. Although Hayne still revered the Union, he insisted that it could only survive if it remained true to these conservative principles. Ultimately, he was determined to "stand or fall with *Carolina*," and when the moment of crisis came, he believed South Carolinians would forcefully defend their freedom.[3]

A few guests bravely pushed back against this radicalism. Planter Henry DeSaussure toasted the United States as "One and inseparable" and called disunion "their only *irreparable evil*." State legislator Hugh S. Legaré declared that, with President Andrew Jackson in power, they had *"no right* to despair of the Republic." In his own speech, Congressman William Drayton refused to endorse nullification, insisting it would violate his conscience and his "duty to God." As long as South Carolina remained in the Union, he explained, the state had to obey the country's laws. Drayton trusted the democratic process and urged the crowd to petition Congress for relief. In the meantime, he insisted that he would rather endure the tariff's burdens than witness the Union's destruction. He prayed that "our star-spangled banner, so often triumphantly unfurled upon the ocean and the land, [would] ever wave, with undiminished lustre, over free, sovereign, and *United* States."[4]

Although Hayne and Drayton both opposed the "tariff of abominations," they defended and prioritized different political ideals. Hayne underscored state sovereignty and claimed the Union only had value if it preserved South Carolinians' freedom. Liberty, for Hayne, was the greatest legacy of the American Revolution—the ideal for which their fathers fought and died. He carefully avoided the word "nullification"; instead, he simply urged the state to maintain its rights and protect its citizens. Drayton shared many of these convictions, but he ranked and defined them differently. He emphasized obedience to the law and trusted rational debate to resolve the crisis. He explicitly denounced nullification and warned that radicalism would provoke disunion and civil war.[5]

Organizers planned this dinner to showcase the state's unity and power; instead, it revealed its deepening divisions. By 1830, two new political parties had begun to coalesce in South Carolina. The State Rights Party—the Nullifiers—readily embraced partisanship, organizing dinners and rallies throughout the state and using the press to mobilize their voters. They evoked the state's Revolutionary history, debated the limits of constitutional power, and kept voters' attention fixed on the "tyranny" of the tariff. They warned that slavery's survival hung in the balance, and they appealed to martial manhood to rally their forces.

Their opponents, who eventually coalesced as the Union Party, were slower to organize and often distrusted partisanship. Many of the party's leaders were moderate men who feared that political division would destabilize the Union and endanger their families. They viewed the Union as the "world's last hope"—a "bright example to suffering humanity"—and they argued that the Constitution preserved both liberty and slavery. They equated Nullifiers' local meetings with the radical Jacobin clubs of the French Revolution and worked to save their state from a new Reign of Terror.[6]

This process of political realignment remained unfinished in 1830. The men who attended the Charleston dinner that July were mostly Nullifiers, yet they greeted Drayton with "long and deafening applause" and celebrated his chivalry, honor, and independence. They praised his decision to obey the "dictates of his conscience," and that October they endorsed his reelection to Congress. The election of 1830 thus represented a moment of transition in which deference and personal politics vied with partisanship to shape voters' decisions—and the destiny of the state.

The political storm briefly subsided in early 1829 as South Carolinians looked to Congress and President Andrew Jackson to lower the tariff. One writer observed that "Tariff fever has subsided" in the state, and even James Hamilton confessed that most South Carolinians viewed the conflict with indifference. Hamilton, however, hoped to galvanize support for nullification, asking the state's editors to "keep up the Fire on the tariff." Columbia jurist David McCord agreed that radicals "must be doing something." Because South Carolina's legislators served for two years, Nullifiers would probably lack the votes to call a state convention until after the next elections in 1830. In the meantime, McCord proposed sending delegates to a national antitariff meeting in Philadelphia that September, hoping to "unite the people of this State" and forge a broader southern alliance.[7]

For these radicals, an insurrectionary panic in Georgetown underscored the stakes of the crisis. In July 1829, militia captain William Vaught heard rumors of a slave rebellion "on the eve of bursting upon them." Local officials filled the jail with suspects and ordered militiamen to patrol the streets day and night to restore "order" and avert the "horrors of insurrection." The assembly granted them $5,000 to establish a town guard, but Georgetown remained on high alert. They executed at least two men, and James Petigru—the state's moderate attorney general—feared they would "hang half the country" before the panic was over. More than a year later, state senators reported starkly that the "spirit of Rebellion has been smothered [but] not quelled."[8]

Residents blamed the conspiracy on northern antislavery reformers, whose liberatory ideals inspired "insubordination among the slaves." The state's editors censored news of the conspiracy, afraid that slaves in other districts would emulate Georgetown's example. In the panic's aftermath, however, radicals defended slavery with even greater urgency. Evoking the "horrors" of the Haitian Revolution, a Columbia editor warned that abolitionists would incite the "savage, St. Domingo spirit" among their slaves. In his annual address, Governor Stephen Miller declared slavery a "national benefit," insisting it enriched the country and shored up the political order. "Upon this subject," he affirmed, South Carolinians could not afford to "speak in a whisper [or] betray fear." Congressman Warren R. Davis agreed, insisting it was unmanly to petition the federal government for relief. Appealing to voters' martial manhood, he explained that no man had ever "obtained justice by whining and whimpering like a great miss from a boarding school." Supplication, he insisted, was a sign of weakness: *you cannot respect a thing that creeps and licks the dust!!!*" Instead, Davis urged South Carolinians to defend their honor and take a decisive stand against tyranny.[9]

With no statewide elections in 1829, radicals focused on Charleston's mayoral contest, which pitted radical editor Henry Pinckney against moderate jurist Thomas Grimké. Pinckney ultimately captured 53 percent of the city's vote. The contest, however, was not a clear referendum on nullification. Grimké was a deeply principled politician often out of step with his own state. He promoted pacifism, temperance, and educational reform, and he walked the streets of Charleston in tattered clothing, explaining that every "dollar saved in this way is an additional sum for the poor." He supported the American Colonization Society, and his sisters Sarah and Angelina Grimké would soon become leaders in the national abolition and women's rights movements. Thomas Grimké viewed colonization as a moderate alternative, hoping it would ameliorate African Americans' condition and de-escalate the divisive debate over slavery. During the campaign, he praised the ACS and confessed that, if he lived in the North, he would "take an active part in promoting [its] objects."[10]

While radicals viewed the Constitution as a compact among sovereign states, Grimké insisted that the American *people* had ratified the document. The Union, he declared, was not a compact but rather "one Nation," and its survival was indispensable to the freedom, peace, and prosperity of its citizens. Opponents labeled Grimké an "enemy within our gates," warning that he would betray the state, uphold the "omnipotence of Congress," and encourage the "murderous schemes of the Colonization Society." Even some supporters expressed reservations, worried that voters' hostility to temperance and colonization would doom his campaign. Grimké, however, refused to compromise his principles, even if they cost him the election. He decried partisanship and insisted that the "only party I shall ever belong to [is] the Party of Principle"—the party of "independent Patriotism, the Party of my Country."[11]

That year's assembly session also failed to provide clear partisan divisions. Radicals, lacking the votes to call a state convention, reluctantly bided their time until the election of 1830 while moderates waited for Congress to convene in December 1829. With native sons Andrew Jackson and John C. Calhoun serving as president and vice president, many South Carolinians hoped the federal government would soon abandon its tariff policy. As a result, state lawmakers largely avoided divisive debates, and a Greenville editor confessed that they accomplished "very little of importance." A Columbia writer agreed that they got "little business done this Session," and a moderate observer rejoiced that "Little is said about Disunion."[12]

When Congress finally convened, a debate over public land sales ignited a dramatic battle over nullification and the nature of the Union. In December 1829, Connecticut Senator Samuel Foot proposed limiting the sale of public land in order to slow the pace of western settlement. As western senators condemned Foot's resolution, Robert Hayne seized the chance to unite the South and West against the Northeast. He entered the debate on January 19, insisting that Foot's proposal would erode the "independence of the States" and "sap the very foundations of the Government itself." Massachusetts Senator Daniel Webster responded the next day, delivering a lyrical defense of the Union. He prayed never to see America's "fraternal stripes . . . severed asunder" or its "happy constellation . . . broken up, and sink[ing], star after star, into obscurity and night!" Forced onto the defensive, Hayne responded with a forceful address on nullification. He argued that Webster's nationalism inverted the Constitution: establishing injustice, ensuring "domestic *discord*," and denying the blessings of liberty. Hayne accused him of "making war" upon South Carolina and seeking to destroy slavery and states' rights. If Webster provoked the state, he warned, "he shall have war." Hayne would meet him at the threshold and "struggle, while I have life, for our altars and our firesides."[13]

In Webster's famous "second reply to Hayne," he passionately refuted nullification, insisting the Union was "the people's government, made for the people, made by the people, and answerable to the people." The American people had preserved the Union for more than forty years, and in this moment of crisis, he hoped they would rally once more to its defense. He prayed he would never live to see the states divided or the land drenched in "fraternal blood." Instead, he hoped that his "last feeble and lingering glance" would behold the American flag without a "stripe erased or polluted, nor a single star obscured." He envisioned the flag floating over land and sea and in "every wind under the whole heaven"—an enduring testament to an ideal etched in "every true American heart—Liberty *and* Union, now and for ever, one and inseparable!"[14]

South Carolina's editors devoted entire pages to the Webster-Hayne debate. Radicals celebrated Hayne's "triumphant vindication of Southern character," and they hoped the whole country would soon embrace nullification. News from Washington that spring, however, underscored the state's growing isolation. The uneasy alliance between Jackson and Calhoun began unraveling almost immediately, as the men disagreed on many of the era's defining political issues. Tensions came to a head in April 1830 at a public dinner celebrating Thomas Jefferson's birthday. Calhoun's allies controlled the program, and they drafted toasts condemning "unequal taxation" and celebrating Jefferson's 1798 Kentucky resolution. Jackson, aware that the "celebration was to be a nullification affair," came prepared with a forceful response. When the official toasts ended, the president raised his glass and declared, "Our Union—It *must* be preserved." Calhoun steadied his hand and defiantly answered, "The Union—Next to our liberties, the most dear."[15]

Three months earlier, Daniel Webster had declared liberty and Union inseparable. Now, Calhoun hinted that they might one day become incompatible—that the Union itself might be conditional. South Carolina's radicals embraced these convictions, accusing the president of betraying their trust and denying their freedom. In response, they brazenly threatened disunion and armed resistance. Editor James Henry Hammond warned Jackson that it was useless to "appeal to our patriotism." For years, he explained, South Carolinians had patiently waited for relief; now, there was "no virtue in any thing but our own firmness." If the Union no longer protected their freedom, another writer insisted, then "the sooner it is destroyed the better."[16]

Edgefield lawyer Francis Pickens agreed, observing that disunion might be the "only means of righting our wrongs." Pickens preferred "any extreme, even war to the hilt" to a world without slavery or free trade. If Congress refused to back down, one radical insisted, "there must be blood letting—the Southern States must stand to their arms." Another writer renounced his allegiance to the Union and urged South Carolinians to secede—"peaceably if we may, forcibly if we must." In Charleston, radicals "openly avow that they not only think it time to calculate the value of the Union—but that they *have calculated* it"—and deemed it no longer worth the price.[17]

As the election of 1830 approached, James Hamilton channeled this anger into a formalized political movement. He helped organize the State Rights Party and worked with dozens of district leaders to establish newspapers, deliver speeches, and host public dinners. One opponent denounced these banquets as "eating caucus[es]," insisting that they maintained "political excitement and influence, under the pretence of hospitality." The dinners' organizers, he observed, invited a distinguished guest—"always a violent partisan"—who delivered a long, fiery speech and offered a militant resolution. Then, fueled by "zeal and wine, the audience clap hands, beat the table, rattle the glasses, and at the hint of the manager, spontaneously rise up and shout aloud . . . It is thus that the great managers of the party create matter enough to keep the columns of a nullifying paper full for a day or two."[18]

In creating this partisan movement, Nullifiers both built upon and broke with the state's political traditions. As historian Lacy Ford observes, the upcountry had long embraced competitive politics. Throughout the early 1800s, candidates actively campaigned for office by speaking at public barbecues, militia musters, and local meetings. Although political campaigns lacked "organizational sophistication," voter turnout reached 70 percent in most upcountry districts, and elections were often personal, boisterous, and competitive. In the lowcountry, however, large planters dominated small parishes with few eligible voters, and politics remained highly deferential. The nullification crisis briefly reoriented these political cultures, providing organizational clarity and replacing personal and deferential politics with partisan competition.[19]

Nullifiers championed free trade, slavery, and states' rights, insisting that South Carolina had the power to declare the tariff of 1828 null and void. Although most still revered the Union, they considered liberty and slavery far more sacred. In their minds, northern manufacturers and abolitionists had corrupted the Constitution, and only nullification could restore it to its "original purity." They appealed to honor and martial manhood and connected South Carolina's struggle to the American Revolution and that year's European uprisings. At stake, they warned, were the survival of slavery and southern "civilization." If they failed to resist, Congress would destroy their economy, emancipate their slaves, and provoke racial warfare across the South.

Union men were slower to mobilize, and they failed to match Nullifiers' organizational power. Many of the state's most prominent politicians opposed nullification, but they proved reluctant to embrace partisan politics. Instead, local leaders and newspaper editors took charge of their districts' campaigns. Editors like Benjamin Perry in Greenville, Constans Daniels in Camden, Aaron Willington in Charleston, and Abner Landrum in Edgefield reprinted and commented on each other's editorials, helping articulate a coherent Unionist ideology. Then, in the summer of 1830, diplomat Joel R. Poinsett returned to South Carolina after four years in Mexico and set about formalizing these connections. He worked with Daniel Huger, James Petigru, and other lowcountry elites to create a Union Party in Charleston, and he met and corresponded with local leaders throughout the state to help coordinate their efforts.

Independence Day offered both parties a chance to reaffirm these principles and mobilize support. The day's public celebrations followed a familiar script across the country. Each town began the morning by beating drums, ringing church bells, and firing salutes. Militia companies led their community in a grand procession, often to a local church, where a minister delivered a patriotic sermon and an orator read the Declaration of Independence.

Afterward, the crowd gathered for a public dinner, where organizers delivered thirteen official toasts celebrating the Union, the Revolution, state and national leaders, and the "Fair Sex." Volunteers then offered several dozen additional toasts, and local politicians delivered speeches celebrating the country's history. These rituals, repeated in towns across the country each year, helped cultivate Unionism and translate the ideals of the Revolution to rising generations. Organizers framed the ceremonies as unifying events and often stressed that "order and harmony prevailed."[20]

In reality, however, the events often served as platforms for communities to contest their political convictions. During the nullification crisis, they helped bring the divisions between Nullifiers and Union men into focus. In Pendleton, for example, one guest toasted the "independence of South Carolina," and another prayed the Union would endure "so long as it is worth preserving, and no longer." In Columbia, organizers declared the Union dearer than life—but "not dearer than liberty." Greenville's Nullifiers framed the American Revolution as a struggle for free trade, and they claimed that anyone who accepted the tariff was unworthy of the founders' legacy. State legislator Waddy Thompson insisted that every "Southern Patriot" should pray for disunion, and other volunteers mourned the "broken Constitution" and threatened to "partition" the Union. At a public dinner in Greenville later that month, Congressman Warren Davis dismissed Unionist beliefs as "philosophical abstractions," confessing that he could not "merge one atom of my affection for South Carolina, in a more extended love for the Federal Union." The state, he insisted, had to rely on "its own energies alone . . . for its salvation."[21]

The state's Union men used these July 4th celebrations to push back against nullification. In towns where Nullifiers controlled the official programs, Union men used volunteer toasts to affirm their principles. In Greenville, Benjamin Perry counseled patience and argued that Jackson would soon strike down the tariff. His ally Benajah Dunham insisted the "best blood of our ancestors" had cemented the Union, and no patriot would ever "estimate its value." Pendleton lawyer Samuel Maverick quipped that Nullifiers could not claim to defend the Constitution when their very principles defied it. A doctor in the same district declared the Constitution the "ark upon which our liberties rest" and prayed that the "rage of passion [would] never effect its nullification." In Spartanburg, where Union men controlled the day's program, guests warned that nullification would dissolve the Union, "blast our independence[,] and ruin our Constitution." If South Carolina left the Union, one speaker declared, Spartanburg District would secede from the state and join the neighboring counties of North Carolina.[22]

For many Union men, manhood demanded moderation, and honor required reason and restraint. They called themselves "moderate and rational men" and argued that Unionism was the only "prudent and manly course." They appealed to fathers and husbands to protect their families, warning that nullification would unleash the chaos of disunion. As Camden editor Constans Daniels explained, Union men were "unwilling to jeopard family and fortune in civil war." A Charleston editor agreed, writing that anyone who "love[d] their firesides, their altars and their children" would remain loyal to the Union. A writer calling himself *A Father* warned Charleston voters that the upcoming election would "decide the fate of your children, and of freedom." An essayist using the pen name *A Householder* agreed, urging voters to defend the Union "in the name of your wives and children, whose safety [Nullifiers] have threatened."[23]

These Union men warned that nullification would shatter the country and the social order, unleashing the chaos of the French Revolution. Nullification, one writer warned, would bring "the reign of anarchy—the temples of your religion demolished . . . your rivers stained with kindred blood, and the chastity of your females violated in their domestic altars." A Charleston essayist agreed that Nullifiers would "convert our pleasant homes into scenes of carnage and misery." Editor Aaron Willington wrote that nullification would "apply a torch to the Temple of Liberty" and destroy the "last refuge of human freedom." Edgefield planter Larkin Griffin added that it would lead to "civil and servile war" and "tear asunder all the holy bands of social life." It would consign South Carolinians' "houses, towns, and cities, to rapine and conflagration" and expose their children to the "worst evils that the mind can conceive."[24]

For Union men, emancipation ranked among the greatest "evils" of nullification. Nullifiers insisted they were defending slavery and states' rights against northern "fanaticism." Union men countered that the Constitution sanctioned slavery and that Nullifiers were emboldening their enemies by eroding the document's power. As Thomas Grimké explained, the Union provided the "only restraint" against fanaticism, and disunion would doom the South to destruction. An essayist using the pen name *A Planter* viewed nullification as a plot to "set fanatics loose among us" and remove the "security which the Laws and Constitution of the Union afford." Another writer agreed, declaring the Constitution the "only barrier" against emancipation. Without its protections, northern states would "aim at liberation" and provoke a "state of war."[25]

These arguments resonated with many voters, who feared slave rebellion and civil war. In response, Hamilton and his lieutenants began reevaluating their party's strategy, playing down nullification and simply calling for a state convention. By doing so, Nullifiers hoped to broaden their appeal, shedding the stigma of radicalism and forcing their opponents onto the defensive. If Union men stood opposed to a state convention, Nullifiers could accuse them of distrusting the people and denying their sovereign power. A Charleston writer claimed that Nullifiers "trust[ed] the people with their own government," and Greenville lawyer Waddy Thompson insisted the "people [could] judge for themselves." Edgefield's Nullifiers agreed, declaring that Union men "oppose a direct appeal to the people, and are afraid to trust them."[26]

Union Party leaders accused Nullifiers of "attack[ing] even truth itself" by disguising their intentions. Editor Abner Landrum emphasized that "Nullification is Disunion, and Disunion is War," while Judge John S. Richardson reminded voters that a convention's power was "absolute and uncontrollable." Nullifiers could use it to revolutionize the state, establish a despotic government, and even dissolve the Union. In many districts, however, Nullifiers' tactics successfully blurred the campaign issues and pressured Union men to endorse the convention. In Pendleton, for example, Union Party leader Jephtha Norton pledged his support, hoping the convention would avoid conflict with the federal government. An Edgefield meeting denounced nullification but called for a "limited convention" to petition Congress for relief. Cheraw lawyer Philip Phillips, a local Union Party leader, insisted a state convention offered the best hope of holding the country together. He claimed it would demonstrate South Carolina's resolve and peacefully pressure Congress to lower the tariff.[27]

Political excitement mounted as the fall elections approached. In Charleston's mayoral election, Union men nominated customs collector James R. Pringle to challenge radical incumbent Henry Pinckney. Hamilton observed that the city had "never seen such an animated contest," and another writer declared it the "hottest election ever contested in Charleston." Turnout soared: 1,592 men voted in the municipal election, compared with only 1,047 the year before. Pringle captured 53 percent of the city's votes, and the Union Party won control of the city council. Union men viewed the outcome as an emphatic rejection of nullification. Editor Aaron Willington observed that Charleston voters had echoed Jackson's defiant call that "Our Federal Union must be preserved." Nullifiers, however, remained confident of victory in the October statewide elections. Pinckney urged voters to "organize for another contest," and Hamilton assured them "we are not beaten."[28]

A few Nullifiers blamed the party's defeat on its tactics, arguing that the "apparent backing out of the question" of nullification had doomed them at the polls. If they had "come out openly for nullification," one writer insisted, they might have defeated Pringle and carried the day. As they prepared for the October elections, the state's most radical Nullifiers refused to temper their rhetoric. At a "great state rights celebration" in Sumter, Governor Stephen Miller declared that South Carolina had three methods of resistance: "the ballot box, the jury box and the cartouch [cartridge] box." If peaceful protest failed, he warned, the state would pursue more decisive action. In Columbia that September, Robert Barnwell Smith raged against the state's passive resistance, arguing that South Carolina had to immediately "settle the question of submission, or resistance." The Union, he thundered, "must be dissolved under its present course of administration," and if that belief made him a traitor, "then gentlemen, I am a Disunionist!—I am a Traitor!"[29]

These Nullifiers underscored the looming threat to slavery. Hamilton declared the current crisis a "battle at the out-posts": if the state "succeeded in repulsing the enemy," he assured voters, then *the citadel would be safe.*" If South Carolinians tamely accepted the tariff, however, then Congress would establish colonization societies in the state, encourage emancipation, and raise the "standard of servile revolt." Hammond warned that the American Colonization Society was growing stronger every day, and "unless soon put down, [it] must ere long deluge this land in blood." He argued that antislavery radicals were watching South Carolina's elections. The Union Party, he said, was unwilling to "protect the rights and honor of the state," and its triumph would embolden northern fanatics to renew their struggle, destroy the South, and inspire the "midnight horrors of a servile war."[30]

To ensure Nullifiers' victory, party leaders organized Committees of Vigilance in every ward in Charleston and tasked them with "defeat[ing] any maneuvers of the opposition party." They urged voters to sacrifice "all personal prejudice and preference" and support the "whole Ticket without division." Although rural Nullifiers could not match the city's political mobilization, they adopted many of the same techniques. They hosted dinners, distributed political pamphlets, and published a torrent of essays and editorials. Among the most famous of these pamphlets was Maria Pinckey's *Quintessence of Long Speeches,* a "political catechism" that distilled abstract principles into accessible questions and answers. Pinckney viewed the federal government merely as an "agent of the Sovereign States," and she framed nullification as a peaceful and constitutional remedy. The moment South Carolina declared itself free, she insisted, the "General Government must recede." She denounced Daniel Webster's nationalist rhetoric, writing that Americans fought the Revolution not so "the colonies might be united, but [so] that the colonies might be free."[31]

Union men responded with their own meetings, pamphlets, and editorials. Greenville's Benjamin Perry published a thousand copies of George Washington's farewell address, which celebrated the Union as the "palladium of [Americans'] political safety and prosperity." In Charleston, the local Union Party urged the "friends of Constitutional liberty and of public order" to fight to preserve the Union. Meetings in Chester, Laurens, Sumter, and Spartanburg overwhelmingly rejected nullification. A Spartanburg writer claimed, with some exaggeration, that only one man in the entire district openly avowed nullification. Upcountry farmers, he observed, "yield to *none* in their devotion to the country—their *whole country,*" and they refused to destroy a Union that had been "cemented with the blood of their fathers." Emphasizing the global stakes of the crisis, a Laurens crowd warned that disunion would prove to the world that "a republic cannot exist ... that the people cannot govern themselves."[32]

Events in Europe that year added greater urgency to the nullification crisis. In July, France's conservative King Charles X issued a series of edicts restricting freedom of the press, dissolving the parliamentary Chamber of Deputies, and disenfranchising three-fourths of the French electorate. In response, Parisian students, artisans, and retired soldiers erupted in protest and struggled to uphold the country's constitutional charter. After three days of fighting, Charles X fled the city, and revolutionaries began creating a provisional government. The spirit of revolution quickly spread across Europe. In August, riots erupted in Belgium, and the country soon declared its independence from the Netherlands. In October, Swiss protestors began organizing assemblies and marches to demand constitutional reform. Poland rebelled against Russia in November, launching an unsuccessful eleven-month war for independence. Protestors in Saxony and Hanover forced their kings to grant constitutions, and central Italy rebelled against the Pope's temporal power and established the short-lived Italian United Provinces.[33]

News of France's revolution reached South Carolina in mid-September, only days after Charleston's municipal election. Editors filled their pages with news of the "transcendently interesting occurrences," and Charleston's French immigrant community hosted a public dinner celebrating the global cause of freedom. Then, on September 23, Charleston held a grand "National Celebration" to honor the revolution. The French Fusilier militia company sang "La Marseillaise" and raised France's tricolor flag over the Battery, and the city's Arsenal fired a 21-cannon salute. Fort Moultrie flew the French and American flags side-by-side, merchants dressed their ships with tricolor banners, and hundreds of men—all wearing revolutionary cockades—marched through the streets toward City Hall. Peter Foyelle, a dance master who had fled from France in the 1790s, hosted a banquet for 300 guests, who raised toasts to "La France," "Les Etats Unis," "La Carolina du Sud," and "l'Union des Peuples."[34]

Men from both parties gathered beneath France's tricolor flag to honor the "holy cause of Liberty." At Foyelle's banquet, Nullifiers James Hamilton and Robert Hayne dined alongside Union men James Petigru and Christopher Memminger and together toasted the French nation and the citizens of Paris. For decades, Americans had imagined the Union as a testament to humanity's capacity for self-government, and many viewed the European revolutions as proof that their ideals were helping liberate the world. These uprisings, however, ultimately heightened the stakes of South Carolina's crisis and intensified the divisions between the State Rights and Union parties. The parties interpreted the revolutions in fundamentally different ways, reflecting their own political and cultural ideas. Union men praised revolutionaries' moderation and restraint. They championed order, stability, and "regulated liberty" both in America and in Europe, and they equated

Nullifiers with the radical Jacobins who launched the Reign of Terror forty years earlier. Nullifiers emphasized revolutionaries' resolve and their fearless defense of freedom. They called upon South Carolinians to emulate this example—to "rise in their sovereignty" and resist the tyranny of their own federal government.[35]

Nullifiers connected their struggle to the July Revolution and encouraged voters to display the same courage and conviction. A South Carolinian visiting Paris marveled that the French people had risen in rebellion without a "single remonstrance or petition, or Convention." While southerners had endured oppressive tariffs for more than ten years, he observed, the French people had refused to wait even a few days. Hammond prayed America's leaders would "profit by the solemn example," writing that the revolution provided a "solemn warning to the rulers of every nation, that the day of absolute tyranny is past." A Richland militia company agreed, declaring the uprising a "warning to those who encroach upon the liberties of the people" and a "bright example of what citizen soldiers can do."[36]

Union men, meanwhile, used the July Revolution to champion order and restraint. At Foyelle's banquet, Petigru toasted the French people's "moderation in victory," and Memminger praised their "courage and moderation." A Charleston writer observed that "France has avoided ruin by a speedy submission to lawful government," and he pleaded with South Carolinians to do the same. Charleston merchant Rene Godard, serving as chairman of a "Meeting of the French," insisted the revolutionaries were fighting not for "licentious liberty which always degenerates into despotism; but [for] rational liberty, founded on Constitutional laws." Union men equated Nullifiers with the radical Jacobins of the first French Revolution. A Columbia writer argued that Nullifiers possessed the "ardour of Robespierre, Danton, and Marat." Another writer imagined Nullifiers abolishing habeas corpus and "dragging citizens to dungeons," like "Danton, Barras, and Robespierre over again."[37]

Party leaders fiercely contested the election of 1830. One Charleston writer called the city's workers to "come up with all your tools, to defend the sacred Union," and another urged "every man [to] come forward to the standard of his country." Violence erupted across the state as the election approached. James Henry Hammond challenged Congressman James Blair to a duel, and he later struck Camden editor Constans Daniels in the face with a bludgeon. In October 1830, a large mob surrounded Charleston editor William Gilmore Simms's office, and several men attacked him with clubs. On election day, a Charleston Nullifier attacked a Union Party voter outside the courthouse, causing blood to stream from his face. At another polling station in the city, Nullifiers "assailed" and insulted a Union man after he accused them of committing voter fraud. For Union Party leaders, this violence illustrated the vast difference between the two parties. While Nullifiers vented their "unbridled passion," Union men "conducted themselves in the most orderly and peaceful manner." Union men, they claimed, filled out their ballots at home with their families, and after casting their votes, they returned to their "domestic duties."[38]

Statewide, the election results were largely inconclusive, as the process of political alignment remained incomplete. Between 1820 and 1828, turnout in Charleston's legislative elections averaged 2,072; in 1830, it soared to 2,575. Charleston's Nullifiers, however, nominated a senatorial candidate who opposed calling a convention, and both parties endorsed William Drayton's reelection to Congress. In the contest for the city's sixteen assembly seats, four men appeared on both parties' tickets, blurring the distinctions between them. Three of these candidates easily triumphed, along with eight Union men and five Nullifiers.[39]

Election results in other districts were equally ambiguous. Many candidates refused to take a stand on the convention issue, and others supported a state convention but opposed nullification. At least seventeen of the state's forty-four districts and parishes elected candidates from both parties. Observes agreed that these results showcased the lingering power of deferential politics. In Greenville, where the Union Party gained a clear majority, Benjamin Perry still insisted that the election was not a "fair test of the strength of the two parties," because many men voted "without regard to the question." Hammond admitted that Nullifiers owed their victory in Columbia to "many local causes" and "personal considerations." An Edgefield writer went even further, suggesting that most upcountry districts were too large for "any common District feeling" to form. As a result, every "neighborhood goes for itself," and the "election is the result of a combination of the narrow feelings and prejudices of twenty-two neighborhoods." One voter, he claimed, had even told an election official to "put down the name of my neighbor, and then fill up the ticket as you please."[40]

Nonetheless, clear partisan alignments were beginning to emerge. Large gaps often separated each party's strongest and weakest candidates; in Greenville, popular Union man Wilson Cobb received 1,256 votes, while his allies Micajah Berry and John Harrison received fewer than 1,000. On the ground level, however, both parties were becoming stronger and more cohesive. At a Richland polling station, for example, the Union Party candidates each received 72 votes, while the Nullifiers each received 14. At a nearby station, Union men received 83 or 84 votes, while their adversaries all secured 9 or 10.

In the antebellum era, political parties often printed and distributed ballots themselves, with the names of their candidates already filled out. The compactness of these election results suggests that voters had adopted party tickets throughout much of the state. Both parties urged voters to act upon principle rather than deference, and many men apparently took this message to heart. In the past three state elections, turnover in the lower house averaged 56 percent. In 1830, it rose to 67 percent, and several popular lawmakers lost reelection bids after falling out of step with their constituents.[41]

When the state assembly convened in November 1830, Nullifiers controlled both houses but fell short of the two-thirds majority needed to call a state convention. The final vote came in as 23 to 18 in the senate and 60 to 56 in the house. Nonetheless, Nullifiers easily elected James Hamilton as governor, Stephen Miller as US Senator, and Henry Pinckney as state speaker of the house. One Union man observed that the "Convention party is well disciplined, and carry almost every election, from that of US Senator down to those for Tax Collectors." Another writer complained that, "if a doorkeeper is to be elected, an enquiry will be made whether he is for or against Convention." While one lawmaker optimistically believed the "friends of peace and the Union have the majority," he confessed that Union men were "not organized and drilled so well as the ultras."[42]

Daniel Huger led the Union Party's resistance in the lower house. On the second day of the session, Nullifiers moved to unseat Charleston Union man Rene Goddard, whose landholdings fell short of the legislature's 500-acre requirement. Huger eloquently defended him but to no avail. When Nullifiers proposed creating a standing Committee on Federal Relations, Huger once again objected, denouncing the measure as a plot to advance nullification. Robert Barnwell Smith dismissed these fears as a "mere chimera, conjured up by [Huger's] heated imagination," and the house overwhelmingly approved the committee. Pinckney filled it with Nullifiers, who drafted a series of resolutions calling for action. The first three—passed unanimously—reaffirmed South Carolinians' "warm attachment" to the Union. The committee then declared that each state could "judge for itself" whether Congress had violated the Constitution and could choose the "mode and measure of redress." This passed by a vote of 93 to 31. A final resolution warned that, once the state had "lost all reasonable hope of redress," it had the "right and duty to interpose in its sovereignty" and resist oppression.[43]

Huger responded with a set of Unionist resolutions, insisting that individual states lacked the power to nullify federal laws. He reminded legislators that the eyes of the world rested upon them. Their fathers had fought the Revolution to prove that "man might be free, and was capable of self-government." Nullification, however, would demonstrate that "freedom was but a phantom," and that "liberty must degenerate into licentiousness." Huger defended majority rule and warned that nullification would give a small minority the power to paralyze the government. South Carolina, he observed, stood on the precipice: "one step forward, and we are lost—lost forever to the Union." He asked lawmakers if they were willing to abandon the "hope of civilized man"—the country that had "lighted our steps to prosperity." If so, he concluded, then "our fathers were the last of American patriots."[44]

Camden lawyer William McWillie echoed these appeals and presented a dire vision of South Carolina's future. He warned that nullification would dissolve the Union and reduce the state to "utter desolation." It would destroy America's prosperity and political freedom and empower tyrants to rise over the "ruins of liberty." The glory and heroism of the American Revolution would "no longer be our history," and the American flag—the symbol of the states' unity and strength—would "no longer be our standard." Nullifiers would trample that flag into the dust, and "all that has been said of it in rhetoric, in poetry, and in song [would] be heard no more." McWillie viewed the Union as the "world's last hope," and he prayed its example would inspire humanity to strive for freedom. If America remained true to itself, he predicted, its fields would produce golden harvests, its commerce would spread to every ocean, and its people would "go forward, gloriously and forever, with freedom's soil beneath our feet, and freedom's banner . . . the banner of the union, proudly streaming o'er us."[45]

As 1830 ended, some Union men expressed hope for the country's future. Greenville editor Benjamin Perry sought to put the year's political excitement behind him, insisting the election had thwarted nullification. In Camden, Constans Daniels agreed that the election results had vindicated the Union Party and ensured the country's salvation. Daniel Huger, however, realized that the crisis was only beginning. He informed a friend that the Union Party "may be permitted to rest for a time, but ... if we do not exert ourselves, we shall yet be beaten." The "attacking party," he observed, always had the advantage, because it could bide its time and choose when to strike. The "defensive" Union Party "must always be ready or we may be surprised and beaten." Many Nullifiers, meanwhile, agreed with James Henry Hammond's assessment: they had "lost their leading measure, but they have fully and triumphantly sustained their principles." Across the state, Nullifiers were "eager for another election." Two years earlier, the state house of representatives had rejected Butler's convention resolution by a vote of 40 to 81; this time, Smith's more radical resolution had secured a narrow 60 to 56 majority. Nullifiers were gaining strength and momentum, and they looked forward to 1832 certain of success.[46]

Despite their confidence, South Carolina remained bitterly divided. The tariff of 1828 had shattered the state's political alliances and given rise to loose radical and moderate factions. Hamilton, Pinckney, and their allies then channeled the state's fury into a partisan organization, establishing committees throughout Charleston and coordinating with local leaders across the state. Nullifiers produced a relentless series of public dinners, speeches, pamphlets, and editorials. Slowly, and often reluctantly, moderates responded with their own Unionist organization. The process of political alignment was incomplete in October 1830, and deferential politics maintained a powerful hold. Even so, that election marked a clear turning point in the state's political history. As the assembly adjourned that December—unable to call a convention—a few South Carolinians hoped that the crisis had passed. Most, however, looked forward to 1832, realizing that the state's greatest test still lay ahead.

3.

Contesting Manhood

Partisanship and Political Violence, 1830–32

As Benjamin Perry paced the dueling ground on August 6, 1832, his mind was "constantly kept on the object in view." His opponent, Turner Bynum, was a Charleston Nullifier who had founded a rival newspaper in Greenville less than two months earlier. The two editors' political debates had quickly grown personal, and on August 4, Bynum had accused Perry of unmanly "subserviency" to Charleston's Union Party leaders. Perry immediately challenged him to a duel, and their choice of seconds underscored the political nature of the dispute. Perry selected local Union men Andrew Crook and Perry Duncan, while Bynum recruited Columbia Nullifier James Henry Hammond. Preparing for death, Perry drafted a farewell letter to the people of Greenville, defending his conduct and accusing local Nullifiers of conspiring to "get rid of me." Too "cowardly to meet me themselves on the field of honor," he wrote, they had enlisted Bynum—a "desperate adventurer without name or reputation . . . who will fight for any one."[1]

They met on an island on the Tugaloo River, on the border between South Carolina and Georgia. Their seconds measured the dueling ground, handed the men their pistols, and commanded them to take their places. Perry later insisted that he felt "cool, firm, and collected, never more so in my life." Bynum fired first, his shot cutting through Perry's coat. Perry returned fire a moment later, striking Bynum just above the hip. The young Nullifier dropped his pistol, reeled backwards, and fell into Hammond's arms. Bynum died the following evening, and Hammond and his friends carried his body to the Old Stone Church in nearby Pendleton. Church leaders refused burial to anyone killed in a duel, so Hammond buried him by torchlight just outside the cemetery walls. As news of Bynum's death spread, Perry fiercely defended his actions, observing that he "could not avoid [the duel] without sacrificing character and usefulness in life." In South Carolina's honor-obsessed culture, he had to "fight for my principles or be disgraced," and he returned home confident that Nullifiers would never "impose on me again."[2]

After the state legislature adjourned in December 1830, both parties redoubled their efforts, consolidating their strength and preparing for the pivotal election of 1832. In village squares and city drawing rooms, they debated the meaning of manhood, the impact of Europe's simmering revolutions, and the fate of liberty at home and abroad. Nullifiers attacked Union men as traitors, Tories, and "submissionists," and their responses revealed deep fractures in the Union Party's gender culture. Many Union men continued to uphold moderate manhood, warning that nullification would provoke "civil and servile war." Others, like Benjamin Perry, espoused martial manhood, fighting back against nullification and violently defending their honor.

These gender divisions intensified the state's political conflict even as they hindered the Union Party's ability to mount an effective organizational challenge to nullification. As they had throughout the crisis, moderate Union men decried partisanship and warned that "Jacobinical" political clubs would destabilize the social order. Martial Union men, however, often embraced partisanship and political violence, insisting they could only defeat nullification by confronting its followers. As the election of 1832 approached, small-scale violence erupted across the state as both parties warned that electoral defeat would herald disaster. Armed mobs roamed the streets of Charleston, political rivals dueled and brawled in the streets, and the violence led one witness to declare that the "war of Nullification has already commenced."[3]

Governor James Hamilton understood the cyclical nature of political engagement, and in the spring of 1831—with the next state election nearly two years away—he feared his party's energies would flag. He urged the state's editors to remain focused on the tariff, reminding them of the "great peril of permitting public feeling to collapse." Nullifiers, he observed, "must have a rally on some firm ground and then stand manfully to our arms." He hoped to maintain an "animated discussion" across the state and ensure the "closest cohesion of our party." Looking ahead to the next assembly session that November, he hoped the state's lawmakers would "take the strongest ground [that] public opinion will justify" but *"not go beyond it."* Although the governor privately believed voters would *"act* as their leaders *think,"* he recognized that party organizers needed to work carefully and deliberately to ensure their victory.[4]

Over the next two years, Nullifiers hosted more than 300 banquets and meetings across the state, creating an almost permanent atmosphere of political excitement. At a dinner in Charleston in May 1831, Nullifiers toasted the "Disciples of Liberty throughout the world" and celebrated the global spirit of reform. Its flame, they observed, "has been kindled in the Old World," and they prayed it would "not be extinguished in the New." One guest urged South Carolinians to defend their rights with cartridge boxes as well as ballot boxes, and another called for "Convention, Nullification, Disunion—any thing rather than submission to tyranny." Congressman George McDuffie, a former nationalist, mocked their opponents for whining that "the Union, the Union, the Union is in danger." The Union, he insisted, had become a "foul monster," and pleas for its preservation only emboldened federal tyrants. Appealing to the crowd's honor and manhood, he asked how South Carolinians could be "terrified by mere phantoms of blood" when their fathers had fought and won a revolution. "Great God!" he exclaimed, "are we men—grown men—to be frightened from the discharge of our sacred duty" by the Union men's "nursery tales."[5]

The Charleston banquet infuriated Vice President John C. Calhoun, who believed that it brought "matters to a crisis." Duff Green, a close ally and editor of *The United States Telegraph,* asked Hamilton if they "were all crazy at McDuffie's dinner" and if they "intended to start into open rebellion." Calhoun had never publicly endorsed nullification, afraid it would destroy his presidential ambitions. He had strongly opposed "active [party] operations that summer," begging Nullifiers to "keep things quiet." Hamilton and his lieutenants, however, refused to back down. By the summer of 1831, with the party pushing for action, Calhoun realized he could no longer remain silent. On July 26, he published his Fort Hill Address, defending nullification and denouncing majority rule as "unjust and absurd." He argued that the Constitution empowered Congress to legislate on national questions but left "peculiar and local" issues to the states. When the federal government overstepped these bounds, he wrote, the states had a solemn duty to intervene.[6]

Nullifiers grew bolder as they built momentum, and in July 1831, they turned many of the state's Independence Day celebrations into partisan rallies. Fifteen hundred Nullifiers paraded through Charleston, carrying banners that demanded "Resistance to oppression" and "Millions for defence, not a cent for tribute." Author Maria Pinckney and two hundred "State Rights Ladies" presented a flag to the crowd, affirming their devotion to the state's "prosperity, safety, and honor." The men then marched to Charleston's Circular Church, where Robert Hayne delivered a fiery address defending state sovereignty. At most July 4 celebrations, local leaders read the Declaration of Independence; instead, Charleston's Nullifiers chose the Virginia and Kentucky Resolutions, a defiant statement of their party's principles. In Barnwell, Edisto, Lancasterville, Pendleton, and dozens of other towns, Nullifiers called for radical action. They drank toasts to "Disunion" and called the federal government an "instrument of oppression." They insisted that patience under tyranny was rebellion against God, and they vowed to resist the "unjust government at any and every hazard."[7]

With the European uprisings still smoldering, organizers often framed nullification as a global struggle for freedom and reform. In Sumter, party leaders devoted three of the thirteen regular toasts to the European revolutions, celebrating Polish patriots for their determination to "live free or die." Columbia Nullifiers claimed that Poland's struggle demonstrated how much a "united People" could accomplish against overwhelming odds. When King Charles X violated his country's constitutional charter, Henry Pinckney observed, the French people had "risen in their might and hurled him from [his] throne." Soon after, Polish and Belgian revolutionaries had launched their own wars for freedom and independence. Now, Pinckney claimed, South Carolinians faced a far greater tyranny, and the only relief lay in their own resolution.[8]

In the ensuing months, Governor James Hamilton worked with district leaders to establish a vast network of State Rights Associations, hoping to achieve the "concert so essential to effective political action." Charleston's chapter first met in August 1831, and dozens of local organizations soon followed. Nullifiers established chapters even in districts like Greenville and Spartanburg, where they had little chance of success. No matter how "fearful the odds against you now are," one writer insisted, the party's principles would eventually triumph. These State Rights Associations distributed thousands of pamphlets and public documents in order to "diffuse correct information" and "promote the blessings of Free Trade." Executive committees in each district managed local party business and corresponded with other chapters, and twice each year they attended statewide party conventions.[9]

Nullifiers called themselves the state's "true Carolinians" and insisted the Union Party was filled with Yankees and traitors. When the "history of the present time is written," Calhoun's niece Lucretia Townes observed, Union men "will be branded as *tories, traitors,* and many other epithets equally deserving." They labeled Aaron Willington's *Charleston Courier* the "Boston Courier published in Charleston" and Jacob Cardozo's *Southern Patriot* the "Northern Patriot." They accused Camden editor Constans Daniels of being a "hireling Yankee editor" and an "Alien enemy." Even Daniel Huger and William Drayton, whose families had lived in South Carolina for generations, were "branded with Northernism" for refusing to support nullification. Greenville Nullifiers warned northern-born residents to act as "Carolinians, not enemies in our camp," and Charleston's party leaders attacked the "enemies of Carolina at home and abroad." They rallied voters with cries to "Rescue Charleston from the imputation of being a Northern city . . . Wipe off the stain of being governed and controlled by Federal officers."[10]

Union men accused Nullifiers of "railing and bandying epithets," using fear, passion, and "wretched sophistry" to manipulate the state's voters. For Nullifiers, they observed, mere "declamation supplies the deficiencies of argument, and reason is lost in . . . vehement eloquence." Union men defended their loyalty and civic devotion, insisting that South Carolina was *"our home."* As a Charleston essayist explained, Union men's "homes, fortunes, and children are a part of Carolina," and they would always uphold the state's true interests. Ultimately, however, they were "also *American,"* and they refused to let Nullifiers shatter the Union or erode their Constitutional freedom. The Charleston essayist fiercely proclaimed that the *"native born, home bred patriots of South Carolina* will amply sustain the Union."[11]

Many Union Party leaders continued to champion moderate manhood. They framed nullification as a generational struggle, insisting that reckless young men without family or fortune were driving the state toward chaos. South Carolina's older, established family men, meanwhile, remained loyal to the Union and pleaded for peace. As one writer observed, men with "large families" and "great property" had more at stake and were therefore more committed to the "peace and welfare of the country." A Charleston worker insisted that anyone who "love[d] your country and its laws, [who] love[d] your families, and their peace and happiness," would rally to the Union Party's ranks. At stake, another writer observed, was the "harmony of society—the security of property . . . the integrity of the Union—all that we hold dear to ourselves and our children." The "cause of rational regulated liberty throughout the world" hung in the balance.[12]

In coastal St. Luke's Parish, Union men draped the American flag over the courthouse and swore to "restrain the impulses of discord" in their state. They rooted their Unionism in moderate manhood, warning that nullification was destroying the social order. Already, they observed, the "ties of friendship are severed—the maternal face is pale with anxiety—and the father trembles for the destiny of his children." While Nullifiers demanded radical action, these Union men hoped to "reason, remonstrate, and take peaceful counsel together." They declared themselves the "constitutional guardians of Liberty," and they stood "forever opposed to Revolution." Rather than organize their parish, however, these Union men warned that "Political Clubs are highly dangerous to liberty," and they vowed to work with "any Party, heart and hand," to lower the tariff.[13]

When Nullifiers taunted them as "submissionists," moderate Union men redefined the term to celebrate their reason and restraint. Camden editor Constans Daniels boldly declared that "We *are* submission men," because they submitted to the law, the Constitution, and the "voice of the majority of the nation." Aaron Willington agreed, writing that Union men's "submission is to the laws, and we deem this the first duty, and the highest honor of a good citizen." Petigru insisted that patriotism made "obedience honorable," and a Columbia editor celebrated the "patriotic submissionist to the laws of his country." A Georgetown writer observed that Union men were "not ashamed to say that we are submissionists," and he described America's fragile republican experiment as the "most successful effort ever made in the cause of rational liberty." For these men, submission to the Constitution did not diminished their manhood; it confirmed it. As true, moderate men, they upheld the social and political order and obeyed the nation's just laws.[14]

These Union men compared the State Rights Associations to the Jacobin clubs of the French Revolution. Petigru insisted that Beaufort's "Jacobinical" planters sought to destroy the social order, and Constans Daniels agreed that Nullifiers would consecrate their victory on the "bloody steps of the Guillotine." William Smith declared the State Rights Associations the "germ of a Revolution." He warned that political clubs had brought the "monster Robespierre into power" forty years earlier and soaked the streets of Paris with blood. Jacobins had "laid waste all Europe, and placed a despot upon the throne of France," and the same fate awaited South Carolina if they allowed nullification to triumph.[15]

This caution exposed fractures in the party's gender culture, as younger, more militant Union men called for action. A Charleston writer claimed that young men were drawn to the State Rights Party because it welcomed their talents and encouraged their ambition. The Union Party, however, was guided by *"prudent old gentlemen"* who "repulsed and rejected" young voters and "chilled [the movement] to the heart." Reminding readers of Europe's smoldering revolutions, he declared the Union the "citadel of regulated freedom" throughout the world, and he insisted that its future "depends not on trimmers and fence men." With a crisis approaching, the Union "must be saved as it was gained, by men who never fear to show their *colors, and nail them to the mast."*[16]

Benjamin Perry, similarly, realized that the State Rights Associations were a "powerful engine" that allowed Nullifiers to build support in every corner of the state. If Union men failed to "make some show of resistance," he warned, they would cede the ground and allow Nullifiers to triumph. He urged every man in Greenville to gather at the courthouse to reject nullification and defend the Union—the "last hope of human liberty." Although William Smith decried the State Rights Associations, he ultimately encouraged Union men to "take up the line of march . . . and call meetings of the people ourselves." Spurred to action, martial Union men like Perry established newspapers, hosted dozens of meetings and public dinners, and created committees of correspondence to coordinate their efforts.[17]

Both parties warned that defeat would herald social and political disaster, and the Nat Turner rebellion vividly demonstrated the stakes of the crisis. In August 1831, Turner launched one of the deadliest rebellions in American history, killing about sixty white men, women, and children in Southampton County, Virginia. Slave panics swept across the South Carolina upcountry, gripping Greenville, Abbeville, York, Newberry, and Laurens, as residents feared that "large bodies of slaves were about to invade the State." Families fled their homes, hiding in fields or forests or village arsenals, and men and women lay awake at night haunted by fears of insurrection. In response, Governor James Hamilton turned over the state's public arms and ammunitions to Major General Robert Hayne for "instantaneous distribution in any quarter of the state." Marion District organized a vigilance company to serve "under arms, day and night," and Spartanburg officials moved a cannon to the courthouse to protect the village. Union District arrested fifty slaves for plotting a "general rise," and Abbeville executed at least one man for allegedly planning to "raise an insurrection."[18]

Nullifiers blamed the panic on northern antislavery "fanatics" and used it to militarize the state. Abbeville's civic leaders asked for money to build a new arsenal, citing the dangerous "situation of the people of this state, with an enemy at their very firesides . . . prompted to mischief by [abolitionists]." Hamilton claimed that "incendiary newspapers" had inspired Nat Turner's rebellion and undermined slavery throughout the South. In his annual message, he asked lawmakers to increase military spending to help maintain "good order" in the state. He hoped to create a "Corps of Dragoons" in each district and add additional cavalry companies in the lowcountry's slave-dense parishes. The cavalry, he observed, could move at a "moment's warning," and within twelve hours, a half-dozen companies could concentrate their forces with "overwhelming power and effect."[19]

Union men, meanwhile, blamed the 1831 insurrection panic on the "discussion of nullification at barbecues, dinner speeches, stump speeches, court yards, and every meeting of a few neighbors." As one writer explained, the "high toned language of liberty or death, shouldering of muskets, &c" had "excited effects in either race . . . that might end in serious consequences." While Nullifiers claimed that northern "fanatics" were inspiring rebellion, Union men countered that most northerners opposed abolition. Northern editors and statesmen, they observed, had decried Nat Turner's rebellion and offered to send men and money to help Virginia restore "order." Some Boston residents, for example, pledged to "march at a moment's warning" and "fly to [southerners'] aid." For Union Party editors, these responses proved that the Union's affective bonds were as strong as ever—that the cooperative spirit of 1776 would "prevail whenever it is called for."[20]

Nonetheless, the insurrectionary panic emboldened Nullifiers and fueled partisan tensions. With no statewide elections in 1831, Charleston's municipal elections became a test of party strength, and voter turnout reached new heights. Both parties ran complete tickets, with Henry Pinckney once again challenging incumbent James Pringle for city intendant. By all accounts, the campaign was the "most animated political struggle" the city had ever witnessed. As one writer observed, the parties held so many banquets that "a man might have lived comfortably for a week or ten days preceding the election, without being a cent out of pocket." The previous year, 1,600 men had cast ballots, with Pringle capturing 53 percent of the vote and the Union Party gaining control of the city council. This time, turnout soared to 1,972, and Nullifiers swept the election. Pinckney mobilized nearly 300 new voters, giving him 53 percent of the city's vote.[21]

Union men accused Nullifiers of stealing the election through bribery and fraud. The State Rights Party, they insisted, preyed on poorer voters—the men "least able to assert their independence." While both parties paid men to vote, Petigru complained that Nullifiers bought "those that were sold before"— dishonorably bribing men who had already pledged their votes to the Union Party. Nullifiers also practiced "new and unheard of means," keeping men drunk and locked up until election day or breaking into houses to drag reluctant voters to the polls. They hired men devoted to the "craft of electioneering" who possessed few "scruples of conscience." Even some Nullifiers believed their party had gone too far. Disgusted by his party's tactics, Baptist minister Basil Manly refused to vote in the election, and his church excommunicated one member for being a "violent partisan and bully in the late election."[22]

Taking stock of the Union Party's defeat, Petigru confessed that Nullifiers "outdid us in maneuvering." A Charleston editor observed that Nullifiers had "gain[ed] by discipline what they [lacked] in numbers," and Benjamin Perry agreed, hoping the election would "inspire the Union party with more zeal and activity." Another writer urged Union men across the state to build up their own political network. The "violent party," he observed, employed "every sort of machinery" and formed State Rights Associations in "every nook and corner of the State." The Union Party had a duty to respond—to "rouse itself to a concerted and energetic action." He asked local leaders to found district-level organizations and elect delegates to a statewide party convention, which would allow them to "harmonise in action and meet the enemy with a concert as united as its own."[23]

February 22, 1832—George Washington's one hundredth birthday—gave both parties a chance to reflect on the crisis and contest the Union's history and ideals. Nullifiers organized a party convention in Charleston, drawing representatives from almost every district in the state. Several thousand people filled the city's amphitheater, which party leaders had adorned with flags, Palmetto trees, and portraits of the state's political leaders. Addressing the crowd, James Hamilton laid claim to Washington's legacy, insisting that his "life [is] our vindication." He imagined Washington as a paragon of martial manhood, emphasizing his Revolutionary War service rather than his time as president. He reminded the crowd that Washington fought a war against "unjust and unconstitutional taxation," and he hoped that same "invincible spirit of resistance" would guide Nullifiers through the crisis.[24]

That same day, Thomas Grimké dedicated a political pamphlet to the American people, celebrating their "good sense, love of order, and unchangeable devotion to the Union." The United States, he declared, "must and shall be perpetual," and he urged readers to "cultivate the spirit of peace" and the "law of love." Union Party lawyer Hugh Legaré, meanwhile, delivered an eloquent speech in Charleston's St. Philip's Church. While Nullifiers made Washington a symbol of martial resistance, Legaré imagined him as a model of moderation and statesmanship. After the Revolution, he observed, Washington and his "discontented army" could have plunged the country into civil war. Instead, the general resigned his power, presided over the Constitutional Convention, and helped forge a more perfect Union. Washington's life had proven that "people [were] capable of self-government," and Legaré urged Union men to uphold those same principles of peace and patriotism.[25]

Then, in July 1832, Congress passed a new tariff law, lowering average import duties from 50 percent to 25 percent. The bill received a two-thirds majority in both houses, and South Carolina's three Union Party congressmen—William Drayton, James Blair, and Thomas Mitchell—all voted in favor. Mitchell pleaded for moderation, denouncing Nullifiers and protectionists alike for allowing "abstract principles" to endanger the Union. He argued that statesmen had a duty to "soothe, to reconcile, and to satisfy"—to find peaceful resolutions to the country's struggles. Drayton compared nullification to the "ravages of a whirlwind" and felt a responsibility to "stop the torrent, which threatens to sweep away the very foundation of social and civil union." He hoped the new tariff would restore harmony and give hope to the "friends of rational liberty, in the old and in the new world."[26]

Although the new tariff still protected northern manufacturing, most

Union men viewed it as a reasonable compromise. They recognized that ending protection altogether could wreak havoc on the northern economy, and they assured voters that the law heralded the return of peace and "national happiness." Local leaders organized dinners and rallies honoring Drayton, Mitchell, and Blair and praising their "manly" and "fearless" votes. Nullifiers, however, viewed the tariff as an unmanly concession of principle. By voting for the tariff, Greenville's Tandy Walker explained, southerners had "yield[ed] the whole ground" and sealed the region's fate. Congressional Nullifiers drafted an address declaring that all hope of relief had "finally and forever vanished," and Calhoun observed that the "question is no longer one of free trade, but liberty and despotism." Across the state, party meetings denounced the Union Party congressmen as traitors and defiantly vowed to accept "no compromise."[27]

Officially, the State Rights Party continued to champion nullification as the "great conservative principle"—the only means of safeguarding liberty within the Union. Most Nullifiers still hoped to preserve the Union as they understood it: as a loose confederation of sovereign states. The political center, however, was shifting closer to radicalism. Two years earlier, party leaders tried to broaden their appeal by playing down nullification and calling only for an unpledged convention. Now, Nullifiers in most districts openly demanded nullification, and a growing number contemplated disunion. One lowcountry politician, for example, warned that the "first drop of Carolina blood that is spilt dissolves the Union forever." Robert Turnbull confessed that nullification could lead to civil war and declared that anyone too scared to fight for their liberty lacked "souls big enough for the crisis." Pendleton's Armistead Burt agreed, insisting that anyone who "count[ed] the cost of being free" deserved to be enslaved.[28]

A Columbia writer proclaimed unequivocally that "THIS UNION MUST BE DISSOLVED." Sectional tension, he explained, had grown too intense, and any attempt at compromise would only "prolong the life of tyranny." He looked to France's July Revolution for inspiration. In three days, he observed, France had thrown off its despotic government and secured constitutional freedom, and the same glorious destiny awaited South Carolina. He promised that "less than three days are sufficient for you to effect all you desire." If South Carolinians rose "in their sovereignty and [spoke] the fiat 'We will be free,'" then the chains of tyranny would fall at their feet.[29]

Nullifiers' Independence Day celebrations echoed these defiant calls for revolution. In Charleston, Robert Turnbull prepared his audience to hazard disunion by invoking America's War for Independence. The state's Revolutionary heroes, he observed, had braved every danger in defense of freedom, preferring the "tempestuous sea of liberty" to the "calm of despotism." He quoted Patrick Henry's stirring call for resistance, thundering, "Give me Liberty or give me Death." A Camden volunteer toasted the "Boston Nullifiers" who threw British tea into their harbor and helped launch the Revolution, and he assured the crowd that the spirit of liberty would lead them to the "same triumphant results." In Walterboro, the official toasts celebrated George Washington as a "Rebel, a Disunionist, a Revolutionist" and declared the Union a chain binding political slaves to their oppressors. In another lowcountry parish, two guests announced that they preferred disunion and civil war to submission. Seven men in a row offered toasts to "Nullification—the rightful remedy," with each receiving nine boisterous cheers.[30]

With the election of 1832 approaching, Nullifiers spared no expense in their efforts to mobilize the state. In the spring of 1832, Governor James Hamilton embarked on a six-week inspection tour of the state's militia companies, and he turned the reviews into a series of partisan rallies. In every village, huge crowds turned out to watch the militia parade and hear local leaders deliver speeches. Hamilton consciously adopted a "plain style," framing his arguments about liberty and sovereignty in terms every voter could understand. His lieutenants produced monthly pamphlets, and Hamilton advised them to pursue a "more popular and less abstract character . . . [so] that they may be brought down to the comprehension of every freeman in the South." In 1831, for example, they began publishing a *State Rights and Free Trade Almanac* to ground political resistance in domestic duty. The almanac provided "moral and political maxims" alongside the "usual astronomical calculations and local information." Marriage advice and cures for smallpox vied for space with discussions of free trade and taxes. Tables listed the duties on "articles of daily consumption" and calculated that a family of five now paid $1 per week to "support a few overgrown manufacturers." These statistics demonstrated that the tariff was not a harmless abstraction but a tangible threat to South Carolina's families.

The almanac used gendered parables to underscore this point. In one story, a woman scolded her husband for refusing to resist the tariff. By raising duties on blankets, cloth, forks, and knives, she explained, Congress made it harder for them to feed and clothe their children. Why, she asked, "are you fool enough to let them pick your pockets in this manner?" She encouraged him to "shut the door and have no more to do" with these northern thieves. Persuaded—and shamed—the husband admitted that a "man's first concern" was his family, and if "a man neglects them, he is worse than a heretic or an infidel." He encouraged readers to "Pluck up your courage and defend your property like a man, or you are no man."[31]

Martial Union men responded to these insults by fighting back and defending their honor. Although Union men "submit to the proper government of the country," John Chesnut observed, they were "not submission men by nature." A Charleston writer swore, "*so help me God* I will never submit to the dictations of Hamilton, Hayne, McDuffie, or Calhoun." If Nullifiers "call us cowards," one essayist declared, "we answer, *try us* ... we defy you." A Union man in Camden warned that they "may yet have the opportunity to convince [South Carolina] that we are not cowards." In Columbia, Union men created an effigy of Nullification and shot it apart, and one observer declared that they would gladly fire at real Nullifiers when the time arrived.[32]

These men helped mobilize and organize the Union Party, and by the summer of 1832, they emulated many of Nullifiers tactics. They established several newspapers of their own, and editors distributed thousands of pamphlets throughout their districts. Party leaders urged men to run for office even when they were hopelessly outnumbered. Even Petigru hoped to "run a ticket in every District ... to ascertain the [party's] numerical strength" and prove to Nullifiers that "there is a minority." Chapman Levy, a Jewish lawyer and veteran of the War of 1812, reported that Camden's Union Party was "up and doing," and he encouraged lowcountry allies to focus attention on "every part of the state." In August, Levy arranged to publish an additional 12,000 newspapers each week to help "disseminate information among the people."[33]

Union men arranged their own Independence Day celebrations to push back against nullification. Twelve hundred Union men marched through Charleston that morning, with 24 stewards symbolizing the states in the Union. A choir sang an original ode celebrating the Union's inspirational power: "Even now, while all Europe is wrapt in commotion, / And the brave bleed or conquer, refusing to bow, / [Freedom] Shines forth like a beacon across the broad ocean." A minister delivered a "manly and fervent prayer," and Daniel Huger read Washington's Farewell Address, which the Union Party had embraced as a statement of party principle.[34]

At dinner afterward, ten toasts referenced the European revolutions. One guest insisted that America's example was "revolutionizing the world," and he prayed that South Carolina would not "throw an obstacle in the way." They toasted the country's republican experiment as the "world's best hope" and the "last refuge of the persecuted patriot." When the empires of Europe crumbled into dust, they hoped the Union would still "stand unshaken, the home and the refuge of liberty." President Andrew Jackson wrote a public letter for the meeting, observing that Revolutionary soldiers had pledged their lives to guarantee liberty *and* Union. He warned that disunion would lead inevitably to civil war and "colonial dependence on a foreign power," and he urged all South Carolinians to cherish an "immovable attachment" to United States.[35]

Political violence had been part of the nullification crisis from the beginning, particularly among editors and politicians. This violence, however, increased in pace and scale in 1832. A Charleston writer reported in September that duels were "frequent in these days," and Julia Brown confirmed that Nullifiers in Camden were "venting their rage in quarrels—and challenges, &c." A New England visitor believed the crisis had gone so far that reconciliation—between the parties and between the state and federal government—was impossible. In Greenville, he reported, almost every man carried a dagger and pistol, "and what is worse, they use them." Duels and brawls had become "daily occurrences." In July, after Nullifier William Choice called Benjamin Perry a coward, the young editor caned him in the street. The next day, Choice attacked Perry at the courthouse, and in the ensuing brawl Perry stabbed him three times in the chest. Then, in August, Perry killed rival editor Turner Bynum in a duel on the border between Georgia and South Carolina.[36]

In April 1832, after trading insults in their newspapers for months, Sumter editors Maynard Richardson and John Hemphill waged a "real club and dirk fight" in the streets. Spectators quickly joined in, and the scuffle devolved into a riot. Richardson stabbed Hemphill three times, and a few other participants suffered "[c]onsiderable injury." Despite Hemphill's injuries, the young Nullifier was undeterred; he continued publishing militantly partisan editorials, and his sister Eliza predicted he would soon "kill some person or be killed himself." Union Party newspapers across the state reported on the fight with headlines declaring "the war of Nullification has already commenced."[37]

One Union Party editor dismissed this "uproar and excitement" as the product of a few lazy "village politicians." He argued that farmers, merchants, and mechanics spent their peaceful days "unimpeded by political jarrings and contentious disputes about moot points." Many South Carolina voters, however, were deeply invested in the crisis and shared these political passions. Charleston Nullifiers, for example, attacked a store belonging to German immigrant (and Union man) John Shachte, throwing bricks through his windows and threatening to tear down the building. When the city guard refused to intervene, Shachte and his friends fired into the crowd and forced the men to disperse. He blamed Nullifiers for the violence and warned that, if the crowd returned, he would perform his "duty to protect myself & property."[38]

In Williamsburg, one writer later recalled, "many bloody scenes [were] enacted by the fists at the court house, at public dinners and on public highways." In the fall of 1832, the district's parties held public dinners on the same day within earshot of each other. At first, everything went smoothly, with "much talking and joking between the two factions." Before long, however, a Nullifier began taunting Union man Robert Fulton, and Fulton responded by punching him. A brawl erupted, as men from both parties rushed to their aid, and the sound of "cursing, swearing and ranting" soon filled the air. A Union Party militia captain finally broke up the fight by riding his horse through the crowd, swinging a stick and yelling at men to "Get out the way, you d——n sons of bitches."[39]

With the statewide elections only a month away, both parties looked to Charleston's municipal contest as a referendum on the crisis. Tensions flared throughout the city, and on election day, armed gangs prowled the street delivering "broken shins and bloody noses" to their enemies. One resident feared a riot would break out and that "many persons [would be] slain." He resolved to "go to the polls *prepared* and if I am assaulted I shall defend myself to the *uttermost*." Benjamin Gildersleeve, who edited a Presbyterian newspaper, reported with alarm that "bribery, and drunkenness, and perjury, and violence and fraud" had consumed the city. Laws prohibited the city guard from voting, but Intendant Henry Pinckney allegedly discharged dozens of guards the day before the election to allow them to vote. Both parties bribed men to support their candidates and locked up rival voters to keep them from the polls. The city narrowly avoided a partisan brawl after a drunken Nullifier jumped or fell to his death from the third floor of a Union Party headquarters.[40]

Nullifiers carried the day, electing their entire ticket by about 160 votes. In private, some Union men worried that the "idea that we are the weaker party has great influence in making us still weaker." Publicly, however, they vowed to redouble their efforts and challenge Nullifiers in every district and parish in the upcoming state elections. They organized countless local meetings and hosted a party convention in Columbia with delegates from across the state. They hoped to cool the "rage and passion" consuming the state, and they repeated the warnings of Washington's Farewell Address. Disunion, they insisted, would "sound the knell of Liberty in the world" and "echo through every clime, that man is unfit for self government."[41]

Events in Europe lent greater urgency to the Union Party's efforts. By 1832, Russia had overpowered the Polish kingdom, Austria had crushed the Italian provinces, and France and Belgium remained constitutional monarchies. For some observers, these events confirmed America's exceptionalism, thus proving that only the Union could harmonize law and liberty. Others, however, drew a darker lesson from the "wreck of European liberty." The Austrian and Russian Empires, they observed, had emerged from the upheaval as powerful as ever, and England and France had refused to come to the revolutionaries' aid. Tyranny, they insisted, had triumphed in Europe, and it could just as easily destroy America's republican institutions. They feared the Union might fail at the very moment that Europe most needed its example. Events in Europe underscored the fragility of America's freedom, and many feared the triumph of nullification—the failure of their republican experiment—would herald the death of liberty in America and around the world.

At stake, a Charleston lawyer warned, was "our bright example to suffering humanity." The Union, he explained, was "an asylum to all nations," offering freedom and hope to "every inhabitant of the world." Nullification, however, threatened to destroy America's "invaluable institutions" and expose its citizens to "oppressions ... far greater than those we suffer." Hugh

Legaré, a Charleston legislator who became America's first ambassador to Belgium, argued that nullification did "more to strengthen the thrones of Europe than all the armies and arts of despotism put together." Thomas Grimké added that the tyrants of Europe would "glory and exult" over the Union's destruction, and their palaces would echo with the "mockery of freedom."[42]

In September 1832, a scuffle broke out between Nullifiers and Union men over the symbols of France's July Revolution. A band of young Union men marched through the city, playing music and waving France's tricolor flag. Nullifiers intercepted and surrounded them, and the two parties wrestled for control of the flag. A city officer intervened, and Union men reluctantly surrendered the flag. Nullifiers accused them of disgracing the banner and proving unworthy of liberty. In response, a Union Party editor published an appeal to the city's French community, insisting the flag could never be "disgraced at the hands of true American Citizens."[43]

Then, days before October's statewide election, a Nullifier mob gathered outside a Union Party headquarters wielding clubs and bricks. Robert Hayne, hoping to avoid bloodshed, urged the Union men to leave the building along an empty adjacent street. When Drayton put the motion to a vote, however, the men refused to back down. They armed themselves with bludgeons and marched through the angry crowd "amidst every species of insults and abuse." Nullifiers hurled bricks and stones at them, striking Drayton, Poinsett, and Petigru, but the Union Party's leaders chose not to fight back. Retaliation, Petigru explained, would only escalate the cycle of violence. They might have "cleared the street" and won the battle, but "doubtless the parties would have met the next time with muskets."[44]

Turnout in the state elections reached at least 75 percent, and it soared as high as 90 percent in some heavily contested districts. Nullifiers received about 26,000 votes—about 60 percent of the state's total—and drew their greatest strength from the western districts between Columbia and the Georgia border. They secured at least 85 percent of the votes in Newberry, Orangeburg, Fairfield, and Lexington Districts. The Union Party, meanwhile, secured about 17,000 votes and polled particularly well in the state's northern districts along the border with North Carolina. The party won at least 58 percent of the vote in Greenville, Spartanburg, Lancaster, Chesterfield, Darlington, Kershaw, and Horry (Table 2).

TABLE 2. Election Results, 1832

District	Nullifier Votes	Nullifier Percentage	Union Party Votes	Union Party Percentage	Estimated Turnout (%)
Abbeville	1,666	64	946	36	78
Anderson	1,503	73	562	27	78
Barnwell	1,101	65	595	35	76
Beaufort	622	86	105	14	51
Charleston	2,028	55	1,675	45	69
Chester	1,096	59	757	41	82
Chesterfield	343	38	559	62	77
Colleton	433	67	212	33	51
Darlington	497	42	698	58	81
Edgefield	1,629	72	640	28	72
Fairfield	1,747	94	103	6	82
Georgetown	348	61	221	39	104
Greenville	500	28	1,311	72	77
Horry	58	14	363	86	57
Kershaw	358	37	603	63	83
Lancaster	439	41	632	59	78
Laurens	1,482	60	985	40	90
Lexington	624	100	0	0	56
Marion	772	61	500	39	82
Marlboro	271	100	0	0	29
Newberry	1,156	89	137	11	63
Orangeburg	873	86	145	14	61
Pickens	991	59	694	41	73
Richland	783	75	259	25	76
Spartanburg	833	31	1,839	69	78
Sumter	983	56	776	44	84
Union	1,352	71	549	29	83
Williamsburg	283	50	283	50	88
York	1,116	51	1,062	49	86
Total	25,887	60	17,211	40	75

Sources: 1830 United States Census; issues of the *Charleston Mercury, Charleston Courier,* and *Greenville Mountaineer* for October 1832.

Methodology: Using the 1830 census, the author estimated the total number of voters in 1832 by adding up all men in the "20 to 29," "30 to 39," "40 to 49," "50 to 59," "60 to 69," "70 to 79," "80 to 89," "90 to 99," and "over 100" categories and prorating the "15 to 19" category.

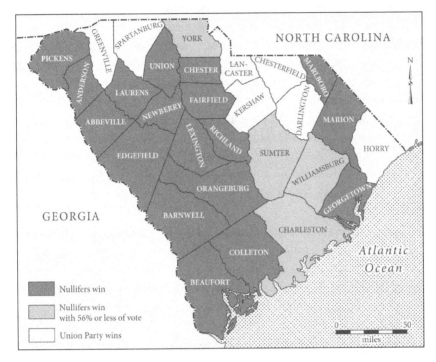

South Carolina Election Results, 1832

The state's partisan reorientation, incomplete two years earlier, had now solidified. Pendleton editor Frederick Symmes reported that, for the first time in living memory, the election had "turned exclusively on a political question." The "compactness of the vote throughout the district," he observed, "proves this to have been the case." In most districts, voters had clearly adopted party tickets. In Richland, for example, the four Nullifiers received between 776 and 783 votes, while three Union Party candidates received between 232 and 237 votes. In Charleston, the parties fielded tickets for the state legislature as well as for local elections like the commissioner of the poor and commissioner of crossroads.[45]

Governor Hamilton wasted little time, ordering a special session of the new legislature to convene on October 22—only two weeks after the elections. On October 26, lawmakers called for a state convention: elections would take place on November 12, and the convention would come together a week later. The house approved the convention bill by a vote of 96 to 25, and the senate concurred 31 to 13. Four years earlier, less than one-third of the state's legislators had supported a state convention; now, nearly 77 percent approved it. While Columbia's Nullifiers celebrated and fired cannon blasts from the state house steps, Union Party legislators drafted an address to the citizens of South Carolina. They encouraged Union men throughout the state to continue their resistance and nominate candidates for the state convention. This election, they declared, could "decide the fate of the Union," and they pleaded with voters to "resist the current of public opinion" and "make another determined effort to save their liberty, the Constitution and the Union."[46]

Some Union Party leaders, however, refused even to nominate candidates, fearing their participation would legitimize the state's proceedings. Charleston politicians claimed the convention was illegal, arguing that Governor Hamilton had no power to call the new legislature into session until the old members' terms had expired. If Union men took part in the convention, they warned, they would "lend [a] sanction" to the proceedings and "commit the party to abide by its decrees." Other Union men, particularly in the upcountry, insisted on contesting the election. Perry declared that the convention embodied the voice of the people, and it was essential that "the people, and not a party, be represented." He urged readers not to "give up the contest too soon" and to rally across the state to preserve the Union. Constans Daniels prayed that the "friends of order—the Union party will hold on to their organization," and a Charleston editor called Union men to "hold fast steadfastly to our principles—to our union as a party."[47]

These Union men remained fiercely loyal to South Carolina, and some confessed that they would "fight with her, although in a bad cause" if civil war erupted. Nonetheless, they often embraced a more national conception of the Union. They viewed it not as a compact of states but as a sacred nation that commanded their allegiance and devotion. One writer, for example, viewed South Carolina as "only an integral part or portion of the United States." Another writer insisted that South Carolinians "owe allegiance to the state . . . only as a member of the Union." A meeting in Charleston declared that "our allegiance to these United States is immediate and direct, and of the most sacred obligation." As long as South Carolina remained in the Union, Benjamin Perry agreed, "our true allegiance is due the United States."[48]

The election for convention delegates took place on November 12, and Nullifiers secured an overwhelming majority. Union men won in only eight districts, most of them concentrated in the upcountry. Turnout plummeted, even in districts where both parties contested the election. Party discipline, however, remained remarkably high. In Spartanburg, for example, turnout fell by 24 percent, but all six Union Party candidates received nearly identical vote totals. When the delegates arrived in Columbia, one writer confessed that the Union Party was "weak indeed" and could do little to stop nullification. Nullifiers, meanwhile, "feel their strength and are in high spirits," prepared to "do precisely as they like."[49]

The convention opened on November 20. Delegates promptly elected Governor Hamilton to preside over the convention, and they formed a committee to draft an ordinance of nullification. Only four of the twenty-one committee members were Union men, and nullification seemed a foregone conclusion. Fault lines, however, emerged among the committee's Nullifiers. Radicals like Pierce Butler hoped to nullify the tariff immediately and openly threaten disunion. Other "lukewarm Nullifiers" sought to delay implementation for ninety days to give Congress time to resolve the crisis. In the end, the committee softened the language of the draft, avoiding the words *nullification* and *secession* and agreeing that the ordinance would not take effect for another two months.[50]

When the committee presented this draft, however, Nullifiers on the convention floor immediately strengthened it. They inserted the word *nullify* and struck out an appeal to the other southern states. The draft had expressed "full confidence" that southerners would "nobly follow and sustain us." Robert Turnbull dismissed this plea, insisting that South Carolina would rely "not on them, but on herself alone." Despite their small numbers, Union Party delegates worked diligently to resist nullification. They voted against Nullifiers' reports and addresses and offered amendments to democratize the state government. Henry Middleton, a former governor, motioned for the convention to adjourn, insisting that it did not fairly represent the people of South Carolina. Representation, he observed, was based on "population and property," giving slave-dense lowcountry parishes more delegates than they deserved. He asked lawmakers to call a new convention, with representation based on the number of white men in each district. The inevitable delay, he hoped, would allow tempers to cool and buy Congress time to lower the tariff. Nullifiers, however, defiantly dismissed the motion.[51]

The convention adopted the Ordinance of Nullification on November 24, 1832, by a vote of 136 to 26. The ordinance declared the tariffs of 1828 and 1832 unconstitutional and therefore null and void within South Carolina after February 1, 1833. It also demanded that all civil and military officers in the state swear an oath to "obey, execute, and enforce this ordinance." As Nullifiers know, this provision would force Union men to resign from office or betray their convictions. As one observer bragged, the provision "amounts to . . . a disenfranchisement of the Union people—those for the lost cause." Nullifiers also boldly threatened to secede. If the federal government tried to enforce the tariff, they resolved, they would "henceforth hold themselves absolved" from their allegiance to the Union. They would declare their state a sovereign nation and proceed to organize a separate government.[52]

Pinckney rejoiced that the "knell of *submission* is rung," and Governor Hamilton proudly observed that the "die has been at last cast." After four years of village meetings and editorial battles, the State Rights Party had nullified the tariff and threatened to destroy the Union. Nullifiers succeeded, in large part, because they organized more effectively and outflanked their opponents in the war of words and symbols. They convinced voters that submission would degrade and dishonor them and destroy "everything that is dear to us as men, as freemen, and as fathers." At stake, they insisted, was their manhood and mastery and the freedom they had inherited from the founding generation. Having passed their ordinance, Nullifiers projected confidence, insisting the process would peacefully restore the Constitution to its "original purity." As the long "nullification winter" set in, however, many South Carolinians feared the simmering violence would erupt into civil war.[53]

4.

Imagining Disunion

The Nullification Winter, 1832–33

The civil war, Joel Poinsett predicted, would begin in Charleston. The governor had called for volunteers to defend the state against federal "tyranny," and as many as 25,000 men had responded. While these volunteers prepared for battle, officials stockpiled arms and built supply depots along the state's major roads. At the governor's word, they would converge on Charleston, overwhelm the small federal garrison, and declare the city a free port. They would confiscate or destroy Union men's property and drive them from the state. The conflict in Charleston would provoke secession and civil war, and the spirit of rebellion would tear the Union asunder. In the ensuing struggle, armies would pillage the southern countryside, brothers would slaughter each other on the battlefield, and slaves would massacre their owners. Great Britain would rush to South Carolina's aid, and the state's "forts would be garrisoned, her soil defended and her harbors filled with British troops and British fleets." The waters would "run red with American blood," and the Union's fragile experiment in self-government would fail.[1]

Poinsett imagined this political apocalypse during the nullification winter of 1832–33, between the passage of the ordinance in November and its scheduled implementation in February. Scholars often gloss over these months or play down the possibility of disunion. At the time, however, the prospect appeared terrifyingly real, and South Carolinians grasped for words to make sense of their uncertain future. Charleston lawyer Mitchell King found the suspense intolerable, confessing that the "present uncertain state is almost as bad as an active commotion." A "brave man," he explained, "would often rather rush on danger than live in constant expectation of it." As the "fatal 1st" of February approached, writer Caroline Howard Gilman observed that it was "utterly impossible" to foresee how the crisis would end. She feared that any small confrontation would "cause the flame to burst out" and consume the state. Artist Charles Fraser agreed, writing that only God knew "how much of what is now wrapt in the gloomy uncertainty of the future will . . . become sad realities." Writers across the state echoed these observations, and the weeks of waiting stirred anxieties and inspired frantic rumors and premonitions.[2]

Nullifiers depicted the president as a "blood-thirsty monster" leading an army of "hired butchers." These "federal mercenaries," they claimed, were massing along their borders and planning to slaughter innocent South Carolinians. Faced with this looming horror, they argued that nullification was the state's only hope of salvation. By volunteering en masse—by defying federal tyranny—they sought to demonstrate South Carolina's unity and resolve. Publicly, they insisted this show of strength would force Jackson to back down. Privately, however, many believed civil war was inevitable, and they trusted "impartial history" to immortalize and legitimize their struggle. The most radical Nullifiers even welcomed the prospect of war and began imagining a future beyond disunion.[3]

The Union Party, meanwhile, blamed Nullifiers for provoking the crisis and imperiling the Union. For years, they had insisted that "Nullification is Disunion, and Disunion is War," and events that winter seemed to confirm their fears. As Nullifiers volunteered en masse to defend the state, Union men warned that any "slight collision" would propel South Carolina toward chaos. They imagined the future in vivid detail, describing disunion in three distinct but overlapping ways: as a political crisis, a military conflict, and a social catastrophe. Fueled by these fears, countless families fled the state. Seeing little chance of averting disaster, they hoped only to escape and survive it. Thousands more, however, chose to stay and defend their right to the "soil of South Carolina." These Union men used their fears as a political weapon, galvanizing support by imagining the future that nullification would create. They evoked the "horrors of a civil and servile war" and envisioned the global death of liberty. By contesting the future and imagining the Union's destruction, they hoped to ensure its survival.[4]

In his final annual message, Governor James Hamilton emphasized the "pacific character" of nullification and prayed for a peaceful end to the crisis. He warned, however, that the "final issue may be adverse to this hope." South

Carolina, he observed, had endured years of oppression, and now Jackson was threatening to coerce the state into submission. In response, Hamilton urged the state assembly to prepare for war, proposing a 2,000-man "Legionary Corps" to protect Charleston and a "State Guard" of 10,000 additional volunteers. He also encouraged lawmakers to reinforce Charleston's artillery defenses, reclaim the city's arsenal from the federal government, and pass a bill of pains and penalties to "compel obedience" from the state's Union men.[5]

Lawmakers went even further, authorizing the governor to mobilize the "whole military force of this State." In addition to calling out the militia, he could organize "all free white men" into volunteer companies to repel invasion and suppress insurrection. Legislators allocated $200,000 to prepare for war, allowing the governor to purchase 10,000 guns and as much powder and lead as necessary. They required all civil and military officials to swear an oath to uphold nullification—seeking to purge Union men from power and enforce loyalty to the state. They defended the right of secession and called upon all South Carolinians to "sustain the dignity and protect the liberty of the state." If Jackson tried to intervene, they vowed to "repel force by force" and "maintain [their] liberty at all hazards."[6]

Legislators elected Robert Y. Hayne as the state's new governor and chose Calhoun to replace him in the US Senate. In his inaugural address, Hayne swore to uphold the state's sovereign power and defend its soil from invasion. Nullifiers, he claimed, hoped to redeem the Union and preserve the Constitution "as our fathers framed it." He warned, however, that they would rather hazard disunion than endure submission. In the approaching struggle, Hayne hoped South Carolina would stand united against tyranny. He denounced Union men as parricidal traitors and insisted that true Carolinians would stay loyal to their "common mother." Let "others desert her if they can," he raged, "let them revile her, if they will—let them give aid and countenance to her enemies, if they may—but for us, we will STAND OR FALL WITH CAROLINA."[7]

South Carolina, however, was dramatically unprepared for war. Upon taking office, Hayne found the state "deficient to a lamentable extent in arms, ammunition, and every description of the munitions of war." The militia was undisciplined and poorly organized, and after years of peace its "military spirit . . . was at a low ebb." Losing no time, Hayne dispatched agents across the country to purchase supplies, began building a factory in Charleston to produce cannon balls, and established an armory and ordnance department in the city. Officials across the state began repairing weapons, mounting cannons, and placing their districts in the "best posture of defence." They spared "neither pains nor expense" and ultimately purchased or produced nearly 10,000 rifles and muskets, 70 cannons, 50,000 cannon balls, 40,000 pounds of gunpowder, and "an abundant supply of lead."[8]

On December 21, Hayne appointed twenty-eight aides-de-camp to raise, inspect, and grant commissions to the state's volunteers. He asked these men to "sacrifice all private considerations to the public good" and serve the state with "zeal, and energy, and devotion to the cause." Building on Hamilton's plan, Hayne hoped to recruit a 10,000-man "Volunteer force" as well as 2,500 "Minute Men," who could respond to sudden emergencies across the state. These soldiers would serve as South Carolina's first line of defense. If war broke out, however, Hayne planned to supplement their numbers by calling out the remainder of the militia—the men who had chosen not to volunteer. He mapped out several routes "from the mountains towards the sea," all converging on Charleston, and he instructed his aides to build supply depots every thirty miles across their districts. He told them to stockpile weapons and secure supplies of corn, bacon, and fodder to feed the marching armies.[9]

These aides traveled across their districts, attending militia musters and local meetings to encourage men to enlist. They appealed to the honor and martial manhood of their audience, urging men to "protect their firesides from the footsteps of the oppressor." At a battalion muster in Pendleton, aide Edward Harleston asked the assembled men to "obey the maternal call of South Carolina" and defend their "firesides from pollution." In Columbia, state legislator William Preston warned that Jackson was raising an army of "hired butchers" to invade the state. The president, he claimed, planned to march through South Carolina slaughtering its citizens and inciting slave rebellion. The other southern states had refused to intervene, and South Carolina's only hope lay in the "moral courage" of its men. Preston appealed to the "party of the state" to enroll their names and pledge their lives to liberty.[10]

These appeals proved highly successful, and Nullifiers across the state marveled at the rush of enlistments. Within days of Preston's speech, the small state capital had furnished 500 volunteers, all determined to transform the "gallant little state [into] an encampment or a battle field." By early

January, a Columbia writer observed that "almost the entire population is volunteering": 1,000 men in Laurens, 1,200 in Fairfield, and 1,200 in Edgefield. An Abbeville doctor praised the "spirit & patriotism" of his district, where Nullifiers had volunteered en masse to defend the state. Barnwell organized an entire regiment, and the district's widespread excitement amazed one witness, who had never seen "more enthusiasm or unanimity." The "military spirit of the people," he observed, "is beyond all expectation."[11]

These scenes repeated themselves across the state and by March 1833 as many as 25,000 men—50 percent of the state's white military-age population—had volunteered (Table 3). In the midland districts around Columbia, the proportion was even higher, reaching 60 percent in Newberry and 75 percent in Edgefield. In Fairfield, 79 percent of eligible men volunteered, and 600 "alarm men" stood ready to suppress slave rebellions in the district. Even men ineligible for service were swept up in the military fervor. Several districts organized reserve units of "Volunteer veterans" too old for active duty. Edgefield enrolled 100 men between the ages of fifty-five and eighty, Richland organized a company of "Silver Greys," and Pendleton accepted 200 "elderly volunteers." One Nullifier confessed that these men were "not very warlike," observing that many carried walking sticks instead of rifles. Still, he viewed them as a powerful symbol of South Carolina's cause, writing that the "fire of liberty . . . still burns bright and steadily in their noble old hearts."[12]

Thousands of children and adolescents also embraced nullification and were drawn to the movement's spectacle and excitement. They eagerly sported blue cockades and Palmetto buttons—the badges of the State Rights Party. They paraded through towns waving banners, playing music, and singing revolutionary songs like "La Marseillaise." The rhetoric and imagery of the crisis infused the culture in which they grew up. As their fathers enlisted in the state army, for example, young boys formed "little regiments" and "marched about the Streets." Henry Tupper, who was four years old during the nullification winter, later vividly recalled the "preparing of cockades and sticks, the smuggling in of boxes of arms, the drilling of the boys, the street fights, and the popular songs." In Newberry, a young girl named Ellennor Arnold practiced her penmanship by scrawling Nullifier rhetoric. "I am a strong Nullifier," she wrote, "and I hope the patriotic state will offer up her most choice sons to pour out there blood on the alters of there country for free trade and states wrights."[13]

TABLE 3. Governor Robert Y. Hayne's "Volunteer Force," 1832–33

District	Artillery	Cavalry	Infantry	Additional Volunteers	Total Volunteers	Military-Age Men	Mobilization (%)
Abbeville	73	102	1,113	—	1,288	2,966	43
Barnwell	—	55	870	—	925	2,065	45
Beaufort	—	—	467	—	467	1,211	39
Charleston	333	—	1,103	114	1,550	4,762	33
Chester	—	75	925	—	1,000	1,926	52
Chesterfield	—	—	130	—	130	1,004	13
Colleton	—	—	400	—	400	1,097	36
Darlington	—	—	224	—	224	1,279	18
Edgefield	—	130	2,020	—	2,150	2,865	75
Fairfield	50	200	1,900	—	2,150	1,967	109
Georgetown	—	30	140	—	170	495	34
Greenville	—	—	120	—	120	2028	6
Horry	—	—	—	—	0	625	0
Kershaw	—	65	125	—	190	1,038	18
Lancaster	—	—	64	96	160	1,235	13
Laurens	40	120	700	—	860	2,477	35
Lexington	—	—	440	—	440	1,011	44
Marion	—	—	144	—	144	1,342	11
Marlboro	—	—	70	—	70	817	9
Newberry	—	130	970	—	1,100	1,859	59
Orangeburg	50	44	450	—	544	1,463	37
Pendleton	—	180	1,120	—	1,300	4,300	30
Richland	120	120	400	—	640	1,281	50
Spartanburg	—	56	630	—	686	2,991	23
Sumter	—	45	360	695	1,100	1,799	61
Union	—	120	850	380	1,350	2,010	67
Williamsburg	—		263	—	263	542	48
York	—	60	840	—	900	2,186	41
Total	666	1,532	16,838	1,285	20,321	50,449	40

Note: Hayne listed no volunteers from Greenville or Horry Districts, but contemporary newspapers indicate that at least 120 men volunteered in Greenville. Fairfield reported 1,550 volunteers (79 percent), plus an additional 600 "alarm men," bringing its total to 2,150 men. As Hayne explained, "The exact number of volunteers organized I am not even now able distinctly to state. The incompleteness of the returns and the fact that the organization of many of the Corps was arrested by the compromise bill, puts it out of my power to be minutely accurate on this subject. My returns show upwards of 20,000 organized Volunteers, and I think the whole number, organized and unorganized, may be safely estimated at 25,000."

Methodology: Using the 1830 census, the author estimated the number of military-age men (18–45) in each district by adding up all men in the "20 to 29" and "30 to 39" categories and prorating the "15 to 19" and "40 to 49" categories.

Sources: "An Account of the Number of Volunteers Raised During the Nullification Crisis," Governors' Messages, SCDAH.

By supporting nullification, adolescent boys laid claim to manhood. As historian Jon Grinspan demonstrates, antebellum voting laws "turned age twenty-one into a sharp boundary between youth and adulthood." These young Nullifiers were unable to vote and therefore excluded from "civic manhood." Many still attended school or college, and few had formed independent households of their own. By debating political ideas or enlisting in the state army, however, they could affirm their rights as men. Charleston's adolescents organized a Young Men's State Rights Association and vowed to "march at a moments warning" to defend their freedom. In February 1833, boys ranging from 14- to 17-years-old met to offer their services to the state. They appealed to the "courage and patriotism of youth" and encouraged all boys capable of bearing arms to prepare for the looming conflict.[14]

Despite this widespread *rage militaire,* however, the state remained desperately short of money and supplies. With some exaggeration, Hayne observed that the "demand for Arms exceeds *five times over*" the number that the state possessed. Barnwell District, for example, raised 850 volunteers—but the men needed proper training and at least 500 additional rifles. Hayne appealed to the volunteers' patriotism, asking Minute Men to serve without pay and urging companies to furnish their own flags and supplies. As Hammond explained, however, many volunteers were too poor to purchase rifles, and the guns they owned were inadequate to the crisis. They might "skirmish in the woods and harass invaders with their shotguns," he wrote, but without proper weapons they could not "stand a moment in the field before a regular force."[15]

Hammond suggested that Hayne borrow money to equip the army. The moment fighting began, he wrote, "negociations should be set on foot for straining our credit to the utmost." In the meantime, Hammond placed his property at the governor's service and hoped that other Nullifiers would do the same. He debated growing a "large provision crop" to feed the volunteer force. His plantation, however, was located near the Georgia border and surrounded by Union men, and he considered it safer to plant cotton and "furnish the State with the proceeds." He also offered the state the use of his male slaves, "to be employed in ditching, fortifying, building as pioneers &c." Hammond clarified that these slaves should only serve as noncombatants, calling it "dangerous policy" to allow them to bear arms. He hinted, however, that the crisis might drive Nullifiers to the "greatest extremities" and compel them to draft slaves into military service.[16]

While some Nullifiers still insisted the crisis would end peacefully, many began to accept—or even welcome—the possibility of war. As Abbeville Nullifier Samuel Townes explained, the crisis had rendered "peacible arbitrament" impossible, and the "fact is now probably obvious that we must fight." Henry Townes—Samuel's brother—marveled at the "determined spirit of resistance" in his district, insisting Nullifiers would "rally as one man & spill every drop of blood tomorrow if their state called them." A Columbia writer observed that South Carolina was quickly becoming a "military nation" as thousands of men prepared for battle. The volunteers, he insisted, were neither daunted nor afraid by "King Andrew the 1st," and they would ensure that "no United States Blackguard soldiers ... set a foot on our soil." If the president dared to invade the state, an upcountry doctor agreed, "he never would get back again."[17]

Throughout the crisis, Nullifiers had condemned Union men as traitors and Tories, comparing them to the men who remained loyal to England during the American Revolution. Those labels assumed greater meaning as civil war loomed. Hammond encouraged the governor to "annihilate instantly the first show of resistance to our laws," whether from federal tyranny or Unionist treason. If fighting broke out, a Camden writer swore, Nullifiers in his district would "deal first with our enemies at home." At a public dinner in Charleston, one guest prayed South Carolina would exile Union men and "no longer permit them to pollute its soil," and a Georgia visitor assailed the "traitorous enemy within your borders." An upcountry Nullifier vowed to "subdue the yankees" in his own district, explaining that he considered native-born "submission men" the same as northern invaders. If the "Tory party" dared to fight against the state, another writer agreed, "we will *crush* them in the dust."[18]

Hayne and his aides devised a flexible military strategy to respond to threats along the state's borders and coasts. He kept volunteers in their own districts, built supply depots across the state, and organized companies of mounted Minute Men to respond to emergencies. Wherever the conflict broke out, he could have 1,000 soldiers ready within twenty-four hours, and "at least 1,000 more every day afterwards for twenty successive days." Nullifiers remained confident that the South would rally to their cause. Hayne reported receiving "liberal offers of assistance from other States, of men, money, and even of vessels." A Columbia editor assured readers that thousands of volunteers from Alabama, Georgia, North Carolina, and Virginia would rush to the state's aid, and another writer declared that two-thirds of Georgia's men would "fight for us tomorrow."[19]

Most Nullifiers imagined the looming war and its aftermath in only the vaguest terms. Rebecca Motte Rutledge, for example, confessed it was "impossible to guess at the result of the crisis." Even if the country avoided war, she wrote, the North and South could "never return to their former harmony ... we shall be no longer brothers, but rivals." Many writers recognized that their resistance might fail, and they looked to history to vindicate their struggle. A Charleston woman observed that, "successful or not, [nullification] will form a noble page in History," and Waddy Thompson declared that "impartial history will say of us, that we did not make the crisis, but met it." Lucretia Townes, the niece of John C. Calhoun, agreed that Nullifiers' names would "live forever" and hold a proud place in the pages of history. Their "children's *children,*" she exclaimed, would read the Ordinance of Nullification and "know that their ancestors were not *voluntary* slaves."[20]

While Samuel Townes could not imagine the struggle itself, he remained confident that South Carolina's volunteers would triumph. From the beginning, Nullifiers had insisted that liberty and Union were *separable,* and Townes reaffirmed that conviction. Glimpsing a future beyond disunion, he declared that "our *liberties* at all events will survive this conflict of arms & the dissolution of this Union." Legislator William Preston dared the president to invade the state. Nullifiers, he insisted, would emerge triumphant even if the entire South abandoned them and Jackson's "hireling soldiery" flooded their borders. In his final annual message, James Hamilton declared that South Carolinians would "rather have every house on the fair surface of our territory razed to the ground and every blade of grass burnt than surrender to the despotism and injustice" of the federal government.[21]

President Andrew Jackson, however, remained determined to crush nullification and preserve the Union. In September 1832, he began working with his cabinet to monitor the growing crisis. He asked Navy Secretary Levi Woodbury to "keep a steady eye to the South" and *"have all things ready"* in case the state tried to secede. Concerned that Nullifiers had compromised the military officers in Charleston, Jackson replaced them with "men who cannot be corrupted." In November, he sent his private secretary to Charleston to uncover the "real intentions of the nullifyers," assess the condition of the city's forts, and meet with Union Party leaders. Poinsett responded with a bleak assessment of the garrison's defenses. The forts were designed to protect Charleston from foreign invasion, not to resist an assault from the city itself. Fort Johnson contained "no works at all," while the sand hills towering over Fort Moultrie left it vulnerable to attack. Castle Pinckney was in "fine order," but it contained "no works in the rear, as all the defences are Seaward."[22]

In 1832, the entire federal army contained about 6,300 soldiers. Less than half belonged to the Eastern Department, which stretched from Florida to the Michigan Territory. Nonetheless, Jackson acted quickly and decisively to maintain federal authority in South Carolina. Between September 1832 and January 1833, he increased the Charleston garrison from 180 men to 635 men—10 percent of the American army. He also ordered the *Natchez,* the *Experiment,* and a small fleet of revenue cutters to patrol the city's harbor. Major General Alexander Macomb urged the officers in Charleston to remain on guard day and night and defend the forts "to the last extremity." Treasury Secretary Louis McLane ordered James Pringle—still serving as Charleston's customs collector—to display "unshrinking firmness and fidelity in the discharge of your duties." McLane authorized him to move the custom house into the forts and use the revenue cutters to enforce the tariff.[23]

By November, Jackson recognized that a "crisis is about to approach, when the Government must act." Hesitation would destabilize the country and destroy the "best hopes of the freedom of the world." He viewed the Union as the source of America's prosperity and the safeguard of its liberty, and he vowed to preserve it—or die in its defense. Many Americans shared these convictions, and thousands offered to help crush the incipient rebellion. Letters poured in from "officers[,] commanders[,] [and] volunteer corps" from across the Union, and the "tender of volunteers" exceeded 150,000 men. Within two weeks, Jackson estimated, he could send 15,000 well-organized troops to Charleston and another 30,000 men into the South Carolina upcountry. After forty days, he predicted, he could march the entire force southward to defeat "every insurrection or rebellion that might arise to threaten our glorious confederacy."[24]

On December 10, Jackson delivered his Nullification Proclamation, articulating a powerful nationalist vision of the Union's nature and purpose. The Union, he insisted, predated the Constitution. It was forged in the colonial era, strengthened during the American Revolution, and cemented by the nation's founding documents. While Nullifiers viewed the Constitution as a revocable compact among sovereign states, Jackson argued that the American *people* had ratified it to perfect and perpetuate the Union. Nullifiers looked to history to legitimize nullification, invoking the Revolutionary struggle against "unjust taxation." For Jackson, however, American history repudiated nullification and affirmed the permanence and supremacy of the Constitution. Had nullification "been established at an earlier day," he observed, "the Union would have been dissolved in its infancy"—torn apart by the Whiskey Rebellion or the War of 1812. The Revolutionary generation instead created a "permanent constitutional compact," forged through "mutual sacrifice" and "formed for the benefit of all." Jackson declared that "disunion, by armed force, is TREASON" and swore to preserve the Union even at the cost of war. If South Carolinians persisted, he warned, they would endure the "misery, of civil strife" and soak the state's fertile fields in blood.[25]

Jackson placed his confidence in the state's Union men, hoping they would "put down this rebellion themselves." The crisis, however, placed tremendous strain on these men, bringing their loyalties to state and nation into conflict. Some responded by renouncing South Carolina altogether. If Nullifiers triumphed, a lowcountry orator declared, "Carolina was no longer his country, and not entitled to his allegiance." Former Governor Richard Manning insisted that his loyalty to South Carolina "consisted only through her free Institutions, and when those are destroyed I owe my allegiance to none but the Gen[era]l Government." Another writer agreed that South Carolinians had a duty to obey the federal Constitution in defiance of all state laws.[26]

Between 1820 and 1860, roughly 200,000 white South Carolinians left the state—most pushed by soil exhaustion and pulled by the promise of cheap land in the Old Southwest. The nullification crisis contributed to this trend by driving some Union men from the state. In 1833, an Arkansas editor reported tens of thousands of South Carolinians fleeing from "political violence," and a North Carolina writer agreed that "thirty or forty thousand have left the State during the reign of terror." Although these reports vastly exaggerated the number of political refugees, they captured the experiences of countless families. Poinsett observed many Union Party leaders wrestling with the decision to leave the state, and William Gilmore Simms predicted that nullification would drive Union men to "arms or emigration en masse." Many families carried out these plans, and an upcountry writer described a "great many people moving to the Ohio [River]" to escape political persecution. Another reported entire families "emigrating to the western wilds" to escape nullification. In December 1832, a Camden writer remarked that he had never witnessed such "rapid and increasing migration from the state."[27]

For many men, the decision to leave was an affirmation of moderate manhood—a desire to protect their families from civil war and slave rebellion. When Charleston merchant John Ravenel's wife left to visit her family in New Jersey, for example, he encouraged her to stay there until the crisis had passed. He began making arrangements to move their family "*ultimately north of the Potomac*," explaining that "troubles await this Land— from which I hold it my duty to protect my Children." Charleston lawyer John W. Mitchell's relatives encouraged him to leave the state, warning him that the "doomed land" was no longer safe for his three young children. He resisted for months, reluctant to leave his home and his ailing father, but he finally moved the family to New York in 1833.[28]

Thousands of Union men, however, chose to stay in South Carolina and contest the state's future. While Nullifiers condemned them as traitors and Tories, these men defended their rights as South Carolinians. Judge John B. O'Neall declared himself a "freeman standing on the soil of his birth," determined to protect the "safety and honor of the State." Charleston legislator Daniel Huger observed that his family had lived in the state for four generations, and the "recollections of the past, entwined with the hopes of the future, bind me to Carolina." He distinguished between the state and its government, insisting that Union men did not view the "Nullification Party as South Carolina, but [rather] as her oppressors." In Abbeville, Union men declared that they owed allegiance to South Carolina but not to the demagogues "now wielding her sovereignty." Affirming their devotion to the state, they refused to let Nullifiers strip away their rights and reduce them to "aliens in the land of our birth."[29]

In December 1832, Union men held a party convention in Columbia with more than 180 delegates from across the state. Divisions quickly emerged between moderate and martial Union men: while delegates like Richard

Manning preferred "more silent and moderate measures," martial men like Joel Poinsett and Christopher Memminger favored decisive action. The delegates ultimately denounced nullification as a revolutionary conspiracy and a threat to Union men's homes and families. The state legislature, they observed, had empowered Hayne to call out the militia to repel federal invasion, "forc[ing] the citizens of the State from their firesides, and their homes, to take up arms and incur the pains and penalties of treason." At Memminger's urging, they began preparing for armed resistance to nullification. They called for Union men in every district to create paramilitary organizations, with a network of local branches spread throughout the countryside. While Nullifiers' volunteer companies were explicitly military organizations, these "Washington Societies" or "Union Societies" were hybrid civic institutions. They allowed Union men to communicate, coordinate, and begin preparing for war. The moment fighting began, however, commander-in-chief Joel Poinsett could convert them into military companies.[30]

Charleston established its Washington Society in early December, and other districts quickly followed suit. Benjamin Perry observed that Nullifiers had stormed to power through "concert and union of action," and he urged Union men to "fight the Nullifiers with their own weapons." He encouraged Union men across the upcountry to organize societies to protect their families and preserve the "Government of our fathers." Jackson called upon the state's Union men to work together and prepare for "every emergency." He reminded them that they were waging a global struggle for liberty, defending not only the American Constitution but also "free institutions throughout the world." Ultimately, at least 9,000 South Carolinians joined these paramilitary societies—18 percent of the state's white military-age population (Table 4). In Charleston alone, almost 1,500 men enrolled. Outside the city, the Union Societies drew their greatest strength from the districts along the North Carolina border, with 50 percent of military-age men in Lancaster, Marlborough, Greenville, and Spartanburg enrolling. In Horry District, where Nullifiers failed to organize a single company, 78 percent of white men volunteered to defend the Union.[31]

As local Union Societies spread across the upcountry, they adopted increasingly militant resolutions. The Spartanburg chapter drew 1,500 members and warned that nullification would provoke anarchy and civil war and "destroy our Republican Institutions." They vowed to do everything in their power to preserve the Union, insisting that "it shall *never* be dissolved . . . *it shall last forever.*" In Greenville, Union men swore never to fight beneath the "bloody flag of Anarchy" or the "single star" of South Carolina. They declared themselves the "disciples of Washington" and resolved that "we are FREE, and will be FREE." Meetings in the district's northern mountains rejected moderation and embraced the possibility of war. The Paris Mountain Union Society, for example, resolved that "argument is exhausted—the period of action is arrived." The region's Union men had "drawn our swords and flung away the scabbards," and they vowed to preserve the Union or "perish in the attempt." When Nullifiers called them cowards and submission men, they offered only two words in response: "Come on."[32]

Dozens of meetings adopted identical resolutions, denouncing the tyranny of nullification and refusing to fight against the federal government. In February 1833, roughly 150 Union men met in Pickens to raise a "Hickory Pole" and fly the American flag. They insisted they would rather "live one day under the Stars and Stripes which now wave over us, than to live a long life without union and liberty." Horry District held a similar ceremony that winter as Union men raised a 57-foot pole and flew the "starry Flag of their Country." In Abbeville, a militia colonel unfurled the American flag and asked his men to rally around it "as a test of principles and patriotism." All but five men stepped forward and circled the "glorious emblem of Union and Liberty," vowing pointedly to defend it against all "foreign and domestic enemies."[33]

Some Union men were reluctant to take up arms without the official sanction and protection of the federal government. If they failed, they feared that Nullifiers would hang them as traitors, confiscate their property, and perhaps target their families. If Jackson called them into service, however, they were "willing to take the field in defence of their liberties at a moment's notice." Novelist William Gilmore Simms reported that Charleston's Union men were eagerly preparing for war. Years of partisan tension, he wrote, had produced a "deep & deadly hostility & hate" between the parties, and Union men now raged with the "manful desire" for vengeance. He warned that the slightest provocation would lead to a merciless hand-to-hand struggle and the "utter extermination of one or the other party." Another writer actively desired civil war, insisting that only military intervention could resolve the crisis and restore "permanent peace and tranquility."[34]

TABLE 4. Paramilitary Union Society Membership, 1832–33

District	Membership	Military-Age Men	Percentage
Abbeville	262	2,966	9
Barnwell	—	2,065	—
Beaufort	—	1,211	—
Charleston	1,457	4,762	31
Chester	900	1,926	47
Chesterfield	800	1,004	80
Colleton	150	1,097	14
Darlington	—	1,279	—
Edgefield	300	2,865	10
Fairfield	—	1,967	—
Georgetown	—	495	—
Greenville	1,000	2,028	49
Horry	487	625	78
Kershaw	—	1,038	—
Lancaster	700	1,235	57
Laurens	—	2,477	—
Lexington	—	1,011	—
Marion	450	1,342	34
Marlboro	—	817	—
Newberry	—	1,859	—
Orangeburg	—	1,463	—
Pendleton	200	4,300	5
Richland	—	1,281	—
Spartanburg	1,500	2,991	50
Sumter	—	1,799	—
Union	—	2,010	—
Williamsburg	—	542	—
York	800	2,186	37
Total	9,006	50,449	18

Sources: Joel R. Poinsett to Andrew Jackson, 22 February 1833; issues of the *Charleston Courier* and *Greenville Mountaineer* for January and February 1833.

Union men described the looming crisis in vivid detail and envisioned disunion as a military, political, and social catastrophe. Nullifiers often portrayed it as a clear sectional conflict, with the Potomac River forming the boundary between North and South. A Columbia writer, for example, appealed to the "States south of the Potomac" to resist the tyranny of their "Northern masters." Union men, however, imagined the crisis as a political apocalypse that would shatter the Union. As diplomat Hugh Legaré explained, America would "go to pieces . . . no two parts will hold together." An upcountry writer agreed that the Union would be "torn to pieces and its fragments [would] be scattered to the four winds." Like the Latin American republics, another writer predicted, the states would fragment endlessly, and "regulated liberty" would disappear from the world.[35]

While the Union guaranteed Americans' liberty and independence, these "disunited States" would be powerless to protect them. The political chaos of disunion would destroy America's republican institutions and ensure the rise of tyranny. In order to survive, legislator William McWillie imagined, the fragmented states would ultimately form stronger governments, raise larger armies, and levy higher taxes. Inexorably, these small republics would become monarchies, and "all the beauty of our institutions would gradually fade away." A meeting in Pickens agreed that nullification would dissolve the Union and replace the "mild and rational system of government" with a military despotism. Another writer insisted that disunion would destroy and discredit the global cause of liberty: "with the dissolution of our Union, must perish our prosperity and the hopes of rational Liberty throughout the world."[36]

Union men also imagined disunion as a military conflict—a civil war both *within* South Carolina and *between* the state and federal government. A Greenville orator confessed that the "very word [nullification] had horrors for him, that it would produce disunion, civil war, bloodshed, revolution and every calamity that the imagination can conceive." William Gilmore Simms predicted the federal government would ultimately overrun the state, blot its "name & star place" out of existence, and divide its territory among the "contiguous and more loyal states." Thomas Grimké envisioned South Carolinians becoming a "band of Parricides, [fighting] a war of rebellion against their lawful Rulers." The world would condemn them, God would forsake them, and they would receive only the "reward of the Sword, cruel, remorseless, insatiable." Gazing into the future, Grimké saw the state's coastline blockaded, its towns burned and abandoned, and its soldiers slaughtered on the "battlefield of brothers."[37]

They warned that South Carolina would have to ally with Great Britain to achieve its independence. The kingdom purchased much of South Carolina's cotton and—Union men claimed—had a political and economic incentive to weaken the Union. As early as 1830, Union Party writers accused Governor Stephen D. Miller of sending agents to Britain to secure an alliance "in a war with the Northern states." According to one rumor, the British were sending a fleet with 10,000 soldiers to defend South Carolina from the federal government. Although few Nullifiers expected or desired British aid, Union men eagerly accused them of betraying the country. If the British intervened, one lowcountry planter warned, the kingdom would "recolonize us" and "dismember the [American] empire." South Carolina, dependent on British protection, would become a "smuggling mart" for British goods and a staging ground for its wars. British ships would patrol the state's harbors, and British soldiers would occupy its forts—a direct assault upon South Carolina's sovereignty and independence.[38]

This British alliance, Union men imagined, would also ensure slavery's destruction. Britain was on the verge of emancipating its West Indian slaves, and one planter insisted it was "utter insanity" to entrust the state's "peculiar interests" to British protection. Another writer, signing himself *A Slave Holder,* warned that Great Britain would impose abolition on South Carolina as a condition of their alliance. Poinsett agreed, writing that Britain's parliamentary debates would transform the West Indies into an "Archipelago of free blacks." If South Carolina placed itself under British protection, the kingdom's abolitionists would soon focus their "philanthropic projects" on the state. Faced with "servile war and destruction," their small army would be powerless to "preserve our property and maintain domestic tranquility."[39]

For many Union men, these visions presaged the most chilling consequences of nullification. They repeatedly evoked the "horrors of a civil and servile war," fearing that disunion would unleash a social and racial apocalypse. Images of the Haitian Revolution still haunted their imaginations. One writer accused Nullifiers of inciting another "Santa [*sic*] Domingo Massacre," and legislator William McWillie argued that nullification would unleash the "horrors of St. Domingo." Disunion and civil war, they feared, would present even greater challenges to slavery's survival. By drawing men away from their homes, civil war would leave wives and children more vulnerable to the "ravages" of an insurrection, and the presence of an invading army would encourage slaves to seek liberation. Union men viewed slavery as an "inherent weakness" in the event of war, and they feared slaves would seize the opportunity to "cut their throats." An upcountry writer even feared that Nullifiers would "arm the slaves and put them forward in the front of battle."[40]

In these visions of disunion, slave rebellion reflected a broader breakdown of social order. As Jackson explained, disunion "reduces every thing to anarchy & strikes at the very existence of society." A writer in Sumter agreed that nullification would sound the "death-knell to all law, all government, all restraint." Union men warned that nullification "strikes at the very root of social order" and threatened to "sweep away the very foundation of social and civil union." Already, they observed, nullification had turned friends and brothers against each other and thrown open the "flood-gates of anarchy." Benjamin Perry insisted that "friendship, love of country, the ties of kindred and the feelings of religion have withered." Nullifiers had "substituted discord for peace, not only in the halls of legislation, but in the family circle, and the very sanctuary of God!"[41]

They warned that nullification would destroy marriage and unleash gender radicalism. They viewed the family as a symbol and foundation of the social order, and they equated the integrity of the Union with the inviolability of marriage. Thomas Grimké revered the Constitution as a "sacred covenant" as "hallowed and irrevocable as . . . the marriage bond," and Barnwell residents prayed that the "union of the states"—like the "union of a fond husband with a deserving wife"—would "be separated only by the decision of Heaven." Union men claimed that Nullifiers sought to subvert this sacred marital order. South Carolina was the only state that lacked a divorce law, and throughout the crisis, Union Party editors reported divorce statistics from other states under the headline "nullification."[42]

By eroding the marriage bond, Union men warned, nullification would encourage women to transgress their "proper" sphere. A Charleston editor, for example, imagined a "regiment of Old Women in Breeches" fighting against the state's Union men. In January 1833, Nullifiers in Clarendon paraded and took target practice in front of their community. A Union man in the crowd watched in horror as several women asked to fire the rifles themselves. Militiamen held the weapons steady as the women pulled the triggers, and one woman tried holding a rifle against her own shoulder. The shock, however, proved too much for her "delicate nerves," and she dropped the rifle. The spectator mocked the proceedings, claiming that the women "instantly offered themselves as volunteers" and predicting that Governor Hayne would "accept... their services with alacrity, and allow each of them a [male] gun-holder, to support her Rifle in the day of battle." Should northern soldiers dare to invade the state, he quipped, they would surely never be "so ungallant as to resist the Amazons of Clarendon."[43]

Union men used these stories to mock their political opponents, and few expected women to actually volunteer. Nonetheless, these stories reflected deep anxieties about women's political participation in the crisis and their "proper" place in society. As the state mobilized for war, some Nullifier women threatened to disown their sons or reject their suitors for refusing to volunteer in the state army. If nullification corrupted and politicized women, Union men feared, it could destroy "domestic peace"—a term that encompassed the emotional harmony of the household as well as the political stability of the Union. A writer calling herself *A Carolina Mother* warned that civil war would lead to fratricidal slaughter, and she insisted that any woman who supported nullification was a "disgrace to your sex... only fit to consort with the wolves and tigers."[44]

Union men blended political and religious imagery in an apocalyptic vision of South Carolina's future, imagining "war, famine and pestilence" consuming the state. Grimké, adopting the Bible's rhythm and rhetoric, warned that the state's wives and mothers "shall have for their portion, weeping, and lamentation, and griefs," and the "gray hairs of her aged men, shall be brought down with sorrow, to the grave." Nullification would tear families and friendships apart and devastate the countryside. The Union's prosperity would evaporate, one writer imagined, and "you will behold your fields untouched by the hoe or by the plough, your threshing floor gaping with emptiness." The "mangled corpse[s]" of parents and friends would haunt their "blood-satiated imagination," and their vacant houses would serve as cruel reminders of the "by-gone days" of happiness.[45]

Joel Poinsett provided one of the most detailed visions of the impending conflict. Rumors swirled that Jackson planned to seal off the state, blockading its ports and stationing soldiers along its borders. Poinsett warned the president that such a blockade would provoke a "desperate and protracted" war between the state's political parties. The Union would ultimately survive, but only after "great loss of life and the total destruction of the property of the State." Nullifiers, he wrote, would occupy Charleston almost immediately, and it would "cost much blood to dislodge them." Union men owned many of the city's most elegant houses, and they feared Nullifiers would burn the town rather than surrender it. Poinsett admitted that Charleston's Union men were too weak to defeat the Nullifiers alone, and in many inland districts they would struggle even to protect themselves.

Instead of sealing off the state, Poinsett urged the president to invade South Carolina at once and overwhelm Nullifiers' scattered recruits. The "blustering volunteers," he wrote, "ought to be stopped at the threshold." He asked Jackson to reinforce the 600 soldiers in Charleston with enough men to "take and hold possession" of the city. At the same time, the president could march volunteers through North Carolina into the state's northwestern districts, which remained staunchly loyal to the Union. Union men in Charleston and across the upcountry would rally to these liberating armies, and together they would "suffocate this rebellion" with one blow. The state's Union men would then "take upon themselves the civil government of the State" and restore harmony to the country.[46]

American observers around the world warned that the global cause of liberty hinged on the outcome of the crisis. Writing from Belgium, Hugh Legaré reported that European monarchs rejoiced at the Union's "approaching downfall," viewing nullification as proof of the failure of self-government. James Buchanan, the American ambassador to Russia, agreed that the "advocates of despotism throughout Europe beheld our dissentions with delight." If Nullifiers triumphed, Buchanan informed Jackson, "constitutional liberty throughout the rest of the world would receive a blow from which it might never recover." By striving to preserve the Union, Daniel Webster declared, Americans were acting "not for ourselves alone, but for the great cause of Constitutional liberty all over the globe." The failure of the European revolutions gave greater urgency to America's mission. Among the "desolated fields and still smoking ashes of Poland," Webster explained, "prayers are uttered for the preservation of our Union."[47]

Fueled by these convictions, most states—including Georgia, North Carolina, Alabama, and Mississippi—passed resolutions denouncing nullification. Maryland insisted the federal government had a duty to protect South Carolina's Union men and stop the state from seceding. Mississippi declared the Union "precious above all price" and vowed to sustain Jackson in striking down nullification. Alabama lawmakers observed that nullification would produce "anarchy and civil discord" and "make shipwreck of the last hope of mankind." They called for the "instant exertion" of patriotism and forbearance, insisting that the affections of the American people represented the "only bonds of our Union, and the sole preservatives of rational and constitutional liberty."[48]

As a "last resort," Alabama proposed a "Federal Convention" to meet in Washington in March 1834. The yearlong delay, lawmakers hoped, would allow tempers to cool and give the nation's leaders time to forge a compromise. Georgia also called for a "Convention of the people" and suggested eleven constitutional amendments to define the balance of state and federal power. Mississippi's lawmakers, however, rejected plans for a convention, insisting it was "madness to expect . . . calm deliberation" amid the political crisis. Despite the "turbulent spirit of the times," they observed, the Constitution still guaranteed "freedom of laws, of order, of security and peace." If politicians tried to amend it, they would unleash "malignant passions" that might transform the country's "peaceful freedom" into a state of "fraternal wars, of bloodshed and desolation."[49]

Virginia governor John Floyd sympathized with South Carolina's resistance and vehemently denounced Jackson's Nullification Proclamation. If the president tried to coerce South Carolina into submission, Floyd swore, he would "oppose him with a military force." Although he expected to die in the looming civil war, he vowed to "do the best I can to save the liberty of my country." Other prominent Virginians shared these sentiments, and meetings across the state's eastern tidewater declared their support for South Carolina. The Virginia General Assembly, however, struck a more moderate tone, urging South Carolina to rescind the Ordinance of Nullification and calling upon both sides to back down. Lawmakers appointed Richmond lawyer Benjamin W. Leigh as a commissioner to South Carolina to help mediate the crisis.[50]

Isolated and divided, South Carolinians now faced the prospect of defying the federal government alone. Despite Nullifiers' herculean efforts, the state remained unprepared for war, and Hayne confessed that the supplies he procured were "insufficient for the defense of the State." On January 21, party leaders held a public meeting in Charleston and agreed to "pause with honor," postponing nullification until March to give Congress more time to lower the tariff. As William Freehling observes, this decision was a "strategic retreat rather than a final surrender." Poinsett warned that the delay gave Nullifiers more time to galvanize their followers and consolidate their strength, and a Charleston writer agreed that it gave them "a chance to proclaim disunion" and "find favour with the other Southern States."[51]

At the Charleston meeting, Nullifiers affirmed the right of secession and swore to "volunteer en masse" in the state army. Hamilton had ordered a shipment of sugar from Cuba, and he agreed to let it sit in the custom house rather than "produce unnecessary collision" with the federal government. If Congress refused to lower the tariff, however, he hoped South Carolinians would *go even to the death with him for his sugar.*" Thousands of Nullifiers greeted his words with "overwhelming acclamations." One writer insisted the entire state was up in arms, prepared to "pour in a torrent into Charleston" and *"die honorably if we did not conquer."* Another Nullifier agreed that South Carolinians were "armed and in the trenches for the support of liberty, and we coolly and fearlessly await the blow."[52]

As the "Fatal First" of February dawned, Union Party writers rejoiced that the country remained at peace. Samuel Cram Jackson observed that "all is calm—no bloodshed—a beautiful day." Mary Chesnut reported that things stood "just as they were," and she hoped the Union Party would "yet save the state." A meeting in Pickens joyfully declared that the "1st of February, 1833, has arrived! We are yet Americans!" Jasper Adams, president of the College of Charleston, marveled that the tenuous peace still held firm, and that "no one is yet harmed." A rush of rumors, however, suggested that civil war remained imminent. Throughout the state, Adams heard, Union men were building a "complete military organization," while Nullifiers were still preparing for war.[53]

The State Rights Party continued to hold meetings and enroll volunteers. In Sumterville, for example, 600 men volunteered at a local militia muster, including several disillusioned Union men. At least one lowcountry parish celebrated February 1 as a milestone in the state's resistance to tyranny—an event "sacred to constitutional liberty." Villagers marched to a local Liberty Tree and shared a public dinner, where they swore to support "Carolina—the whole of Carolina—and nothing but Carolina." That evening, students from South Carolina College paraded down Main Street in Columbia with an effigy of King Andrew the First. They carried it to a Union Party newspaper office, where they triumphantly shot and burned it.[54]

As tensions escalated in South Carolina, politicians in Washington worked frantically to forge a compromise. In January, New York Congressman Gulian Verplanck proposed lowering the tariff to its 1816 levels over the next two years. The bill met widespread opposition: protectionists opposed any reductions, northern Democrats desired specific protections for local industries, and southern radicals denounced the bill for maintaining the principle of protection. Its failure, Webster confessed, left congressional moderates "heartless & desponding," uncertain of the Union's survival. In early February, however, Calhoun and Clay set aside their bitter political rivalry to attempt to avert civil war. Clay introduced a bill to gradually lower the tariff over the next nine years, after which Congress would levy duties only to raise revenue for the federal government. While a few senators objected, Calhoun immediately rose to support the plan. Amid tumultuous applause, he declared that anyone who "loves the Union must desire to see this agitating question brought to a termination."[55]

While Jackson encouraged tariff reform, he also asked Congress to grant him military power to enforce the laws. The resulting "Force Bill" enraged many southerners, and fifteen senators voted unsuccessfully to table its discussion. Nullifiers denounced it as a "bill to dissolve the union" and threatened to secede immediately if it passed. Many congressmen, however, viewed it as an essential element of compromise. As Clay explained, the two bills represented an "olive branch" and a "flaming sword," offering South Carolinians the choice between peace and war. By tempering power with mercy, Clay hoped to save the country from his own vision of disunion: cities looted and burning, fields devastated by marching armies, and "streams of American blood shed by American arms!" When Congress passed the bills, on March 1, 1833, Clay celebrated it as "perhaps the most important congressional day that ever occurred."[56]

Although the compromise tariff fell short of their demands, most Nullifiers claimed it as a victory for the state. A Columbia editor rejoiced at the "glorious triumph of Nullification," and an upcountry writer agreed that "we have gained a great and glorious victory." Robert Barnwell argued that Nullifiers had attained the "substantial object of [their] resistance" by forcing Congress to lower the tariff, and Hamilton assured supporters that "there is neither dishonor nor inconsistency in our acceptance of this compromise." They claimed the crisis as a vindication of martial manhood, insisting they had defended their freedom in the face of overwhelming odds. A woman in Sumterville, presenting a flag to a local regiment, observed that South Carolina had struggled "almost alone" against the tyranny of the federal government. Hamilton agreed that Nullifiers had contended against "tremendous odds." If war had broken out and the state's volunteers had "retired from the field, with nothing more than the credit of a drawn battle, we should not have been dishonored."[57]

The state convention met again on March 11 and voted 153 to 4 to rescind the Ordinance of Nullification. Nonetheless, delegates remained unbowed and unrepentant. Robert Turnbull proudly observed that Nullifiers had "tamed the pride of this arrogant Federal Government" and "foiled the barbarian fury of General Jackson." McDuffie viewed the compromise as a temporary victory, warning that slavery—the state's "deeper cause"—remained in jeopardy. He argued that South Carolina had more to fear from northern abolitionists than from foreign armies and that a "thorough system of defence" was indispensable to their safety and freedom. The state's militia, he insisted, should be as highly trained as Napoleon's armies, and its citizens should always act "as if the day were at hand, when they must defend their freedom." Robert Barnwell Smith agreed that slaveholders were "worse than mad" if they "do not hold their destinies in their own hands." Although Nullifiers had momentarily "beaten back" their northern oppressors, they would soon "pour upon you, with thicker numbers, and redoubled fury."[58]

Nullifiers denounced the Force Bill as an assault on constitutional freedom, and the convention voted 132 to 19 to nullify it. While scholars have viewed this as a "purely symbolic gesture," many Nullifiers were deeply committed to resisting the law. A month after the compromise, Hammond reported that the military spirit in his district remained as strong as ever, and a Columbia orator urged listeners to stay armed and "ever ready" to resist the "bloody bill." At a public dinner that July, an upcountry guest condemned the law and declared that only the "spirit that animated the Nullifiers" could save them. Calhoun warned that the Force Bill heralded the end of liberty and limited government, and he viewed nullification as the state's only salvation. The federal government, he declared, could never enforce the law in South Carolina. The other states "may live under its reign, but Carolina is resolved to live only under . . . the Constitution. There shall be at least one free state."[59]

On March 27, Charleston's Nullifiers hosted a military ball at the Arsenal to celebrate their "victory" over federal tyranny. Organizers lined the square with cannons and palmetto trees and draped the state flag from muskets above the crowd. Transparencies celebrated the state's radical leaders and declared "paramount allegiance to the state." Several thousand guests attended, and one witness compared the ball to the medieval "days of chivalry and romance"—a sight that had "never been seen in America." The spectacle and symbolism "inspire[d] the spirit of patriotism in every heart" and "excite[d] the warmest devotion to the rights of man."[60]

Five days later, 1,300 Charleston volunteers gathered on Meeting Street and marched to the Arsenal, where the artillery greeted them with a 124-gun salute. As a "glorious array of ladies" looked on, Governor Hayne presented the men with a flag and delivered a proud and defiant address. The other states, he observed, had abandoned South Carolina, leaving it to confront the "colossal power" of federal tyranny "unaided and alone." Despite their isolation, Nullifiers had rushed to defend their freedom and save their state from destruction. Hayne warned, however, that the crisis had only begun: until Congress repealed the Force Bill, "there can be no safety for the rights of the states." He urged the volunteers to stay vigilant and prepare to defend their rights at "any and every hazard."[61]

Union men, meanwhile, celebrated the country's survival and enjoyed a brief moment of political peace. Camden writer William Blanding marveled at the "first quiet Saturday I have seen in months," observing young men playing ball on the field where Nullifiers had drilled the week before. Benjamin Perry rejoiced that the "Union is safe for the present," and he prayed that partisan strife would finally give way to harmony. He resigned as editor of the *Greenville Mountaineer*, and his successor promised to devote less time to politics. Charleston's Union Party organized an elegant ball for the American officers stationed in the city. Twelve hundred guests gathered at a plantation north of the city, where the scent of spring flowers and the sound of patriotic music filled the air. The *USS Experiment* lay at anchor in the river nearby, and the American flag—the "holy banner of our union"—floated triumphantly above the crowd.[62]

Most Union Party writers, however, still feared for the future. Blanding warned that "this quiet may last but a few days," and Perry predicted that another crisis lay ahead. Nullifiers had threatened to pass a treason law and a new oath of allegiance. If they succeeded, Perry wrote, Union men would have only three options: "fight, quit the state, or become the vassals of the nullifyers." Poinsett reported that Nullifiers still hoped for secession, and Petigru agreed that the State Rights Party was laying the groundwork for a southern confederacy. These fears for the country's survival, however, only fueled Union men's resolve. John Chesnut declared that they remained "as firm in support of their principles as ever," and if another crisis arose, they "will be more united in action." Although the immediate danger had passed, the future remained uncertain, and the Union remained in peril. With new conflicts looming over the nature of loyalty and the fate of slavery, Union men despaired that "we are not yet to have quiet."[63]

5.

Swearing Allegiance

The Test Oath Controversy, 1833–35

The compromise tariff of 1833 defused the national crisis and helped avert secession and civil war for a generation. Within South Carolina, however, partisan tensions simmered for another three years, and the state remained on the verge of war. Nullifiers still dominated the state legislature, and they enacted a series of laws meant to consolidate their power and unify the state. They condemned Union men as traitors and demanded that all public officials swear an oath to bear "true allegiance . . . to the State of South Carolina." When the state's Court of Appeals ruled the oath unconstitutional, they amended the state constitution and threatened to abolish the court itself. Preparing for the next sectional crisis, they strengthened and reformed the militia and removed Unionist symbols from their flags and uniforms.

The Union Party fiercely resisted these "reforms," challenging Nullifiers at the ballot box, in the courtroom, and in the streets. Their responses, however, exposed the unresolved divisions between martial and moderate Union men. Lowcountry moderates like James Petigru and Thomas Grimké hoped to work within the political system, trusting court rulings and legislative discussion to restore harmony. They parsed and reinterpreted "allegiance" to reconcile the oath with their political convictions. Martial Union men, including a young William Lowndes Yancey, grew increasingly impatient with these abstract legal debates. In a series of massive Union Party meetings, thousands of men rejected the test oath and resolved to "die [as] freemen" rather than "live [as] slaves." South Carolinians shifted their anxious attention from Charleston to the upcountry—to the rebellious "state of Greenville"—where martial Union men prepared to resist oppression with the very stones of their mountains.[1]

Nullifiers taunted them as hypocrites and opportunists. After opposing nullification for five years, they observed, the Union Party now called for open resistance to their own state's laws. Throughout the crisis, however, Union men remained consistent in their commitment to the United States. Nullifiers insisted that sovereignty ultimately—essentially—resided in the states, and that South Carolina therefore demanded the "paramount allegiance" of its citizens. Most Union men, however, believed in dual sovereignty. They understood themselves, fundamentally, as South Carolinians *and* Americans, viewing the bonds between state and nation as mutually reinforcing. As one writer explained, "true patriotism" entailed devotion to *both* the state and federal constitutions, because "the State is made up of those two Governmental compacts." This belief fueled their resistance to nullification and the test oath. Convinced of the Union's transcendent, liberating power, they refused to sever its bonds or to allow Nullifiers to "drive them from the land of their birth."[2]

The spring of 1833 brought a brief and anxious peace to South Carolina. Congress had approved the compromise tariff, and Nullifiers had rescinded their ordinance. The *Natchez* and *Experiment* left Charleston in April, and the army quickly reassigned most of its soldiers. By July, only three artillery companies—158 men—remained. After months of patroling the harbor, the revenue cutters rested off the city's wharves, where men and women from both parties could tour them. Union men throughout the state rejoiced that partisan strife had given way to "quiet and harmony." As a Charleston writer observed, the "demon of discord has been stayed," and the "God of peace reigns triumphant." The Union Party indefinitely postponed its statewide convention, and local leaders held few meetings or public dinners that spring. Many sought to put the crisis behind them and heal the state's political divisions.[3]

Harmony, however, remained elusive. Although the immediate danger had passed, one writer explained, the "germ of discontent" had "struck deeply, very deeply, into the public mind." Enraged by the Force Bill, Nullifiers encouraged this disaffection and continued to rail against federal tyranny. They argued that the law was "incompatible with freedom": that it effectively abolished the states, tore apart the Constitution, and turned the president into a despot. While South Carolina had nullified the "Bloody Bill," it remained in force throughout the country, and only constant vigilance and military preparation could ensure liberty's survival. Nullifiers called upon South Carolinians to resist the law at all hazards, ominously insisting that "Any thing is better."[4]

Most Nullifiers still viewed the congressional compromise as a glorious victory, insisting the state had forced the federal government to back down. Party radicals, however, rejected the settlement and denounced their own allies for accepting it. A lowcountry writer, for example, judged the new tariff *"a Defeat,"* observing that the state's congressmen and convention delegates had traded away their liberties. South Carolina's volunteers, he insisted, were more radical and resolute than their leaders—ready to fight to "sustain the State." Thomas Cooper agreed. Geographer George Featherstonhaugh visited Columbia shortly after the crisis and found the college president unrepentant. Cooper believed Nullifiers were "quite in the wrong to make peace with the Union men," insisting they had surrendered everything they "might have brought forth at a future day." Instead of compromising, Cooper argued, South Carolinians should have "taken the field against General Jackson" and "fought all the power he could have brought against them."[5]

In March 1833, a week after the Nullification Convention adjourned, Poinsett observed that Nullifiers were still "animated with the zeal of fanatics." They maintained their partisan organization, and they were working tirelessly to "disseminate their doctrines and destroy the Union." A New England editor visited Charleston that month and found Nullifiers still wearing their blue cockades and "nullifying badges" as "proudly and fearlessly" as ever. Nullifiers marched through Columbia carrying effigies of William Drayton, James Blair, and Thomas Mitchell—the state's Union Party congressmen. They displayed the figures throughout town, playing music and huzzahing wildly, before ultimately hanging and burning them. Charleston's Irish Volunteers celebrated St. Patrick's Day that year with speeches and toasts demanding resistance. The company enlisted to serve the state during the nullification winter, and Nullifiers celebrated the men as the champions of constitutional liberty throughout the world. Captain William P. Finley toasted the "Palmetto and the Shamrock," praying they would "flourish forever . . . on shores unsoiled by the footsteps of tyranny."[6]

When Robert Turnbull died in June 1833, Nullifiers across the state hosted meetings and delivered tributes—serving both to honor his memory and to galvanize the party. They wore black crape armbands for a month as a sign of mourning and vowed to uphold Turnbull's constitutional principles. They viewed his death as a "national calamity," lamenting the irreparable loss to the cause of human freedom. In Charleston, a large crowd escorted his body to St. Philip's Episcopal Church, where a military company fired a long salute. That November, Governor Robert Hayne laid the cornerstone for a grand monument to Turnbull's memory. Hamilton delivered a riveting eulogy, declaring Turnbull's 1827 pamphlet *The Crisis* the "first bugle-call to the South to rally." He celebrated South Carolina's glorious triumph, observing that "six weeks of impending nullification" had accomplished more than ten years of idle petitioning. Although Nullifiers had accepted the compromise, Hamilton said, they had not abandoned their principles. The moment Congress trampled their liberties, they would return to the trenches and nullify the law again. South Carolinians remained in the Union "under an act of permanent nullification," and they would resist the tyrannical Force Bill until Congress tore it from the statute books.[7]

Nullifiers' Independence Day meetings reaffirmed their partisan resistance. At a military festival in Columbia, guests toasted South Carolina as "Our only Sovereign" and proclaimed the Union worthless without liberty. If Congress refused to repeal the Force Bill, they insisted, then South Carolinians would tear down the American flag and "cease to celebrate this day." In Lexington, the Richland Nullifiers militia company declared that nullification had stemmed the tide of tyranny, and if it ever failed, they would respond with fixed bayonets. The Calhoun Hussars swore to dissolve the Union rather than submit to tyranny, while an officer in the Hayne Riflemen urged the state's volunteers to remain in arms indefinitely. Throughout the state, Nullifiers equated the Ordinance of Nullification with the Declaration of Independence and declared February 1, 1833, as sacred and significant as July 4, 1776.[8]

Union men, meanwhile, used their Independence Day meetings to celebrate the country's survival. Some foregrounded their own party's role in defeating nullification, insisting that Union men would always fight to sustain "liberty, order, and good government." A Greenville resident vowed never to forgive or forget Nullifiers' treasonous actions, while a Charleston orator declared that anyone who sought to "obliterate one star" from the American flag deserved a traitor's death. Most speakers, however, prayed that the spirit of partisanship would rapidly fade away. A Sumter artilleryman, for example, hoped that "party strife will soon be forgotten, and peace and harmony again reside among the sons of South Carolina." Charleston editor Aaron Willington rejoiced that America's "glorious experiment of rational liberty" survived and continued to give hope to the world.[9]

They recognized, however, that the Union remained vulnerable. To ensure its permanence, they needed to foster patriotism and cultivate a spirit of compromise and conciliation. Union Party leaders in Chester and York arranged for local women to sew American flags and present them to militia units. Charleston painter Susan Belcher presented Greenville District with a flag depicting an eagle encircled by twenty-four stars and soaring above the "transient clouds" of partisanship. A Charleston writer encouraged "Union ladies" across the upcountry to return the favor by sewing a flag for the city's "Union soldiers," who "stood firm at their post" in the hour of crisis.[10]

At the same time, Charleston's Union Party began raising money to commission a painting glorifying the American flag. In the late 1820s, while Joel Poinsett served as Minister to Mexico, General Vicente Guerrero marched on Mexico City after a disputed election. Many residents took refuge in Poinsett's house, which became a target for Guerrero's army. As the rebels gathered outside the building, Poinsett appeared on the balcony and unfurled the American flag, demanding protection for everyone inside. The soldiers reportedly "cheered the standard of our Union" and placed guards outside the house to protect it from attack. Union Party leaders insisted that the story had no parallel in human history, and they sought to preserve its "moral beauty and grandeur . . . on the page of the historian and the canvass of the painter."[11]

For Union men, this painting was part of a much larger vision. With "sectional excitements" eroding devotion to the Union, they hoped to create a series of paintings, songs, and celebrations to "excite and perpetuate National enthusiasm." These nationalist paintings would remind Americans—and teach the "rising generation"—of the "unseen but highly moral" power of the Union. By mass producing engravings of these scenes, every family in the country could display them in their homes, and children could "learn before they can read, to love and reverence the emblem of our country's power." Newspapers as far away as Vermont, Louisiana, and Ohio reprinted this appeal, and subscriptions soon poured in from across the country.[12]

Despite their pleas for "vigilance and firmness," Charleston's Union Party leaders decided not to contest the congressional election of 1833. As Poinsett explained, they were only willing to challenge Nullifiers for power when the Union's survival hung in the balance. They believed "no sacrifice [was] too great" to sustain the "majesty of the laws" and save the country from anarchy. The congressional compromise, however, had achieved those goals, and now they sought to "restore order and harmony" to the community. By contesting the election, they feared, they would only heighten the political excitement—degrading the state's political institutions and tarnishing the city's character and credit. Nonetheless, Poinsett insisted, the party was "unbroken in spirit [and] in numbers," and it would never waver in its devotion to the Union.[13]

Just before the election, a group of Union men and disaffected Nullifiers formed an Independent Ticket, headlined by James Petigru and Daniel Huger. While some residents viewed the ticket as a symbol of reconciliation, others saw it as a cynical attempt to prolong partisan strife. The Union Party's Central Committee disavowed the ticket and refused to enter the fray. Only 1,537 people voted in the municipal election that September—down from 2,070 the year before. Turnout among Nullifiers fell 17 percent, but party discipline remained strong, and most voters submitted straight-party tickets. Although the Independent Ticket framed itself as bipartisan, it drew most of its candidates—and voters—from the Union Party. Nonetheless, turnout among Union men plummeted by 38 percent, and Nullifiers swept the municipal elections.[14]

Statewide, the congressional elections demonstrated both the strength and the ambivalence of Unionist partisanship. Party leaders in three congressional districts chose not to contest the election. In Charleston, editor Aaron Willington observed, Union men were "almost entirely passive and inert"; he had never seen them "more listless than on this occasion." Lancaster Union man James Blair, however, ran unopposed, and elsewhere the party fielded candidates even in districts where it was hopelessly outnumbered. In the northwestern corner of the state—Pendleton, Greenville, Spartanburg, and York—both parties contested the elections with as much urgency and excitement as ever. Turnout in these districts *increased* from the previous year, and one editor declared it the "most exciting and animated" election he had ever witnessed. Nullifiers won both elections in this part of the state by razor-thin margins: 51 percent in one district and only 50.6 percent in the other. Nullifiers captured eight of South Carolina's nine congressional seats, and they insisted that Union Party strength had collapsed throughout the state.

The results, however, were deceptive, and overall, both parties remained healthy and vibrant across large portions of the state. In the five contested congressional districts, turnout for both parties essentially matched its 1832 levels. As one editor explained, the "friends of Union though beaten are not discouraged—theirs is the cause of truth, and will at last prevail."[15]

In these congressional elections, nullification itself was rarely at issue, although memories of the previous winter still bitterly divided communities. Instead, the political contests focused on the test oath and the nature of allegiance. The Ordinance of Nullification required all civil and military officers in the state to swear an oath to "obey, execute, and enforce this ordinance." Although the Nullification Convention rescinded the ordinance in March 1833, Nullifiers debated enacting a new oath of allegiance. One proposal— ultimately rejected—required all state officials to declare South Carolina a "Free and Sovereign State" and renounce "all other allegiances." Union men in the convention vehemently opposed the test oath, insisting it would prolong and intensify the political crisis. Nullifiers, however, claimed it was necessary to unify the state. They ultimately pushed through an act requiring officers to swear allegiance to South Carolina and "obedience only" to the federal government. When it passed, by a vote of 90 to 60, a Union Party judge advised Benjamin Perry to "go home and convert your plowshares into swords and your pruning hooks into spears, for we shall have to fight."[16]

Most Nullifiers celebrated the oath, hoping to purge Union men from power or bring them "into the line of patriotism and duty." The Force Bill, they observed, still hovered over the state, empowering President Jackson to tear South Carolina apart. As one Nullifier warned, a "storm is rising in the political horizon," and "every officer and seaman must be faithful in his post." South Carolina, he wrote, had to ensure the loyalty of its citizens, and anyone who swore allegiance to another power was unworthy of its trust. A Charleston writer agreed, insisting it was essential for the state to "ascertain its friends from its foes." With civil war still looming, South Carolina could not allow its weapons to fall into the hands of its enemies.[17]

Although the Nullification Convention had approved the oath, the state legislature still needed to codify it into law. When the assembly reconvened in November 1833, Nullifiers quickly moved to consolidate their control. They held commanding majorities in both houses, and a former congressman observed that the party now *was* the state. In his annual message, Governor

Hayne asked lawmakers to ensure South Carolina's "permanent protection and security." He proposed reorganizing the militia, bolstering Charleston's defenses, and stockpiling 10,000 muskets and rifles to meet "any sudden emergency." South Carolina, he observed, had made great strides during the nullification winter, and they could not afford to "lose all the ground we have gained."[18]

Nullifiers drafted an amendment to enshrine the test oath in the state constitution. After days of debate, the house approved it by a vote of 90 to 21, and the senate concurred 30 to 13. Union Party Senator Alfred Huger tried to alter the wording, clarifying that South Carolinians could swear the oath without renouncing their national allegiance. The senate, however, overwhelmingly rejected his proposal. The constitutional amendment would not take effect right away. In order to alter the state constitution, two successive sessions of the South Carolina General Assembly needed to ratify an amendment—delaying action until the following year.[19]

Undeterred, Nullifiers added the test oath to a bill reorganizing the state militia, which they passed on December 19. The militia bill immediately removed all generals from command and empowered the legislature—dominated by Nullifiers—to appoint their successors. All other officers would lose their commissions in April 1834, and their companies would hold elections to replace them. Every officer would then have to declare "true allegiance" to South Carolina. Anyone who refused would face court martial and forfeit his commission, and his commanding officer would appoint someone to take his place. In a symbolically rich gesture, the bill replaced the American eagle on the militia buttons with the state Palmetto tree. Legislators also appropriated almost $70,000 for the governor to publish manuals of military tactics, reinforce Charleston's arsenal, and purchase 14,000 guns fit for "immediate use."

Union men fiercely resisted these "reforms." They insisted that the oath violated their freedom of conscience and forced them to choose between their allegiance to state and country. If another crisis erupted, and an officer remained faithful to the Union, the state could execute him for treason. If, instead, he stayed true to his oath and sided with South Carolina, he would become a traitor to the United States. With the oath in place, no Union man could conscientiously hold military office—a dilemma that effectively disenfranchised every Union man in the militia.[20]

In response, some Union men left South Carolina altogether. In one upcountry village, the "triumph of nullification" prompted several prominent families to abandon the state. In another community, soil exhaustion and the "prevalence of nullification" drove countless Union men westward, until "scarcely a single family" remained. Other moderate Union men favored peaceful protest, hoping to work through the state courts to overturn the militia bill. Some even argued that Union men could swear the oath without violating their consciences. A lowcountry writer calling himself *Walterborough* insisted the oath was "perfectly harmless." South Carolina's constitution already required officers to swear to uphold the state and federal constitutions, and *Walterborough* claimed the new oath was essentially the same. By taking the oath, he merely swore allegiance to the state "as known and recognized by my country."[21]

Martial Union men, however, rejected these passive responses and organized massive meetings in protest. In York District, the militia bill caused an "unprecedented uproar," and one observer feared "there will be blood shed yet." Adopting a "high chivalric tone," a local leader threatened to wage war against every Nullifier in the state. In Chester District, the oath "roused the indignation of the whole union party," and 700 men assembled in the rain to declare their opposition. They refused to obey anyone who swore the test oath and resolved to elect their own officers regardless of the consequences. They would "maintain the supremacy of the law at the point of the bayonet," and if the Constitution "must perish they too will perish with it." Spartanburg's Union men supported "a revolution by appeal to arms," and they denounced the moderate members of their own party as "traitor[s] to the cause."[22]

As the state's northwestern districts erupted in protest, one writer insisted the "excitement in the Mountains is beyond description." Unionist outrage was stronger and more widespread than ever before, and party leaders declared that Nullifiers could never enforce the militia bill. Greenville's Union men "welcome[d] Revolution" with all its consequences and vowed to free themselves from tyranny or "let their bones whiten and their blood enrich their hills." They urged their militia officers to defy the bill and maintain their commissions, vowing to "stand by [them] to the death." They began gathering arms and ammunition to defend themselves, and they asked Union men throughout the state to help them save the Constitution—"or die with it."[23]

This unprecedented political excitement spread throughout the state. Darlington's Union men favored "the most determined resistance," while those in Spartanburg prepared to "resist by an appeal to arms." A Yorkville writer agreed that they would "take the battle field" rather than submit to tyranny. At a meeting there that February, 1,000 men gathered to fly the American flag and declare their opposition to the law. They resolved to maintain their freedom against every enemy—even their own "tyrannical Legislature." As a Lancaster meeting explained, Nullifiers had transformed the state into a military camp, disenfranchising Union men and spreading "discord and hatred" throughout South Carolina. Having tried everything in their power to maintain peace, these Union men now prepared to "try what virtue there is in bullets!" Meeting after meeting echoed these sentiments: denouncing the test oath, pledging only to serve under their own officers, and vowing to resist the law "even to the death."[24]

Some Nullifiers recognized the gravity of the crisis. George McDuffie informed Greenville Nullifier Waddy Thompson—now a brigadier general—that the Union men in his district would "disregard your orders & erect the standard of open rebellion." Others, however, relished the opportunity to fight. After a militant Union Party meeting in Abbeville, Henry Townes "laugh[ed] at their folly" and insisted that Nullifiers "would be very glad to have a good excuse to shoot some of them." If Union men "become insurgents and make war," a Charleston writer insisted, Nullifiers would rally to defend the state and enforce the law. If necessary, he threatened, they could even call upon President Jackson to "employ the forces of the Union to 'suppress the insurrection.'"[25]

The political fury horrified moderate Union men, who worked to rein in their martial allies and peacefully resolve the crisis. James Petigru observed that the "whole mountain region is in a flame," and he warned that a "border war" would erupt unless Nullifiers backed down. Another writer feared that the state's mountains would "soon be crimsoned with the blood of brethren." The oath, he insisted, would rekindle the "fires of civil commotion," and no matter which side won, the state would become a charred ruin of "domestic desolation." Spartanburg lawyer James E. Henry believed most party leaders—even in the upcountry—were "opposed to violence," but the political fury among rank-and-file Union men would "never permanently subside until they have tasted blood—and felt some of the horrors of civil war."[26]

By early 1834, even Benjamin Perry recognized the need for moderation. Exhausted and hoping for peace, he had largely retreated from public life after the nullification winter. Even the test oath failed to move him, and he privately insisted Union men could take it without violating their principles. With "great reluctance," however, he reentered the "turmoil of party strife" to help save the state from war. He found the district's Union Party on the verge of revolution. In February 1834, fifteen hundred Union men gathered in Greenville, many prepared for armed resistance. Undeterred, Perry presented a series of moderate resolutions and desperately encouraged the crowd to accept them. After a spirited discussion, they agreed to remain "peaceable citizens" and work through "legal and proper" channels before resorting to arms.[27]

A meeting in Spartanburg the same day followed the same pattern. One observer insisted the meeting "exceeded any thing I ever beheld—there was no speaking—we concluded it was best not to speak—*the excitement was too great.*" Twelve hundred people attended, and most favored "going ahead" and "plac[ing] the Union party on the offensive." A party committee, however, drafted moderate resolutions that encouraged the crowd to resist "*first,* by legal means." Several committee members dissented, but the "cool-headed" moderates ultimately prevailed. They hoped to maintain law and order, preferring to "await the attack from the nullifiers." Nonetheless, they agreed that Nullifiers could never enforce the test oath in the district, and they warned that—if peaceful measures failed—"we know what follows."[28]

Greenville's leaders called for a statewide Union Party convention to meet the following month—an attempt to "moderate the inconsiderate rashness of some of the party." The plan quickly gained momentum, and meetings across the state began appointing delegates. The convention met in Greenville on March 24, with 110 delegates from at least thirteen districts. They appointed Charleston lawyer Daniel Huger as president, and in his two-hour opening address, he raged against the militia bill and test oath. He was prepared to "risk every danger" to ensure the Union's survival, insisting that only "strong measures . . . could arrest the [Nullifiers'] revolution." A local Nullifier reported that Huger was "embittered to a degree approaching madness," and Petigru confessed that he was "far ahead of the rest" of Charleston's delegates.[29]

Several upcountry delegates rallied to Huger's leadership, preferring to fight rather than "turn the quarrel into a law suit." Poinsett, however, served as chairman of the convention's Central Committee, and he drafted a series of moderate resolutions intended to "make the Nullifiers the aggressors." He had seen civil wars and revolutions devastate the Latin American republics, and he feared the country's freedom would not survive the struggle. He had gone to Greenville to "calm the troubled waters," and he urged the delegates to exhaust every "peaceable and constitutional remedy" before resorting to violence. He trusted the courts to strike down the test oath, and if the state's judges sustained it, he would appeal to the Supreme Court. At the same time, he urged the state's Union men to stand by their principles: to reject the oath, elect their own officers, and refuse to serve under any officer "*appointed* to command them."[30]

The delegates ultimately approved Poinsett's resolutions, and many party leaders rejoiced at the convention's moderation. Martial Union men, however, were ready and eager to fight. Two Charleston delegates reported that the "excitement in the upper districts was spontaneous with the people, and almost incontrollable [*sic*]." If Nullifiers tried to enforce the test oath, an Abbeville delegate observed, "you will certainly hear of bloodshed." Even Poinsett was ultimately willing to resort to violence to maintain his freedom. If necessary, he wrote, he would set aside his personal feelings and lead his party into battle. He urged Union men not to abandon the state, assuring them that they "had a right to the soil." He resolved to live and die in South Carolina, with the Star-Spangled Banner as his shroud.[31]

Even before the Union Convention met, party leaders had begun challenging the test oath in court. In February 1834, Charleston's Washington Light Infantry, a predominantly Unionist militia company, elected Edward McCready as a first lieutenant. He refused to swear the new oath and sued to receive his commission—but Judge Elihu H. Bay denied him. In April, when Lancaster colonel James McDonald sued for his commission, Judge John S. Richardson sided with him and declared the oath unconstitutional. The Union Party appealed Bay's ruling and Nullifiers appealed Richardson's, and the state Court of Appeals agreed to hear the cases in Columbia later that spring.[32]

Robert Barnwell Smith defended the state—and the test oath—while James Petigru and Thomas Grimké represented the Union Party officers. They debated for hours, contesting the nature of sovereignty, liberty, allegiance, and judicial review in a series of powerful speeches. Nullifiers argued that sovereignty was indivisible and that South Carolina remained a "free, sovereign, and independent state." The state therefore had a right to demand "exclusive allegiance" from the men entrusted to serve it. By refusing to swear the oath, they maintained, their enemies denied the state's sovereign power and proved themselves "unworthy of liberty." Most Union men, however, believed in dual sovereignty, insisting the state and country both deserved their allegiance. As a Charleston meeting explained, they "owe[d] allegiance to the State which gave us birth and obedience to the laws which protect us." They refused, however, to "renounce their allegiance to the United States," which protected them from foreign invasion and preserved their republican institutions.[33]

Historian David Potter contends that nationalism flourishes not by overpowering other loyalties but by incorporating and subsuming them, and this dynamic characterized nullification-era Unionism. Union men's love for their families, communities, and state helped sustain their devotion to the country. Benjamin Perry observed that men's devotion to the Union could not diminish their love for South Carolina, because the two emotions were "not only consistent, but seem to strengthen and invigorate each other." State and country were "equally dear to me; and in fact, are but one and the same," because they were "both the governments of the people." Drayton agreed that "Federal and State Allegiance are perfectly consistent: instead of interfering with, they mutually strengthen each other." Sumterville Judge John S. Richardson agreed that being "for the State, properly means 'for the State' in the Union, under both the Federal and State Constitutions. The State is made up of those two Governmental compacts."[34]

Three judges served on the Court of Appeals: Union men John B. O'Neall and David Johnson and Nullifier William Harper. Predictably, the court ruled the test oath unconstitutional in a 2 to 1 vote, declaring that South Carolinians owed dual allegiance to state and country. Nullifiers denounced the ruling with a fury that "far exceeded" anything Union men expected. Some urged Governor Hayne to call the state legislature into special session and impeach O'Neall and Johnson, while others encouraged him to ignore the court altogether. Although Hayne viewed the ruling as a "monstrous outrage," he recognized the danger of impulsive action. It would be "worse than useless," he concluded, "to attempt to legislate with a partisan Court ready to arrest your Laws." Instead, he looked ahead to the fall elections. If Nullifiers secured another two-thirds majority in the state assembly, they could add the test oath to the state constitution and outflank the Court of Appeals. To ensure a decisive victory, Hayne encouraged Nullifiers to employ "all the means heretofore found so successful": reorganizing local State Rights Associations, hosting meetings, and flooding the countryside with pamphlets.[35]

A special congressional election that June provided a test for both parties. In April 1834, James Blair—the Union Party's only representative in Congress—committed suicide in Washington in a fit of drunken despair. Party leaders lamented Blair's death as a national tragedy, observing that his seat represented the "last and only citadel of our principles" in Washington. They nominated former Governor Richard Manning to replace him while Nullifiers countered with Colonel Benjamin Elmore. In May, a Union Party writer reported that the "agitation of the people and the struggle of the parties" exceeded "all that we have experienced in the past." Nullifiers, in particular, were publishing pamphlets, circulating handbills, and "moving heaven and earth" to defeat Manning. Ultimately, however, the Union Party triumphed by about 650 votes.[36]

That spring, Union men also contested militia elections throughout the state, and one upcountry writer rejoiced that the party was steadily "turning back . . . the torrent" of tyranny. These victories helped energize the party, and in their Independence Day meetings they reaffirmed their resistance to the test oath. If Nullifiers amended the state constitution, one meeting declared, Union men would "rush upon [them], and slay them at the cannon's mouth." In Abbeville that day, twenty-year-old William Lowndes Yancey delivered his first major public address: a fiery appeal for Union. Yancey studied law in Greenville under Benjamin Perry and quickly absorbed his mentor's Unionist principles. In his speech, he celebrated the "cords of affection" that united all Americans and warned that Union men would fight with swords and muskets to hold the country together.[37]

Meetings across the upcountry portrayed the test oath amendment as part of a conspiracy to destroy republican government. As Greenville editor Charles D'Oyley explained, Nullifiers began by seizing control of the state legislature. Because lawmakers elected the governor, this gave them control of the executive branch as well. Nullifiers then imposed a test oath to gain control of the militia and purge Union men from office. When the Court of Appeals struck down the oath, Nullifiers resolved to amend the constitution and perhaps even abolish the court. If they succeeded—if they triumphed in the upcoming elections—Nullifiers would control the entire state government and perhaps tear the state from the Union. Some writers pushed the conspiracy even further, claiming that Nullifiers were plotting to murder Union Party leaders. Rumors swirled that Nullifiers were infiltrating Unionist militia companies in order to assassinate their officers or that Nullifiers were bribing Union men's slaves to kill them. Although these stories likely had little foundation in fact, they underscored the anxieties that still divided the state.[38]

Both parties redoubled their efforts as the October elections approached. Nullifiers founded Whig Associations or reorganized their old State Rights Associations to "disseminate correct political intelligence." Union men responded with massive petitions against the test oath: 350 men signed in Edgefield, 600 in York, 900 in Spartanburg, 900 in Pendleton, and more than 1,400 in Greenville. In Clarendon, Union men accused Nullifiers of "conspiring to destroy the institutions of the country." They vowed to resist with "spirit and determination" and to "brave death, rather than perjury." At a meeting in Greenville that September, William Lowndes Yancey invoked the state's Revolutionary history to affirm the power and majesty of the Union. Turning to the district's Revolutionary War veterans, he asked if any man would march alongside traitors while the "single Star, Palmetto, and Rattle Snake waves over him, against that banner which he once fought for, bled for, [and] gave up fortune for?" He urged the crowd to demand their rights as citizens of the United States—to lodge one more protest against injustice and then fight their oppressors with the very stones of their mountains.[39]

Many observers believed South Carolina was on the verge of an intrastate civil war. If Nullifiers refused to back down, one writer declared, "we will fight." Union men had the "best marksmen in the State," and if fighting broke out, they would "clean the coasts of our enemies" in a "short and bloody" campaign. On October 12, the night before the election, Nullifiers in Charleston broke into a Union Party house on Queen Street, demolishing windows and beating several Union men. The following night, when 300 Nullifiers besieged a Union Party headquarters, the outnumbered Union men opened fire on the crowd and wounded six men. Enraged, Nullifiers rushed to the city arsenal and demanded weapons, but the guards refused to release them. Hayne and Hamilton arrived and struggled to restrain the crowd, urging them to "wait till [they] had got the law on their side." When the time was right, Hamilton swore, he would lead the party to "victory and revenge."[40]

In the election of 1834, James Petigru reflected, Union men "made great efforts and rallied the whole of our party, but the majority retained an unbroken phalanx." Nullifiers captured three-fourths of the seats in the state legislature, ensuring they had enough votes to amend South Carolina's constitution (Table 5). Union Party editors described this as the "most important Election which has ever taken place in this country" and warned that it could be the state's last free election. These appeals resonated with voters, and the Union Party *gained* ground on their opponents. In the twenty-two districts for which complete election returns exist, turnout among Nullifiers fell by 10 percent between 1832 and 1834. Union Party turnout, however, declined by only 2 percent. Both parties remained reasonably healthy and cohesive throughout much of the state. The Union Party elected two congressmen—Yorkville lawyer James Rogers and Clarendon planter Richard Manning—and Benjamin Perry fell about 70 votes short of unseating Nullifier Warren R. Davis.[41]

For many Union men, the election results illustrated the injustice of South Carolina's political structure. The state constitution granted each parish and district equal representation in the senate, giving St. James Santee (with about 100 voters) as much power as Pendleton (with roughly 5,000). These "rotten burroughs" helped give Nullifiers an insurmountable 75 percent supermajority in the state legislature. Union men argued that the test oath amendment violated the spirit of the constitution, since less than two-thirds of the state's voters supported it. They vowed to resist this "fearful tyranny," refusing to "fold their arms and suffer themselves to be trampled on." A Charleston writer declared that "all bonds of brotherhood are broken—all ties of fellow-citizenship are severed," and Union men and Nullifiers "must be foes." William Lowndes Yancey thundered that upcountry Union men had "planted the emblem of their faith—the Star Spangled Banner" in the soil of their mountains, and "no force shall tear it down" while they lived to defend it.[42]

A Georgetown editor declared that Union men had "lived [as] citizens of the State and the United States—freemen under both, and we have resolved

TABLE 5. Election Results, 1834

District	Nullifier Votes	Nullifier Percentage	Union Party Votes	Union Party Percentage	Estimated Turnout (%)
Abbeville	1,354	57	1,033	43	65
Anderson	1,730	72	658	28	81
Barnwell	—	—	—	—	—
Beaufort	679	88	92	12	50
Charleston	1,765	54	1,507	46	56
Chester	1,001	58	739	42	70
Chesterfield	148	27	406	73	43
Colleton (Incomplete)	375	59	261	41	—
Darlington	441	42	611	58	65
Edgefield	1,563	90	172	10	50
Fairfield	—	—	—	—	—
Georgetown	304	54	260	46	97
Greenville	419	22	1,509	78	74
Horry	31	8	363	92	49
Kershaw	143	30	338	70	38
Lancaster	261	31	579	69	55
Laurens	1,365	61	861	39	74
Lexington	421	52	390	48	65
Marion	689	63	410	37	65
Marlboro	495	96	22	4	52
Newberry	—	—	—	—	—
Orangeburg (Incomplete)	406	84	78	16	—
Pickens	775	53	688	47	57
Richland	718	75	244	25	63
Spartanburg	840	31	1,875	69	72
Sumter (Incomplete)	532	56	415	44	—
Union	1,152	68	538	32	67
Williamsburg	310	49	318	51	90
York	1,039	49	1,067	51	76
Total (Incomplete)	18,957	55	15,434	45	—

Note: Election results unavailable for Barnwell, Fairfield, and Newberry Districts. Election results incomplete for Colleton, Orangeburg, and Sumter Districts.

Sources: 1830 United States Census; issues of *Charleston Mercury, Charleston Courier,* and *Greenville Mountaineer* for October 1834.

to die so." If the state legislature passed the amendment, he argued, Union Party lawmakers should "secede" and organize a convention in Charleston. They should issue a proclamation denouncing the state government and declaring South Carolinians "absolved from its laws." They should then order a "military organization of the whole party" and prevent all state elections until Nullifiers rescinded the test oath. The writer recognized the radicalism of these plans. The test oath, however, would subject Union men to taxation without representation and degrade them to the level of Russian serfs. Yancey, now serving as editor of *The Greenville Mountaineer,* reprinted the resolutions and insisted that they "express the sentiments of the great mass of the *people* in the Mountains."[43]

By the time the state legislature opened in November 1834, tensions neared a breaking point. Union men introduced a resolution stating that "true" allegiance to South Carolina did not imply "exclusive" allegiance; Nullifiers countered with one confirming that the oath demanded exclusive allegiance. On December 4, Abbeville legislator Armistead Burt proposed a new treason bill declaring that anyone who levied war against the state or gave comfort or aid to its enemies would "suffer death without benefit of Clergy." Nullifiers also drafted a bill to abolish the Court of Appeals and consolidate the assembly's power over the state. Union men pushed back against every measure, but they were hopelessly outnumbered. The senate passed the test oath amendment on December 5, and the house followed soon after—easily surpassing the necessary two-thirds majority.[44]

While legislators debated and voters prepared for battle, James Petigru traveled to Columbia to avert the impending catastrophe. He hoped to persuade both parties to back down—to agree that the oath "leaves the question of divided allegiance to the judgment and conscience of every man." He expected his efforts to fail. Union men, he observed, were "running wild" and refusing to swear the oath, while Nullifiers were working to make its wording *stronger.* When he arrived in Columbia, he confessed, "things looked pretty dark," and Union men were "breathing nothing but war." He feared that mediation would fail and South Carolinians would soon find themselves "knee deep in blood."[45]

To his surprise, however, several Nullifiers appeared willing to work toward peace. Hamilton delivered a conciliatory speech in the senate, and David McCord offered to meet with Union men to "bring about a pacification." At a Union Party caucus on December 4, moderate and martial Union men debated the merits of compromise and whether "the oath was capable of an innocent construction." Ultimately, they crafted an ultimatum. They would accept the test oath only if Nullifiers tabled the treason bill, abandoned their plans to abolish the Court of Appeals, and clarified that allegiance to the state was consistent with allegiance to the Union. Petigru met with Hamilton the following day, and after a long discussion, the former governor "expressed himself satisfied with the terms." Hamilton served on the state's committee on federal relations, and he agreed to draft a report acceding to the Union Party's demands.[46]

Rank-and-file Nullifiers still sought to strengthen the test oath, and Hamilton feared a "rebellion in the ranks" if news of these meetings leaked. Over the next few days, he struggled to pacify the militant members of his party. He called a party caucus for 10:00 a.m. on December 9, hoping to conclude the debate before his belligerent allies began drinking. After four hours of discussion, Hamilton persuaded most legislators to accept the compromise. The house approved the committee's report by a vote of 91 to 28, and the senate concurred 36 to 4. The assembly "resounded with applause," followed by "shaking of hands, warm congratulation and wonderment and rejoicing." David McCord ordered 500 copies of the report printed, and moderates in both parties hoped the compromise would finally bring peace to the state. Calhoun observed that the "restoration of harmony is complete," while Petigru reported hopefully that the "spell of party is broken and Nullification in Carolina is no more than a recollection."[47]

The "most violent" Nullifiers, however, refused to accept reconciliation. They made up about one-third of the party's legislators: in the house, twenty-eight men voted against the compromise report, thirty-four voted to take up discussion of the treason bill, and thirty-five voted to reform the judiciary system. Martial Union men in the state's northwestern districts also rejected the compromise. William Lowndes Yancey "*dissent*[ed] from every principle contained in it," insisting the test oath still demanded exclusive allegiance to the state. He thundered that Nullifiers had surrendered nothing while the Union Party had given up everything. Greenville's Union men had resisted the test oath for almost two years, and many believed that their own representatives had betrayed them by accepting it.[48]

In January 1835, several thousand Union men gathered in Spartanburg

District to celebrate the anniversary of the Battle of Cowpens. Here, in 1781, Continental Army soldiers and militiamen had decisively defeated a British army in one of the turning points of the Revolution's southern theater. To mark the occasion, Benjamin Perry delivered a stirring address celebrating the Union as the war's crowning achievement. Now, he warned, Nullifiers sought to destroy that Union—"poisoning and blighting all that is sacred in friendship—all that is patriotic in feeling, and all that is lovely and estimable in society!" Like Yancey, he rejected the compromise, insisting it had not resolved the nature of allegiance.[49]

At a public dinner that evening, guests celebrated the Union Party as the "political salvation of South Carolina." The official toasts endorsed the compromise, and party leaders from Charleston and Columbia wrote letters welcoming the "cessation of party strife." Yancey, however, raged that liberty was too sacred for the party to compromise away, and other guests echoed his resistance. They saluted the "mountain citizens" of Greenville, Spartanburg, and Pickens, who stood united against tyranny in the 1770s and the 1830s. They were "determined to be free," and they would never allow one star to fall from the sacred American flag. If Nullifiers renewed the struggle, Union men would prove themselves worthy of their ancestors and sustain their liberty with their lives.[50]

In July 1835, Brigadier General Waddy Thompson ordered Greenville District's militia officers to assemble for review—igniting a military controversy that tested the limits of the state compromise. By attending the review, they would have to swear the oath of allegiance and adopt the state's new Palmetto buttons. In doing so, many believed, they would violate their principles and betray the trust of their men, who elected them in April 1834 with explicit instructions not to take the oath. After a meeting at Benjamin Perry's house that summer, they decided to boycott the militia muster; by one estimate, 240 of the area's 400 officers chose not to attend.[51]

Thompson ordered the arrest of all field officers and most company officers, but he soon focused his attention on four men: Colonel Thomas Brockman, Colonel Robert Goodlett, Lieutenant Colonel William McNeely, and Major Henry Smith. He charged them with willfully disobeying orders and conspiring to "defy and resist the laws of the state" and scheduled a court martial for September 21. Union men denounced the proceedings, warning that Nullifiers would stack the court against them, and Thompson confirmed their fears by appointing Nullifier Tandy Walker as Judge Advocate. Smith and McNeely published letters reaffirming Union Party principles and declaring the court martial a plot to trample civil liberty. They insisted that Nullifiers, by charging them with mutiny for attending a peaceful political meeting, were effectively denying Union men their freedom of speech and assembly. While Nullifiers demanded paramount allegiance to the state, Smith reflected that he had served state and country together for twenty-five years. He had fought against Britain in the War of 1812, and he fiercely resisted any attempt to divide his allegiance to the state from his devotion to the Union. He would serve forever beneath the Star-Spangled Banner—the "proud emblem of Liberty—whether against foreign or domestic enemies." Despite their efforts, however, the court martial found all four officers guilty, cashiering them from service and disqualifying them from holding office for the next twelve months.[52]

The few elections that year revealed a district and state in transition. In January 1835, Congressman Warren R. Davis died in Washington after a long illness. Governor George McDuffie scheduled a new election for September, and the campaign raged throughout the summer. Yancey endorsed his mentor Benjamin Perry in *The Greenville Mountaineer,* and Nullifiers responded by nominating Waddy Thompson. The campaign centered on four interlocking issues: the approaching presidential election, the oath of allegiance, the legitimacy of nullification, and the nature of the Union. Thompson ardently defended the test oath, insisting he would take it even if it demanded exclusive allegiance to South Carolina. The federal government, he contended, had no power to coerce the states, and any "violation of the compact of Union" would authorize and justify secession. Perry, however, insisted that secession was "at war with the fundamental principles of our Government." He denounced nullification and championed the principle of "divided Allegiance." Reflecting upon his love for the Union, he trusted his actions to speak for themselves: "If my course for the last five years be not a sufficient pledge," he insisted, then "I am incapable of giving one."[53]

Thompson secured a commanding victory, defeating Perry 3,234 to 2,524. For Greenville voters, the partisan battles of the nullification crisis remained salient: 1,922 men cast their ballots in the election (down only six votes from the year before), and 76 percent voted for Perry. The Union Party, however, collapsed in neighboring Pendleton District. Hundreds of Union men failed to turn out, and the party's share of the district's vote fell from 35 percent in 1834 to 28 percent in 1835. Union men attributed Thompson's victory to fraud, violence, and intimidation, claiming that Pendleton Nullifiers had threatened to lynch anyone who supported the Union Party. In reality, however, Pendleton's Union Party leaders devoted little time to the campaign, and many quietly accepted the test oath compromise. In Charleston's municipal election earlier that month, neither party formally nominated candidates, and newspapers published three tickets dominated by incumbents. Turnout plummeted. Only 812 men voted in the city election, down from 1,634 the year before.[54]

Across much of the state, observers agreed, the "din of nullification" had ceased, and the "spirit of party" lay dormant. One upcountry writer confessed that he had "little to write about politicks," because "we have peace [and] quiet in this part of the country." Ominously, however, he reported "some little stir about the abolitionists of the north," observing that South Carolinians were "determined to stop them." For the past two years, the partisan struggle over Unionism, sovereignty, and allegiance had divided the state and kept the wounds of nullification from healing. Nullifiers continued to view the Union as a compact of sovereign states and demanded exclusive allegiance from the men who served South Carolina. Most Union men, however, championed dual sovereignty and insisted that state and country held an equal claim to their allegiance. Although lawmakers forged a compromise in December 1834, tensions lingered in some districts for years. In the summer of 1835, however, the crisis in South Carolina entered a new phase. As abolitionist tracts poured into their post offices and antislavery petitions flooded Congress, Nullifiers and Union men found themselves united against a common enemy. Many South Carolinians felt their state was under siege, with abolitionism threatening to tear apart the fabric of society. Their responses helped to unify the state—and erode the foundations of the Union.[55]

6.

Forging Consensus

The Politics of Slavery, 1835–36

From the beginning of the crisis, Nullifiers traced their defiance of the tariff to their defense of slavery. As a Greenville writer explained, the tariff of 1828 subsidized northern free labor and discouraged southern slave labor—a precedent that could threaten slavery's survival. "Upon the same principle," he observed, Congress could "abolish the one [system of labor] and give bounties to the other." It could liberate and colonize African Americans and "break up the whole domestic policy of the Southern States." With the tariff in force, another writer agreed, "a majority in Congress could sanctify any act whatever." Nullifiers feared that the tariff system would devastate the southern economy: cotton prices would plummet—"your land will become valueless—your slaves will be liberated." As slavery collapsed, they warned, African Americans would rise in rebellion across the South and "deluge this land in blood."[1]

Union men, however, consciously separated these two issues. Although they denounced the tariff and hoped for its repeal, they insisted that slavery remained secure. They argued that the Constitution sanctioned and protected slavery—that the Union provided the "only restraint" against "fanaticism." They realized that few northerners supported abolition, and they trusted the conservative majority to side with the South. For Union men, the most immediate threat to slavery came not from Congress but from their own state's reckless course. Nullifiers, they warned, were undermining the Constitution and drawing slavery into public debate, and their "high toned language of liberty or death" was only encouraging insurrection.[2]

Then, in 1835, the American Anti-Slavery Society (AASS) launched a series of campaigns that made the abolition movement impossible to ignore.

It shipped thousands of antislavery pamphlets across the South and flooded Congress with petitions. National leaders denounced the proceedings and tabled the antislavery petitions. Postmaster General Amos Kendall allowed southern postmasters to censor the mail, explaining that their duty to their communities trumped their obligation to the laws. In the long run, the AASS campaigns helped reframe the national debate over slavery and contributed to its eventual abolition. Within South Carolina, however, they permanently eroded the foundations of Unionism, which would never again be as powerful or unequivocal. For years, Nullifiers had warned that Congress would one day strike against slavery. Now, abolitionists were seemingly using federal institutions to reach into their homes. The anger and anxiety that followed helped unify the state and divide the country, ensuring that South Carolina's political landscape would never be the same.[3]

Virtually all white South Carolinians were deeply committed to slavery and white supremacy. By the 1820s, the state's radicals had begun piecing together a militant, unapologetic defense of slavery. Turnbull insisted it was the most benign labor system in the world, writing that few other laborers "work easier and have more comfort" than southern slaves. A Columbia writer agreed, indicting northern wage labor and contending that "No slavery is so wretched as that which is spent within the walls of a factory." While northern workers endured squalor and starvation, he claimed, southern slaves received paternal care and protection. He argued that slavery "civilized" African Americans, ennobled slaveholders, and ensured the political stability of the South. In his annual message, Governor Stephen Miller insisted that slavery was "not a national evil; on the contrary, it is a national benefit," because it enriched the Union and empowered white men. In the mid-1830s, Calhoun baldly declared the institution a "positive good," and Hammond called it the "greatest of all the great blessings."[4]

While many Nullifiers embraced these convictions, Union men were often more receptive to older "necessary evil" defenses. Greenville editor Obadiah Wells called the institution "an evil and a curse," and Benjamin Perry declared it an "evil ... entailed upon us by our ancestors." Camden governess Julia Brown decried the "curse of slavery" and wept over the "miserably degraded state of the slaves." Nat Turner's rebellion, she observed, had "shown the south, what they may *fear,* and expect at some future [date]." James Petigru freed a few of his slaves, defended freedmen's limited rights in court, and prayed that slavery would eventually die away. Thomas Grimké bravely championed colonization and privately grappled with slavery's morality.[5]

A few South Carolinians, including Grimké's sisters, rejected the institution altogether. Sarah and Angelina Grimké moved to Philadelphia in the 1820s and joined the abolition and women's rights movements. Angelina supported her brother's Unionist convictions and viewed nullification as divine vengeance. Slavery, she explained, was "too great a sin for justice always to sleep over, and this is, I believe, the true cause of the declining state of Carolina." Ebenezer Cooper, a Reformed Presbyterian minister, expressed a similar outlook, insisting God was punishing America for the "national Sin" of slavery. The "guilt of slavery," he maintained, was only increasing, as slaveholders abandoned God's laws and hardened their hearts against justice. Throughout the state, small pockets of religious dissenters shared these moral reservations, and some excluded slaveholders from the congregations. Like the Grimké sisters, however, they found life in South Carolina increasingly "untenable." As the Reverend Hugh McMillan explained, the "hand of slavery was closing the door of emancipation," and sermons against slavery were provoking ever greater resistance. In 1829, McMillan moved to the Midwest with "nearly all his congregation," and Ebenezer Cooper followed three years later.[6]

The overwhelming majority of Union Party supporters, however, "sanction[ed] and tolerate[d]" slavery. As Benjamin Perry explained, most Union men saw it as an essential "part of the social system"—an institution "interwoven with our interest, our manner, our climate, and our very being." Whatever qualms they felt, they insisted they could not "remedy [the situation], without the ruin of ourselves and the injury of [their slaves]." Although Petigru freed a few slaves, for example, he held 125 more in bondage, and he failed to speak out against the institution. Julia Brown pitied slaveholders "almost as much if not more than the slave[s]," and she was "utterly at a loss to know *what can* be done." Emancipation, she feared, would bring only death and devastation. Perry agreed that abolition would ruin southern society, and Wells warned that it would turn the slaveholding states into "one great mausoleum of war, blood, and carnage."[7]

Crucially, anxieties over slavery's survival did *not* lead inevitably to radicalism. During the nullification crisis, instead, these fears reinforced Union men's moderation and their commitment to the federal government. At party meetings and in newspaper columns, they argued that the Constitution sanctioned and protected slavery and that only a handful of "fanatics" sought to abolish it. Constans Daniels, for example, assured readers that most northerners disavowed abolitionism and supported southern rights. He reprinted northern editorials and published news of northern meetings hoping to repair the fraying cords of Union. Other Union men agreed: a Charleston planter insisted the Constitution "protect[ed] the Southern States," and Benjamin Perry observed that northerners had no desire to "interfere with [their] domestic policy."[8]

Nullifiers, however, continued to champion their militant defense of slavery and states' rights. Even after they rescinded the Ordinance of Nullification, they urged voters to remain vigilant, warning that another political crisis was imminent. In July 1833, Pinckney declared that abolitionists were whetting their knives and lighting their torches, preparing to "clothe our fields with desolation, and turn our rivers into blood." These "fanatics," he insisted, hoped to turn "every southern city [into] a St. Domingo, and every village [into] a Southampton"—vivid reminders of the Haitian Revolution and Nat Turner's Rebellion. Pinckney acknowledged that few northerners supported abolition. He warned, however, that the movement would steadily gain strength and that abolitionists would one day wage the "worst of all wars" against them. When that moment arrived, southerners could trust neither Congress nor the northern states—only each other. Richland planter Pierce Butler predicted that the "slave question" would ultimately "Dissolve the ties of this Union. *It will do it.* And if things go on as they begin . . . it *ought to do it.* Every move on the subject cuts one *cord* of this government."[9]

Union men recognized the power of these appeals and worked fiercely to counteract them. Camden editor Thomas Pegues warned that "all this noise about slavery is intended for *political effect.*" Nullifiers, he explained, were using the issue to "inflame the public mind" and undermine the Union. He reminded readers that slavery "will not [and] cannot be touched," and that every major northern politician was on their side. Benjamin Perry warned that Nullifiers were still conspiring to incite civil war and establish a southern confederacy. When the tariff failed to unify the South, he observed, the state's "revolutionists" had seized hold of slavery—hoping to "provoke the

North and inflame the South." Perry, however, trusted northern conservatives to disavow abolitionism, and he appealed to Daniel Webster to uphold the "South, the Union and the cause of republican Government."[10]

These Union Party leaders viewed themselves as moderate men holding the middle ground between northern and southern radicalism. Yorkville residents insisted that only "fanatics and nullifiers" would draw slavery into public debate, and a Charleston writer agreed that abolitionist William Lloyd Garrison and Nullifier John C. Calhoun were "aiming at the same end, public excitement." Aaron Willington published dozens of articles praying for the Union's survival against "Southern discontents" and "Northern fanaticism." Although they saw abolitionists and Nullifiers as two sides of the same coin, the latter seemed to pose a more immediate threat to slavery in the early 1830s. As one writer explained, Garrison's antislavery pamphlets were "smothered almost as soon as they [arrived]," while Pinckney's ravings freely circulated throughout the state. By exaggerating abolitionists' power, Union men warned, Nullifiers were emboldening rebellious slaves and inspiring a "spirit of discontent." They were weakening the bonds of Union and striking a deadly blow at the "vitals of the State."[11]

Then, in the summer of 1835, the American Anti-Slavery Society launched one of the first direct-mail campaigns in American history. The AASS, founded two years earlier, declared slavery "the greatest possible violation of human rights" and published four monthly journals to illustrate its injustice. By 1835, they were printing more than one million pamphlets and periodicals per year, and that May they began a bold campaign to spread their message throughout the South. They collected the names of 20,000 southern ministers, merchants, and civic leaders and bombarded them with 175,000 antislavery tracts. They hoped that "moral suasion" would open slaveholders' eyes to the evils of the institution. As one abolitionist predicted, their pamphlets would inspire "a feeling against which [slaveholders] cannot stand." Some masters, they knew, would "rave and scold and threaten" and "draw closer the cords" of bondage. Ultimately, however, they would welcome abolition to ease their consciences of an "intolerable burden."[12]

On July 29, 1835, the steamship *Columbia* arrived in Charleston Harbor, carrying thousands of these antislavery tracts. Postmaster Alfred Huger, a Union Party leader, dutifully began delivering the mail. As news of the "incendiary" papers spread, however, hundreds of residents gathered to confront him. The crowd contained the "most respectable men of all parties," uniting "Nullifiers and Union men, Jackson men and Clay men . . . men who differ on all other points." Huger himself was deeply committed to slavery, and he declared the pamphlets "inflammatory and incendiary—and insurrectionary in the highest degree." As postmaster, however, he had a duty to uphold federal authority, and he vowed to "defend [the mail] until I am overpower'd." Huger refused to surrender the tracts, and he drafted an urgent letter to Postmaster General Amos Kendall asking for instructions.[13]

Although the city guard eventually dispersed the crowd, residents returned that night and broke into the post office. The following evening, 2,000 people gathered on the parade ground and burned the mail, along with effigies of AASS leaders William Lloyd Garrison, Arthur Tappan, and Abraham Cox. Huger feared the crisis would escalate if the flood of pamphlets continued, and he swore to do everything in his power to "prevent future Excesses." Ultimately, however, he doubted that he could "sustain himself in this position" for long. The entire city was arrayed against him, and only a "military force greater than [Charleston's] Undivided population" could permanently protect the mail.[14]

While Huger anxiously waited for guidance, Charleston's civic leaders rallied to protect the city. On August 3, a meeting at City Hall denounced abolitionists for inciting rebellion and "whet[ting] the knife of assassination." They arranged for guards to protect the mail and empowered a committee to "take all measures necessary to meet the emergency." Observers emphasized the crowd's wealth and respectability, and several ministers legitimized the meeting with their presence. Significantly, men from both parties attended, and the committee included eleven Nullifiers and at least eight Union men. Union Party leader Henry DeSaussure observed proudly that the "spirit of Carolina was rising" to meet the "evil" of abolition, and Robert Hayne urged the entire South to "act energetically and in concert."[15]

The committee presented its report a week later, declaring slavery "inseparable from the existence of the State." They asked the harbor master and railroad president to keep track of everyone entering the city and urged officials to punish anyone affiliated with the AASS. They also demanded that northerners suppress the spirit of fanaticism: silencing antislavery societies and banning "seditious Papers" from the mail. If Congress refused to act, they warned, the southern states would adopt "decisive" measures to defend themselves. They called for a southern convention and vowed to "defend their property against all attacks—be the consequences what they may." Soon after, Charleston's merchants and storekeepers swore to cut off trade with anyone who supported the abolition movement. In doing so, they refused to "add fuel to the fire that is intended to consume us"—to "fold our arms and see our families butchered, and our fire sides deluged with blood."[16]

Similar meetings took place across the South. By December 1835, more than 150 southern communities had hosted militant torch-lit parades and antiabolition rallies. They formed vigilance committees to patrol the countryside, intimidate African Americans, and search stage coaches and steamboats for antislavery tracts. They received support from every level of white society, and in some cities, they commanded enormous resources. New Orleans' "Anti-Fanatical Society," for example, reported a budget of half a million dollars, and another Louisiana parish offered $50,000 to anyone who delivered AASS leader Arthur Tappan—dead or alive.[17]

Dozens of communities across South Carolina hosted antiabolition meetings. Most followed the same pattern and adopted similar resolutions. "Respectable" community leaders called the meetings to order and chose a committee to draft resolutions. Ministers offered prayers and sanctioned the proceedings, while local orators offered fiery speeches denouncing northern fanaticism. The resolutions often struck an orderly but defiant tone. They argued that Scripture and the Constitution both justified slavery, and they refused to discuss the institution "in any manner." They accused abolitionists of undermining the Union's harmony and stability and insisted Congress had a moral duty to stop them. Ultimately, however, they called on southerners to defend themselves, demanding political unity and organizing vigilance committees to stifle dissent.[18]

While some meetings called for "cool and calm decision," others struck a more radical tone. Sumterville residents denounced Tappan and Garrison as "enemies of mankind" and threatened to kill them if they set foot in the state. They vowed to resist abolition until their dying breaths, and they hoped the impending crisis would find all South Carolinians "prepared, with arms in their hands." A Pendleton meeting warned that abolition would make it "unsafe" for South Carolina to remain in the Union, and several lowcountry meetings boldly called for secession. If northerners failed to "put a final stop" to abolitionism, one meeting resolved, the southern states had a solemn duty to secede. Forced to choose between "Union without liberty and property" or disunion with them, they would "make the choice promptly, unitedly, and fearlessly."[19]

Responding to the crisis, Postmaster General Amos Kendall confessed that he lacked the legal power to censor the mail. Nonetheless, he refused to order Huger to deliver the antislavery tracts. The post office, he explained, should serve the American people and bind them together—not become the "instrument of their destruction." Although federal officers "owe an obligation to the laws," he insisted, they held a higher duty to the communities in which they lived. When those duties conflicted, Kendall wrote, "it is patriotism to disregard [the law]." Kendall allowed Huger to decide the issue for himself, writing that he would neither sanction nor condemn the local postmaster's actions. In effect, his message gave southern postmasters license to censor the mail and rid their communities of "incendiary" papers.[20]

Antislavery tracts continued to pour into South Carolina's post offices. Only days after the Charleston bonfire, one writer found thousands of pamphlets piling up in Huger's office, and weeks later a copy of *The Liberator* arrived with "threatening language" scrawled across the margins. Although Huger removed these "offensive" papers from the mail, some slipped through and circulated throughout the state. When a few pamphlets reached Columbia in early August, a mob attacked the post office at midnight and tried to force its way into the building. After a long argument, Postmaster Daniel Faust—an elderly Union man—convinced the crowd to leave. A local vigilance committee, however, interrogated him four days later and demanded that he suppress the pamphlets.[21]

As Huger and Faust discovered, local vigilance committees often took the law into their own hands to preserve "peace" and property. Charleston residents organized a Lynch Club and advertised their actions in the city's newspapers. They threatened to serve "written notice" to anyone who sympathized with abolition and warned that "any person not going away as ordered, will by Lynched." If anyone fought back, the club would hang them "as a public example." On August 20, they targeted local barber Richard Wood for illegally trading with the city's slaves. When Wood refused to leave, the Lynch Club dragged him through the street to a nearby wharf, where they tied him to a post and gave him twenty lashes. After pouring tar over his body and covering him in cotton, they carried him through the market so residents could "take warning by his fate." Officials placed in him jail for his own protection and sent him north several days later.[22]

That summer, local clubs and vigilance committees lynched at least five men across the state. Robert Gage, the son of an upcountry planter, observed that the "whole country is in a state of ferment." Several men, he reported, had been "tried before Judge Lynch [and] condemned & hung without a word." In early September, Columbia's Lynch Club targeted a man for an unspecified crime and "inflicted the punishment" on Main Street at 10:00 a.m. In a small upcountry village, one editor remarked, "Judge Lynch *pinned* it into a chap" after residents discovered him talking to local slaves. Around the same time, Orangeburg villagers "detected" two outsiders, and "Judge Hang presided there and passed sentence on them."[23]

Some Union men spoke out against these proceedings, insisting the accused men deserved full and fair trials. One Camden editor, appealing to moderate manhood, viewed lynching as an expression of "anarchy and misrule" and argued that "every good citizen" had a duty to denounce it. Only the law, he explained, could secure Americans' liberty and property. Aaron Willington agreed that Lynch Clubs would undermine the laws and encourage "fearful abuses." Others, however, condoned or helped provoke the attacks and praised the lynch mobs for their "quietness and order." Union Party editors published advertisements for the Lynch Club and openly called for the murder of abolitionists. "Let such justice be meted out," a Greenville editor declared, and before long "they will keep at a proper distance."[24]

These defenses of lynching reflected a broader shift in South Carolina politics. In the aftermath of the AASS direct mail campaign, many of the state's antiabolition meetings framed themselves as bipartisan, hoping to demonstrate South Carolina's unity and resolve. A rally in Sumter drew "persons of all parties," and men in Abbeville, Greenville, and Camden gathered "without distinction of party." Americans made similar antipartisan appeals throughout the antebellum era, often to serve deeply partisan ends. During the nullification crisis, for example, Nullifiers tried to deny legitimacy to Union men by claiming to speak for all "true South Carolinians." The summer of 1835, however, was a period of transition in the state. The test oath compromise had resolved the most pressing partisan issues, and most South Carolinians were eager for harmony. The direct-mail campaign took place in this moment of political uncertainty and provided a powerful motivation for unity.[25]

For the past five years, public meetings, militia companies, and even church congregations had sharply divided along party lines. Newspapers had served as unofficial party organs, and editors had often only reported their own party's meetings and events. At these antiabolition meetings, however, at least 25 percent of committee members were Union men, and leaders from both parties worked together to draft reports and resolutions. Virtually every newspaper vehemently denounced antislavery "fanaticism" and published news of the meetings, another striking departure from the partisanship of the early 1830s. A Camden editor, for example, warned that abolitionists would "awake[n] a servile war [filled with] murder and rapine and all the darker deeds" and "build the freedom of the slave upon the annihilation of the white man." Although Union men had stood by the country in the "darkest hour of peril," Aaron Willington observed, they would mournfully tear it apart rather than surrender their slaves.[26]

Some political distinctions endured, and some Union men pushed back against the state's growing consensus. While Nullifiers often equated all northerners with abolitionists, Union men were more likely to maintain their faith in northern conservatives. A Charleston Nullifier, for example, warned that the "whole population of the North" supported abolition "directly or indirectly," while another writer insisted that "eight-tenths of the northern people are Abolitionists." Union Party editor Obadiah Wells, however, assured readers that 90 percent of "respectable" northerners rejected abolitionism, and he trusted the Constitution to safeguard slavery and social order. Some Union men viewed the public outcry as yet another political conspiracy. Benjamin Perry believed Nullifiers were using the direct-mail campaign for political effect, because they knew that "Slavery is the only thing that can produce a dissolution of the Union . . . the only thing that will unite the whole South in opposition to the North." Wells agreed, accusing Nullifiers of trying to drain the federal treasury, dismantle the Navy, and leave the country vulnerable to European tyrants. He argued that Nullifiers only decried abolitionists in order to promote a southern confederacy and enable "foreign troops . . . to land upon our shores."[27]

These appeals, however, were largely unsuccessful, and the threat of abolition pushed the Union Party toward the state's political margins. Beaufort Union man Benjamin Allston, for example, tried—and failed—to moderate his district's radicalism. When a meeting that September condemned "*Northern* fanaticism," Allston objected and introduced a new set of resolutions. He insisted that the vast majority of northerners rejected abolition, and he trusted their "patriotism, kindly feeling, and sense of justice" to peacefully resolve the crisis. The crowd, however, overwhelmingly opposed the resolutions, and Allston ultimately withdrew them.[28]

A similar scene took place in Abbeville, where a bipartisan committee reported militantly proslavery resolutions. Most public meetings followed a familiar script, with the crowd "unanimously" endorsing the committee's report. This time, Union man John Pressly objected and forced the meeting to vote on the resolutions one by one. Most passed without dissent, as the crowd declared slavery a "domestic question" and expressed "abhorrence" toward abolition. Pressly, however, protested three resolutions. One declared the Union a compact of sovereign states, united "for special purposes only." Another demanded a federal law barring the Post Office from carrying "seditious Papers," and a third called for a southern convention to "defend our property against all attacks." Despite his pleas, the resolutions passed overwhelmingly. Only three men voted against the sovereign-state and seditious-paper resolutions, and Pressly stood alone in opposing a southern convention. The moment was deeply symbolic, as the resolution declared that South Carolinians stood "united as one man" in defense of southern rights. Pressly's solitary dissent belied the claim, revealing a few lingering doubts and divisions—but it also proved how rapidly Nullifiers' beliefs were hardening into orthodoxy and transforming the state's political culture.[29]

Events in Washington that winter only accelerated that trend. As antislavery pamphlets flooded southern post offices, the AASS began petitioning Congress to abolish slavery in Washington, DC. This tactic was as old as the country itself; in 1790, Benjamin Franklin had petitioned the first Congress to "loosen the bounds of slavery" and ensure "equal liberty" for all Americans. The AASS, however, dramatically increased the scale and frequency of the campaign, sending nearly 200 petitions with 34,000 signatures during the 1835–36 session alone. Initially, Congress dealt with the prayers as it always had, voting to accept and immediately table the first two petitions. When the third petition arrived, however, James Henry Hammond rose to demand a "more decided seal of reprobation." Instead of tabling the appeals, he urged the House not to accept them at all—to stifle discussion before it began. He "wished to put an end to these petitions," refusing to "sit there and see the rights of the southern people assaulted day after day."[30]

Hammond's motion ignited a fierce debate over the limits of constitutional freedom and congressional power. While most northerners opposed abolition, they passionately defended their right to petition the government. As New York Democrat Samuel Beardsley explained, Congress could "decline acting" on certain petitions, but it could not deny Americans' "sacred and invaluable right" to present them. Beardsley sided with the South "against all agitation on this subject" and sought to "put down the fanatics of the North." He reminded Congress, however, that radicals in *both* sections were using antislavery agitation to tear the country apart. Only by accepting and tabling the petitions, he argued, could Americans maintain "peace, quiet, and order, in every part of the Union."[31]

Most southerners, however, saw the debate not as a contest over the right of petition but rather as a struggle for slavery's survival. Hammond framed his demands in the language of southern honor, observing that abolitionists had "assailed" and "assaulted" their way of life. By accepting antislavery petitions, he warned, Congress would legitimize the abolition movement and implicitly grant the federal government the power to regulate slavery. Francis Pickens, a young Edgefield Nullifier, rushed to Hammond's defense, urging Congress to stop the AASS "at the threshold." He viewed the abolition movement as a transatlantic crusade to stifle southern freedom. The "moral power of the world," he observed, was arrayed against them. Great Britain had freed its West Indian slaves in 1833, and France had begun debating emancipation. Now, the AASS had gained a foothold in the North, and its spirit of "fanaticism" would only grow stronger. Pickens argued that southerners would soon face a stark choice: defend their "consecrated hearthstones" to the death or watch their own country become a "black colony."[32]

The debate placed tremendous strain on southern moderates. With the future of slavery apparently at stake, they could not allow Congress to discuss the petitions. Rejecting them altogether, however, could galvanize northern resistance, strengthen the abolition movement, and weaken the bonds of Union. In early February 1836, after weeks of tense debate, Charleston Nullifier Henry Pinckney offered a compromise. He proposed creating a select committee to address the antislavery petitions, instructing it to report that

Congress had no power over slavery in the states and "ought not" to interfere with it in Washington, DC. Pinckney hoped to sidestep the debate's constitutional controversies. He would assert the right to petition while protecting the right to property, and confirm Congress's power over the District of Columbia while ensuring that slavery there remained secure. Congress quickly approved the plan, with southerners evenly divided and almost every northerner voting in favor. Three months later, the committee delivered its final report, agreeing that Congress would receive and table all antislavery petitions.[33]

Pinckney's actions baffled many contemporaries, who questioned why a radical Nullifier would defy his party and craft a potentially Union-saving compromise. Some traced his moderation to a recent religious conversion. As early as mid-January, Hayne advised Hammond to "keep Pinckney *straight,*" warning that he had been "strangely self willed and erratic" since becoming "a *saint.*" Others saw the former editor as a mere political opportunist. Despite *The Charleston Mercury*'s influence, Pinckney remained a second-tier statesman in South Carolina, overshadowed by Calhoun, McDuffie, Hamilton, and Hayne. By working with Martin Van Buren—Jackson's handpicked successor—to resolve the crisis, Pinckney could position himself as a national leader. As Hammond explained, he could become "a second Clay [and] save the Union."[34]

Pinckney, however, viewed his moderate gag rule as an urgent necessity. He warned that Hammond's plan would place the "contest *upon the right of petition,*" which many Americans in both sections considered a "sacred and fundamental" freedom. The debate, then, would only unify the North while dividing the South. It would also strengthen abolitionists' hands, allowing them to "cry out that they were persecuted and disfranchised." Pinckney, by contrast, planned to center the debate on abolition. He recognized that most northerners opposed immediate abolition, and by "letting the right of petition alone," he hoped to unite "all parties" in suppressing the movement. He assured South Carolinians that he had not forgotten the nullification crisis, nor had he forsaken his principles. Then, as now, he sought to defend slavery and southern rights, and he asked his constituents to calmly consider which plan was "best for them, as slaveholders."[35]

Pinckney's plea failed to persuade most South Carolinians, and letters poured into the *Mercury* office denouncing his conduct. One writer insisted that Pinckney had "sacrificed the South" and left the state vulnerable to rebellion. "Dishonor, and ruin, and wretchedness," he warned, would engulf South Carolina, and a "new Act will be added to the West India Tragedy." Writers reached for military metaphors to describe the gravity of Pinckney's betrayal. A Columbia cashier accused him of "surrender[ing] the Citadel," and a Barnwell doctor agreed that he had "desert[ed] his post" on the "Watch Tower of Southern Rights." One essayist observed that Pinckney had struck the Palmetto Banner in surrender. He expressed shock and dismay to hear the congressman "prating about the Union" when his "denunciation of unionism in the days of Nullification yet vibrate[d] upon the ear."[36]

While Pinckney's political fortunes fell, Hammond and Pickens became heroes throughout much of South Carolina. A Charleston editor remarked that they had "done their duty manfully," and another writer agreed that they "would not disgrace [their] manhood by tamely and patiently submitting." Edgefield residents praised the men as "true models of Carolina patriotism" and insisted the federal government had no authority over slavery. The moment Congress tried to regulate or restrict it, they warned, the entire South would secede. Barnwell's citizens shared these sentiments, declaring that the time had arrived for South Carolinians "not only to speak, but to act." Their "very existence [was] in danger," they observed, and only decisive action could save them from destruction.[37]

Dozens of South Carolinians wrote to Hammond that winter, expressing an uncompromising defiance toward abolition. Hayne advised him to "meet the question boldly in every shape ... the more directly the better." He remained confident in southern strength and resolve and "fear[ed] nothing from discussion or excitement." Richland Nullifier Pierce Butler encouraged him to *"Fix bayonets"* and "dispute every inch of ground." By seizing the initiative, he argued, South Carolinians would force every southern congressman to choose a side. Together, they would prove to their enemies that they could vindicate slavery "in the forum and in the field." A Columbia writer agreed that hesitation would prove fatal: every hour of delay strengthened the abolitionists and "weaken[ed] us at home."[38]

Some writers insisted it was already too late to preserve southern freedom. Henry Nott, a professor at South Carolina College, baldly declared that "all is lost." Europe and the North, he explained, had already turned against slavery, and the southern states were full of enemies. He believed the native northerners who filled their towns were only "*feebly* with us," and that many secretly plotted their destruction. When the final crisis arrived, he predicted, poor southerners and religious dissenters would renounce slavery "on the ground of republicanism as well as religion." Another writer agreed that there was little hope for slaveholders' survival. Years of agitation, he observed, had inspired a powerful "spirit of insubordination" in their slaves, and even disunion could not protect them from the impending catastrophe.[39]

Despite their anxieties, most South Carolinians still hoped for victory and vindication. Thomas Cooper welcomed the prospect of disunion, insisting the South "had no safety in any other measure." He connected the state's struggle to Poland's ill-fated revolution. The Russian emperor, he observed, had vanquished the Polish armies and "annihilated" the rebellious kingdom. The "Demon of Discord has shaken his wings over both Continents," provoking a hemispheric struggle between liberty and tyranny. Cooper observed that southerners needed "all the courage we can muster," and he urged Hammond to "force a decision"—to compel southern leaders to choose sides in the looming struggle over slavery. If Congress voted to accept antislavery petitions, he wrote, southern lawmakers should resign en masse and begin working toward secession.[40]

Cooper offered a dramatic vision of South Carolina's future. If the federal government interfered with slavery, he wrote, "separation and war" must inevitably follow. While South Carolinians had temporized and retreated during the nullification winter, this time they would "act decisively" and secede from the Union. The rest of the South would gradually follow, and the loss of tariff revenue and bank credit would devastate the northern economy. The ensuing civil war would "assume a savage character," as southerners slaughtered their enemies without remorse. As Cooper explained, affirming martial manhood, northerners had incited their slaves to "ravish [their] females, & then to cut their throats," and he had "no scruples about the means of putting [them] to death."[41]

Other South Carolinians echoed these defiant calls to arms. A Columbia writer agreed that the state's "only safe reliance" lay in its "swords and muskets." Thomas Twiss, a professor at South Carolina College, vowed to "stand by the south" and "fight to the last in the just and right cause." Nullifier Thomas Stark believed the state "should have dissolved the union when Charleston was blockaded [during the nullification winter]," and he hoped Hammond's resolution would finish the task. Virginia radical Beverly Tucker urged South Carolinians to take the "decisive step" toward disunion. If Jackson allowed the state to secede peacefully, he explained, the rest of the South would quickly follow. If the president tried to stop South Carolina, the other states would rise up against him. Either way, the old Union would collapse, and the resulting southern confederacy would flourish in its freedom. Hammond forwarded the letter to Governor George McDuffie, who "entirely concur[red]" with its contents. South Carolina, McDuffie declared, must "exorcise the demon," even "if the magic circle is drawn in blood."[42]

Across South Carolina, the gag rule debate provoked a faint echo of nullification-era partisanship. The state's Union Party congressmen—Richard Manning and James Rogers—supported Pinckney's moderate resolutions while the remaining Nullifiers sided with Hammond. Union Party newspapers, including *The Greenville Mountaineer, The Camden Journal,* and *The Charleston Courier,* reported Pinckney's actions with nuance and sympathy. Camden editor John West declared the resolutions a "conclusive appeal to the heart and head of every patriot," and a Charleston writer calling himself *Unionist* hailed them as a "patriotic triumph." Aaron Willington viewed Pinckney's plan as the only practical solution. The "whole controversy," he observed, revolved around "whether to reject the petition, or to reject the prayer of the petition." In practice, these tactics were identical, and Pinckney had "wisely and patriotically . . . preferred gaining the practical point, to losing the theoretical one."[43]

Some Nullifiers feared that Pinckney's "defection" would revive the partisan battles of the early 1830s. A Georgia writer warned Hammond that Union men would "use [Pinckney] hereafter to divide the party," and state senator Angus Patterson agreed that the "Union party would sustain him" in order to rise to power. Obsessed with forging a militant proslavery consensus, these Nullifiers viewed the smallest dissent as a signal of disloyalty and division. An upcountry doctor predicted slaveholders would never have peace, because there were "too many amongst ourselves who strengthen the cause of abolitionism, not directly, but indirectly, by their lukewarmness." The crisis over slavery, editor Edward Johnston observed, made it "increasingly dangerous to remain as we are—without any concert throughout the state." Union men, he observed, were "timid" and "incapable of manly and resolute views," and they were "sure to desert us—when it came to the practice, instead of declarations—on the slave questions."[44]

A few Union men tried to revive their party in the summer of 1836, revealing that the tensions and labels of the nullification crisis still carried some weight. In August, party leaders James Petigru, Alfred Huger, Joseph Johnson, and James Pringle met in Charleston to choose a candidate for the fall's congressional election. After a long debate, they decided on Hugh Legaré, who had spent the past four years as ambassador to Belgium. Legaré's long absence had sheltered him from the state's partisan battles, and he had largely avoided "angry collisions with his enemies." At the same time, he was "ardently attached to the Union" and "zealous to defend the Institutions of the State." The following month, forty of the city's most prominent Union men published a call for a party meeting at City Hall, where they formally nominated Legaré for Congress.[45]

Petigru spearheaded the campaign, pledging to "write and battle, and bustle, and do all things." The city's Union Party editors quickly reentered the fray. The "Union Banner is once more unfurled," Aaron Willington declared, and he would faithfully take his place beneath its folds. The flag, he explained, symbolized Union and Liberty—"proclaim[ing] the glory of our nation" and the principles of their party. If voters rallied around it and remained united, they were sure to achieve victory. The editor evoked the memory of nullification to will the party back together. "Let all divisions in our ranks now cease," he pleaded, and "let us, still alive to the sacred associations which knitted our very hearts together in the by-gone season of common peril, rally as a band of brothers under the time honored flag."[46]

Charleston editor Jacob Cardozo insisted that Union men could never vote for Pinckney. The former Nullifier, he explained, had persecuted the Union Party and worked to tear the country apart. Even as Pinckney asked for Union men's support, he disavowed their principles and refused to repent. Alfred Huger agreed, observing that Pinckney had betrayed first his country and then his party. Despite his actions in Congress, Pinckney had "not given up his ground as a Nullifier," and Union men could not afford to trust him. The party's voters needed to rally now or risk their own destruction. If they failed to field a candidate, he warned, "our people would go over to Pinckney and never return." Poinsett shared these sentiments, urging Union men to stand together in the fall campaign. If the party collapsed, he feared, their "scattered force will only strengthen the nullifiers."[47]

Despite these passionate appeals, the election of 1836 signaled the death of nullification-era partisanship. In the early 1830s, Charleston's Union Party meetings routinely drew more than a thousand people. In September 1836, only 193 men turned out, and many of them opposed their party's course. When the meeting began, attorney Benjamin Pepoon urged the crowd *not* to nominate a candidate, igniting a long debate about the party's future. James Petigru and Alfred Huger opposed Pepoon's resolution, and the meeting ultimately tabled it by a vote of 108 to 85. Enthusiastic editors insisted that a "considerable majority" of Union men supported Legaré's nomination. Less charitable observers, however, mocked the proceedings and refused to accept the "party's" decision. As one former Union man observed, there "now exists no political party at all in Charleston," and every voter was free to follow the "dictates of his conscience."[48]

Even men who supported Legaré hoped the election would not "turn on party feeling." Poinsett observed that "Carolina demands repose from political strife," and another writer prayed that "Party heat" would never again endanger the city. A writer calling himself *A lover of peace* urged Union men not to support Legaré. The past two years, he explained, had obliterated the "old party distinctions" and "banish[ed] discord from the domestic altar." Union men had defeated nullification and resolved the test oath controversy, and the "great principles" that united their party—"the preservation of the Union and resistance to domestic oppression"—no longer called them into battle. Instead, he argued, Union men should rally around Pinckney, who had faithfully served the city and boldly vindicated southern rights. He insisted that the gag rule was a signal triumph for the South, protecting slavery more forcefully and conclusively than any Congress ever had. Legaré's nomination could only "reawaken the warfare of party." Pinckney's reelection, however, would foil Nullifiers' "scheme of agitation" and demonstrate South Carolina's unity and resolve.[49]

Pinckney's gag rule also left Nullifiers searching for direction. On September 20, 1836, the State Rights Party held a meeting at City Hall to select Pinckney's replacement. The congressman, they explained, had "compromised our rights" and betrayed the city's trust, leaving South Carolinians vulnerable to antislavery agitation. The party refused to renominate him, instead selecting attorney Isaac Holmes. Crucially, however, only 170 men attended the meeting, and barely 60 percent of them supported their new candidate. In a public letter two days later, Holmes declined the nomination. The party scrambled to nominate another candidate, but he, too, turned them down.[50]

Desperate to defeat Pinckney, some Nullifiers turned to Hugh Legaré, and in early October they organized a meeting "without distinction of party." Leaders from both parties carefully choreographed the event to symbolize civic unity. Nullifier Henry Deas called Union man Thomas Bennett to the chair, and Union man James Petigru nominated Nullifier Edward Laurens as secretary. Together, they declared that the "two great political parties" would no longer "keep alive a spirit of hostility" or exclude their enemies from power. This "United Ticket" nominated Legaré for Congress, Poinsett for state senate, and an evenly divided slate for the state house of representatives.[51]

Pinckney's followers responded by calling a meeting of "Independent Republican Voters." They, too, celebrated the test oath compromise and the "oblivion of party difference." They accused their opponents of reviving the "prejudice of party" and reopening the state's "fester[ing]" wounds. To illustrate their political independence, they nominated Pinckney for Congress and a mixture of Nullifiers and Union men for the state legislature. In the campaign that followed, observers struggled to make sense of the city's shifting alliances. Jacob Schirmer, a Charleston cooper, reported that "the old parties were quite amalgamated and divided into the Union & Pinckney [Parties]." Petigru informed Legaré that Nullifiers were "betting on your election," and he predicted that they would "get nearly as many nullification votes as Pinckney will take away." At the Union Party meeting in September, dozens of Nullifiers lined the galleries and expressed "joy" and relief at Legaré's nomination.[52]

About 2,100 men voted in Charleston's congressional election—down 21 percent from two years earlier. Pinckney captured 55 percent of the city's votes and (according to Petigru) polled particularly well among poor and working-class voters: the "Irish, the mechanics, and the Methodists." In the slave-dense parishes surrounding Charleston, however, Pinckney's support virtually collapsed. Two years earlier, Pinckney captured 88 of 123 votes in the parish of St. John's Berkeley; now, only two men voted for his reelection. With the support of these coastal parishes, Legaré narrowly won the election. *Mercury* editor John Stuart praised parish voters for "do[ing] their duty nobly" and "vindicat[ing] the character of the District," but he lamented that so many city voters remained loyal to Pinckney.[53]

Statewide, election results confirmed the trends in Charleston. Bitter memories lingered in many districts, and some voters remained avid partisans. In Spartanburg, incumbent James Rogers (a former Union man) faced William Clowney (a former Nullifier) in a rematch of their 1834 campaign. Nearly 75 percent of district voters remained loyal to Rogers, despite—or because of—his support for Pinckney's gag rule. Spartanburg, Greenville, and Clarendon all elected full slates of Union men to the state legislature, while other districts elected only Nullifiers. In Kershaw District that August, Daniel Huger prayed for the "integrity of our party," and James Chesnut rejoiced that "our chances for [a] Representative" were steadily improving. During the nullification crisis, Kershaw had been "in the van of the party," and Huger believed Union men were still looking to its example. If the district faltered now, he warned, "confusion must follow."[54]

To a remarkable degree, however, the state's political campaigns blurred or erased the party lines of the early 1830s. Few districts held public meetings, and few candidates declared themselves Nullifiers or Union men. Five of the state's nine congressional races went uncontested, and two others pitted former Nullifiers against each other. Even in Greenville, former Union men refused to challenge incumbent Waddy Thompson, who championed Hammond's stronger gag rule. An upcountry editor observed that the "old party organization in our State is broken up," and a northern writer marveled at the state's profound political calmness. As a Charleston voter explained, "Nullification and Union, once watch-words" that called the parties into battle, were quickly losing their power to mobilize the people.[55]

By early 1835, weary from years of partisan strife, most South Carolinians simply wanted peace. A majority of voters accepted the test oath compromise, and most party committees and organizations quickly disbanded. South Carolinians, however, had experienced this before. In the summer of 1833, an uneasy calm had descended on the state—until Nullifiers began threatening to purge Union men from power. This time, former Nullifiers consciously avoided "renew[ing] the bitterness of party strife." In March 1836, for example, Columbia's local leaders planned a meeting to denounce Pinckney's moderate gag rule. They were careful, however, not to alienate his "Union accomplices." Although Manning and Rogers—the state's Union Party congressmen—supported Pinckney's resolutions, the Columbia writers left them "entirely unmentioned." As a Charleston writer explained, many former Nullifiers preferred to stay "silent rather than exhibit a division on the subject." Throughout the state, they began working *with* former Union men to forge a political consensus and defend slavery and social order.[56]

For nearly a decade, radical South Carolinians had warned that northern "fanatics" would one day turn the federal government into an instrument of abolition. Those anxieties helped fuel the nullification crisis and brought the country to the brink of civil war. They failed, however, to persuade 40 percent of the state's voters, who saw the Union as the greatest guarantor of white liberty and African American slavery. Then, at the same moment that political peace returned to South Carolina, the American Anti-Slavery Society launched its direct mail and petition campaigns. Suddenly, abolitionists seemed to reach into South Carolinians' homes and invade the halls of Congress, inspiring slaves to "cut the throats of defenceless women and children." These events appeared to confirm Nullifiers' warnings, and they helped unify the state as nullification never could. By August 1835, Union men like Aaron Willington were prepared to "root [the Union] from our hearts and . . . tear down its pillars, though moistening its fragments with tears of blood."[57]

As antislavery tracts poured into South Carolina's post offices, John C. Calhoun boldly declared that "Unionism is extinct in our state." National sentiment was far from dead, and many South Carolinians remained conditional Unionists well into the antebellum era. During the sectional crises of the 1840s and 1850s, some state leaders worked to harness federal power to preserve and expand slavery's reach. As an organized political movement, however, Unionism would never fully recover in South Carolina. After 1835, it was always more fragile, more contested, and more conditional, and every crisis found fewer men willing to defend it. By 1860, as South Carolina prepared the tear the Union apart, Benjamin Perry and James Petigru stood virtually alone in resisting secession and praying that the "great and glorious Union" would endure.[58]

Epilogue

The election of Abraham Lincoln in November 1860 provoked outrage across the South. Lincoln was a Republican committed to "free soil, free labor, and free men," and many southerners viewed his election as an assault on slavery and white supremacy. In response, on December 20, 1860, a state convention in Charleston voted to dissolve the Union and declare South Carolina's independence. Throughout the city, one witness observed, "loud shouts of joy rent the air." Church bells tolled and cannons roared, and men and women flooded the street in celebration. Bonfires burned through the night, and firecrackers and rockets lit up the sky. Civic leaders raised the state's Palmetto flag, and merchants hung bales of cotton above the streets, inscribed with the words "THE WORLD WANTS IT." In the days ahead, thousands rushed to volunteer for their new nation, flush with optimism and certain of victory. By all accounts, South Carolinians were "almost unanimous" in their support for independence, and the state convention ratified the Ordinance of Secession by a vote of 169 to 0.[1]

Mississippi followed three weeks later, and by February 1861, seven slaveholding states had withdrawn from the Union and organized a new southern Confederacy. A tense stalemate stretched into early spring as Confederates consolidated their strength and Unionists in both sections struggled to craft a compromise. Then, on April 12, Confederate artillery in Charleston Harbor opened fire on the Union garrison at Fort Sumter. Three days later, Lincoln called for 75,000 soldiers to "suppress insurrection," prompting four additional states to secede. The Civil War that followed lasted four years, cost roughly 750,000 American lives, and ultimately led to slavery's destruction.[2]

As Americans navigated the secession winter of 1860–61, many looked to the nullification crisis for guidance. In a culture steeped in historical memory, the patriotism of Andrew Jackson, Henry Clay, and Daniel Webster provided powerful reference points. As a Maryland orator explained, these men's "deep seated love of country" had saved the Union a generation earlier and "pointed out a path to their successors." Illinois Governor Richard Yates agreed, echoing their belief that America's freedom depended on a "perpetual, unbroken Union." As the secession crisis deepened, an Oregon editor mourned that "[w]e have no Clay or Webster or Gen. Jackson now." The "great statesmen of the last age," he observed, had staved off disunion again and again. Now, no one remained who could "mount the whirlwind and direct the storm." Unionists invoked Clay's spirit of compromise and Webster's lyrical devotion to the Union. Editors and politicians endlessly quoted Webster's second reply to Hayne, proclaiming, "Liberty and Union, now and forever, one and inseparable."[3]

As historian Russell McClintock observes, however, Andrew Jackson became "far and away the most ubiquitous historical reference" during the secession crisis. The Nullification Proclamation appeared in dozens of newspapers, and countless men and women repeated Jackson's defiant toast: "Our Federal Union—It must be preserved." Illinois' out-going Governor John Wood included the phrase in his annual message, and Massachusetts Governor John Andrew used it to end his inaugural address. On January 8, the anniversary of Jackson's victory in the Battle of New Orleans, northern towns celebrated his memory with public dinners and rallies. John Andrew ordered every town in Massachusetts to fire a 100-gun salute, and Pennsylvania legislators marked the day by reading the Nullification Proclamation. A New York editor prayed the entire country would treat "St. Hickory's Day" as a "general fête." A single day devoted to Jackson's principles, he explained, "would do more to revive the spirit of patriotism and Union than a century of compromises."[4]

Many Unionists hoped—in vain—that President James Buchanan would follow Jackson's example and quell the incipient rebellion. General-in-Chief Winfield Scott, who had commanded the federal garrison in Charleston in the winter of 1832–33, urged the president to reinforce the country's southern forts. The Virginia-born general celebrated Jackson's decisive stand against treason, hoping to overawe secessionists and avoid civil war. Another southern Unionist prayed Buchanan would take a "Jacksonian position," and a Pennsylvania writer wishfully praised the president's "Jacksonian spirit." Buchanan's indecision, however, frustrated many observers, who sighed longingly "for an hour of Old Hickory." If Jackson was president, a Tennessee Unionist observed, "this glorious Union of ours would still be intact." An Ohio editor agreed, insisting that an hour of Jackson's "manhood, force and nerve" would instantly restore the fractured country. While Buchanan cowered in the White House, Jackson would *act*—summoning "to the country's aid the courage of her sons, and call[ing] upon THE PEOPLE OF THE UNION North and South" to unite against treason.[5]

Many northerners expressed confidence in Lincoln, hoping he would "prove a second Jackson." A Pennsylvania writer trusted that, "Like Jackson," the new president would "prove himself equal to the emergency" and craft a new Nullification Proclamation. A Wisconsin legislator called him "another Jackson"—a man committed to preserving the Union and punishing the nation's enemies. Francis P. Blair, who had served as one of Andrew Jackson's advisors, hoped Lincoln would issue an "eloquent appeal . . . like that of Genl Jackson in the crisis of 1832." Postmaster General Montgomery Blair (Francis's son) insisted that "rebellion was checked in 1833 by the promptitude of the President," and he urged Lincoln to reinforce the Charleston garrison just as Jackson had a generation earlier. As Lincoln crafted his first inaugural address, he drew upon four documents: the Constitution, Clay's 1850 plea for compromise, Webster's second reply to Hayne, and Jackson's Nullification Proclamation.[6]

In many ways, of course, the nullification and secession crises were fundamentally different. Jackson was a southern planter who championed proslavery Unionism and helped forge the national Democratic Party. Most southerners trusted him to defend slavery and southern rights, and they feared nullification would lead to anarchy. In 1832–33, no other state joined South Carolina, leaving Nullifiers to confront the federal government alone. Lincoln, however, led an essentially sectional party committed to stopping the spread of slavery. Although Lincoln disavowed immediate abolition, many southerners viewed all Republicans as antislavery fanatics. The Reverend James C. Furman, for example, warned Greenville voters that Republicans would make their slaves "the equal of every one of you." He insisted that Lincoln would abolish slavery and send "Abolition preachers . . . to consummate the marriage of your daughters to black husbands!" These racial and gendered appeals proved highly effective. Lincoln won only two southern counties, and ten states excluded him from the ballot altogether. For many southerners, his election proved that slavery was no longer secure within the Union—that "safety, honor and political libert[y]" demanded "a separation of the South from the North."[7]

Many South Carolinians viewed secession as the culmination of a thirty-year crusade for freedom. Since the nullification winter, one editor remarked, they had "looked forward to the present day . . . preparing for the storm that has burst upon us." Convention delegate John Middleton believed it was unnecessary even to debate the state's course. South Carolinians, he explained, had been "debating this matter for the last thirty years, and . . . at last arrived at a true and final decision." After a generation of "agitation, and compromise, and submission," Robert Barnwell Rhett rejoiced, South Carolinians were finally ready to dissolve the Union. As they approached the precipice, secessionists drew inspiration from the nullification crisis, which many remembered as a triumph over federal tyranny. History, one writer explained, vindicated the state's struggle and proved that Jackson had backed down. Camden editor Thomas Warren agreed, observing that "even General Jackson, tyrant as he was, dared not" defy South Carolina.[8]

As radicals mobilized support for secession, the symbols of the nullification crisis became powerful rallying points. Men sported blue cockades, and women displayed their old homespun dresses as sacred "relic[s] of the past." At a military parade in Charleston, cadets proudly unfurled a "State Rights Resistance Flag of 1832." The banner had once belonged to a battalion in Hayne's volunteer force, and it depicted a soldier and cannon sheltered beneath a Palmetto tree. After twenty-eight years, one writer observed, its "tattered folds . . . again waved in triumph" over the streets of Charleston. A week later, another fading flag appeared over a Charleston printing office, and the "nullification flag of 1832" began flying over the Citadel. Veterans of Hayne's army volunteered in the state's new home guard units, and seven men who had served in the Nullification Convention signed the Ordinance of Secession. With the Union dissolved, Charleston's artillery companies fired a triumphant salute, using powder saved from the "stirring times of Nullification."[9]

As secessionists understood, the political calculus had shifted dramatically in the past thirty years. A lowcountry writer rejoiced that South Carolina would become, "as in the days of nullification, an armed camp, only this time we will be almost unanimous." A generation earlier, one editor observed, Nullifiers had challenged the federal government with only a "bare majority" of the population behind them. If the state refused to "recede in 1832," he asked, then "how much less will she do it now, when her people are united to a man?" During the nullification crisis, South Carolinians were "divided amongst themselves, and not a solitary southern State" defended them. Now, "her people act as one man, and four or five States stand ready to . . . share her fate."[10]

Thirty years earlier, partisan divisions threatened to tear the state apart. Nullifiers stormed to power by channeling voters' anger and anxiety into an organized political movement. They framed the tariff of abominations as a threat to slavery and white supremacy and called on voters to defend their freedom "at the threshold." These arguments, however, failed to persuade 40 percent of South Carolinians, who saw the Union as the "world's last hope"—the only safeguard against social and political chaos. Slowly, often reluctantly, they organized a party of their own to resist southern radicalism. From 1830 to 1834, Nullifiers and Union men vied for power across the state, struggling to decide the "destiny of free government."[11]

In 1835, however, partisan compromise coupled with antislavery agitation substantially altered South Carolinian politics. Union men and Nullifiers worked together to denounce the AASS, demand a congressional gag rule, serve in repressive Vigilance Associations, and lynch dissenters and "fanatics." Even after 1835, the road to disunion was neither clear nor direct. Many South Carolinians remained conditional Unionists and worked fiercely to hold the country together on their terms. The debates over the direct-mail and petition campaigns, however, provided a road map for radicalism. South Carolinians condemned *all* northerners as abolitionists, demanded—and enforced—southern unity, and called upon men to defend the racial and gender hierarchy at the heart of their world.[12]

By the fall of 1860, only a handful of South Carolinians dared to publicly defend the Union. Speaking in Anderson that October, Benjamin Perry confessed that he was "still a Union man," and even Lincoln's election could not alter his convictions. The Constitution, he explained, still protected slavery, and Republicans' policy of nonextension "really amounts to nothing," since there was "no territory at present where slavery can be carried."

Secession, however, would provoke "revolution and civil war, and endanger our property, our liberty, and Independence." If civil war erupted, he warned, nothing could stop a northern army from landing in the South Carolina lowcountry and "proclaiming freedom to the slaves who shall flock to their standard." Federal forces would "carry off" thousands of slaves and incite rebellion among those who remained.[13]

A few other South Carolinians resisted secession, most of them veterans of the nullification-era Union Party. Postmaster Alfred Huger maintained "National & Federal" principles and refused to resign his office. The Union, he explained, was "made sacred by Every recollection," and he mourned that he was destined to outlive it. Judge John B. O'Neall spoke out against secession even as his neighbors threw eggs and turnips at his body. Charleston cooper Jacob Schirmer lamented the "dissolution of our glorious Union," and Judge George Bryan declared that he still saw the Union as "the greatest blessing to North and South." James Petigru supported the conservative Constitutional Union Party in 1860 and prayed that secessionists would not "make [Lincoln's] bare election a *causus belli*." He decried disunion and pleaded for South Carolinians to wait until Lincoln committed an "overt act against the Constitution." As Petigru heard the Charleston church bells tolling for secession, he remarked that radicals had "set a blazing torch to the temple of constitutional liberty." South Carolinians, he observed, would "have no more peace forever," and he had "seen the last happy day of [his] life."[14]

In Greenville and Spartanburg Districts, Unionist sentiment lingered in some communities. At Spartanburg Court House, a few residents defiantly denounced secession, and a rural meeting insisted the state was "acting rather hastily." A few Spartanburg residents even organized a "Union Military company" to stem the tide of radicalism. Public outrage, however, forced them to disband several days later, as they "fear[ed] being hanged." As elections for the state convention approached, Greenville moderates nominated a ticket—headlined by Benjamin Perry—opposed to immediate secession. Perry received 225 votes, and he secured a majority at a few rural polling stations. Secessionists, however, carried 85 percent of the district's vote. It was the first time Perry had ever lost an election in Greenville District. When news of secession reached him, Perry wrote mournfully to Petigru that he had "been trying for the last thirty years to save the State from the horrors of disunion. They are now all going to the devil, and I will go with them."[15]

In March 1861, Lincoln sent South Carolina native Stephen Hurlbut to Charleston to investigate the "actual state of feeling in this City & State." A generation earlier, Jackson had done the same thing, sending his secretary George Breathitt to uncover the "real intentions of the nullifyers." Breathitt visited Charleston's federal garrison and met with local Union Party leaders, and he discovered a city and a state divided. Hurlbut, however, found only Petigru. In the entire city, he reported, "Fort Sumter is the only spot where the U[nited] States have jurisdiction and James L. Petigru [is] the only citizen loyal to the Nation." South Carolinians had embraced secession, and a large number hoped to "precipitate collision [and] inaugurate war." Secession, he observed, was a "fixed fact," and South Carolinians had "no attachment to the Union." Every man who remained loyal to the Union thirty years earlier was now prepared to take up arms for the Confederacy. He concluded sadly that political compromise and patriotic eloquence would not avail: "There is positively nothing to appeal to—The Sentiment of National Patriotism always feeble in Carolina, has been Extinguished . . ."[16]

Notes

ABBREVIATIONS

CC   Special Collections, College of Charleston Libraries

CU   Special Collections and Archives, Clemson University Libraries

DU   David M. Rubenstein Rare Book & Manuscript Library, Duke University

HSP   Historical Society of Pennsylvania

LOC   Library of Congress

NYHS   New York Historical Society

SCDAH   South Carolina Department of Archives and History

SCHS   South Carolina Historical Society

SCL   South Caroliniana Library

SHC   Southern Historical Collection, University of North Carolina at Chapel Hill

INTRODUCTION

1. John S. D. Eisenhower, *Agent of Destiny: The Life and Times of General Winfield Scott* (Norman, OK: University of Oklahoma Press, 1997), 134–39; Winfield Scott, *Memoirs of Lieut.-General Winfield Scott*, ed. Timothy D. Johnson (Knoxville, TN: University of Tennessee Press, 2015), 123–35; William W. Freehling, *Prelude to Civil War: The Nullification Controversy in South Carolina, 1816–1836* (New York, NY: Oxford University Press, 1965), 1–3; Andrew Jackson to Joel R. Poinsett, 24 January 1833, Joel Roberts Poinsett Papers, Historical Society of Pennsylvania (HSP hereafter).

2. Winfield Scott to William C. Preston, 14 December 1832, in *The Nullification Era: A Documentary Era*, ed. William W. Freehling (New York, NY: Harper Torchbooks, 1967), 175–77.

3. Jacob W. Bailey to Jane Keely, 24 November 1832, and Jacob W. Bailey to William M. Bailey, February 1833, Miscellaneous Manuscripts, Charleston Library Society, on microform at South Carolina Historical Society (SCHS hereafter).

4. Robert J. Turnbull, *An Oration Delivered in the City of Charleston Before the State Rights & Free Trade Party* (Charleston, SC: A. E. Miller, 1832), 22; *Columbia Telescope*, 16 July 1833.

5. *Greenville Mountaineer*, 12 January 1833 and 9 February 1833; Joel R. Poinsett to Andrew Jackson, 22 February 1833, Andrew Jackson Papers, Library of Congress (LOC hereafter).

6. Andrew Jackson to Maunsel White, 22 December 1832, *The Papers of Andrew Jackson, Volume 10: 1832*, ed. Daniel Feller, Thomas Coens, and Laura-Eve Moss (Knoxville, TN: University of Tennessee Press, 2016); James Madison to Edward Everett, 28 August 1830, *Selected Writings of James Madison*, ed. Ralph Ketcham (Indianapolis, IN: Hackett Publishing Company, 2006); *Register of Debates in Congress*, Senate, 21st Cong., 2nd Sess., 59–80.

7. See Manisha Sinha, *The Slave's Cause: A History of Abolition* (New Haven, CT: Yale University Press, 2016); Van Gosse, *The First Reconstruction: Black Politics in America from the Revolution to the Civil War* (Chapel Hill, NC: University of North Carolina Press, 2021).

8. *New York Spectator,* 24 January 1833; *Charleston Courier,* 12 January 1833; Donald J. Ratcliffe, "The Nullification Crisis, Southern Discontents, and the American Political Process," *American Nineteenth Century History* 1, no. 2 (Summer 2000): 1–30.

9. See Freehling, *Prelude to Civil War;* Lacy K. Ford, *Origins of Southern Radicalism: The South Carolina Upcountry, 1800–1860* (New York, NY: Oxford University Press, 1988); Stephanie McCurry, *Masters of Small Worlds: Yeoman Households, Gender Relations, and the Political Culture of the Antebellum South Carolina Low Country* (New York, NY: Oxford University Press, 1995); Manisha Sinha, *The Counterrevolution of Slavery: Politics and Ideology in Antebellum South Carolina* (Chapel Hill, NC: University of North Carolina Press, 2000). This book describes Union Party voters as "Union men" to distinguish them from the "Unionists" of the Civil War era and more accurately reflect the partisan labels of the time. The label, of course, was explicitly gendered: Union men insisted that women were "Better suited to the domestic than the political circle." See *Greenville Mountaineer,* 12 July 1834.

10. James M. Banner Jr., "The Problem of South Carolina," *The Hofstadter Aegis: A Memorial,* ed. Stanley Elkins and Eric McKitrick (New York, NY: Knopf, 1974), 60–66; *Pendleton Messenger,* 18 July 1832; *Greenville Mountaineer,* 19 January 1833. See Richard Hofstadter, *The Idea of a Party System: The Rise of Legitimate Opposition in the United States, 1780–1840* (Berkeley, CA: University of California Press, 1969); Jeffrey S. Selinger, *Embracing Dissent: Political Violence and Party Development in the United States* (Philadelphia, PA: University of Pennsylvania Press, 2016).

11. In 1832, for example, the Union Party triumphed in three of the four districts where slaves made up less than one-third of the population. Nullifiers, meanwhile, captured all six districts where slaves constituted more than two-thirds of the population. As Lacy Ford observes, however, a more extensive analysis reveals only a weak correlation between a district's political leaning and its "wealth, incidence of slaveholding, average size of slaveholding, ratio of blacks to whites, or severity of economic distress." The partisan battles of the nullification crisis did not break down along clear geographic or economic lines. Instead, he contends, "the crucial decisions were made on the basis of the ideological and tactical choices presented during the campaign." See Ford, *Origins of Southern Radicalism,* 137; J. P. Ochenkowski, "The Origins of Nullification in South Carolina," *The South Carolina Historical Society* 83, no. 2 (April 1982): 121–53; Jane H. Pease and William H. Pease, "The Economics and Politics of Charleston's Nullification Crisis," *The Journal of Southern History* 47, no. 3 (August 1981): 343–45.

12. *Greenville Mountaineer,* 22 November 1834; Carroll D. Wright, *The History and Growth of the United States Census, Prepared for the Senate Committee on the Census* (Washington, DC: GPO, 1900), 17, 31. Demographic data for the Union Party was calculated by compiling a list of names from petitions to the state legislature, then searching for each individual in the 1830 and 1840 censuses. See, for example, "Inhabitants of Abbeville, Kershaw, Lancaster, Greenville, Pendleton, and Union Districts, Petition Protesting against the Proposed Amendment to the State Constitution," South Carolina Department of Archives and History (SCDAH hereafter);

"Inhabitants of Spartanburg District, Petition Opposing the Test Oath and Protesting its Being Included in the Constitution of the State," SCDAH; "Inhabitants of Edgefield District, Petition Protesting the Proposed Alteration of the State Constitution," SCDAH.

13. Cynthia Nicoletti, "Roundtable IV Comment," paper presented at the Power, Violence, and Inequality Collective Fellows Mini-Conference, University of Virginia, April 2019; Elizabeth R. Varon, "Disunion! The Coming of the American Civil War, 1789–1859," paper presented at the Library of Virginia, December 2008, available at http://www.c-span.org/video/?282900-1/disunion.

14. Gary W. Gallagher, *The Union War* (Cambridge, MA: Harvard University Press, 2011), 2.

15. McCurry, *Masters of Small Worlds;* James Brewer Stewart, "'A Great Talking and Eating Machine': Patriarchy, Mobilization and the Dynamics of Nullification in South Carolina," *Civil War History* 27, no. 3 (September 1991): 197–220; *Columbia Telescope,* 11 September 1832; *Winyaw Intelligencer,* 10 November 1832. See also Andrew F. Lang, *A Contest of Civilizations: Exposing the Crisis of American Exceptionalism in the Civil War Era* (Chapel Hill, NC: University of North Carolina Press, 2021). This book adapts the work of Amy Greenburg, who argues that the social and economic changes of the 1830s created "two preeminent and dueling mid-century masculinities." Restrained men, she argues, grounded their identities in family, faith, and financial success, while martial men glorified physical strength, violence, and social and sexual dominance. See Amy S. Greenberg, *Manifest Manhood and the Antebellum American Empire* (New York, NY: Cambridge University Press, 2005).

16. Edward Bartlett Rugemer, *The Problem of Emancipation: The Caribbean Roots of the American Civil War* (Baton Rouge, LA: Louisiana State University Press, 2008); Timothy Mason Roberts, *Distant Revolutions: 1848 and the Challenge to American Exceptionalism* (Charlottesville, VA: University of Virginia Press, 2009); Adam I. P. Smith, *The Stormy Present: Conservatism and the Problem of Slavery in Northern Politics, 1846–1865* (Chapel Hill, NC: University of North Carolina Press, 2017); Caitlin Fitz, *Our Sister Republics: The United States in an Age of American Revolutions* (New York, NY: Liveright Publishing Corporation, 2016); Ann L. Tucker, *Newest Born of Nations: European Nationalist Movements and the Making of the Confederacy* (Charlottesville, VA: University of Virginia Press, 2020).

17. *The Debate in the South Carolina Legislature in December 1830 on the Reports of the Committees of Both Houses in Favor of Convention* (Columbia, SC: S. J. McMorris, 1831), 101.

1. CONTAINING CHAOS

1. *Charleston Mercury,* 3 October 1828; *Daily National Journal,* 5 August 1828; *Aurora & Pennsylvania Gazette,* 31 July 1828; *Augusta Chronicle,* 8 October 1828.

2. George Howe, *History of the Presbyterian Church in South Carolina,* vol. II (Columbia, SC: W. J. Duffie, 1883), 735–37; *Charleston Observer,* 23 November 1833; *Charleston Mercury,* 3 October 1828.

3. *Charleston Mercury,* 3 October 1828; Robert Tinkler, *James Hamilton of South Carolina* (Baton Rouge, LA: Louisiana State University Press, 2004), 94.

4. Freehling, *Prelude to Civil War,* 89–133; Rachel N. Klein, *Unification of a Slave State:*

The Rise of the Planter Class in the South Carolina Backcountry, 1760–1808 (Chapel Hill, NC: University of North Carolina Press, 1990), 257–68. See also Robert Elder, *Calhoun: American Heretic* (New York, NY: Basic Books, 2021).

5. Freehling, *Prelude to Civil War,* 99–101.

6. Tinkler, *James Hamilton of South Carolina,* 36–37; *Statutes at Large of South Carolina: Volume 1,* ed. Thomas Cooper (Columbia, SC: A. S. Johnston, 1836), 226–27; Freehling, *Prelude to Civil War,* 101.

7. Maurie D. McInnis, *The Politics of Taste in Antebellum Charleston* (Chapel Hill, NC: University of North Carolina Press, 2005), 8; Benjamin E. Park, *American Nationalisms: Imagining Union in the Age of Revolutions, 1783–1833* (New York, NY: Cambridge University Press, 2018), 199. In reality, market forces rather than tariff policies contributed to this economic downturn. Cotton prices soared after the War of 1812, and as thousands of white settlers flooded into Alabama and Mississippi, they began cultivating the crop. Cotton production increased fivefold between 1814 and 1826, causing the market price to plummet. At the same time, South Carolina's worn-out soil produced smaller yields than the new plantations in the Old Southwest. See Tinkler, *James Hamilton,* 55–56.

8. Lacy K. Ford, *Deliver Us From Evil: The Slavery Question in the Old South* (New York, NY: Oxford University Press, 2009), 207–78. The court convicted four white men of sympathizing with and offering assistance to the African American conspirators. See Philip F. Rubio, "'Though He Had a White Face, He was a Negro in Heart': Examining the White Men Convicted of Supporting the 1822 Denmark Vesey Slave Insurrection Conspiracy," *The South Carolina Historical Magazine* 113, no. 1 (January 2012): 50–67.

9. Varon, *Disunion!,* 51; Michael P. Johnson, "Denmark Vesey and His Co-Conspirators," *William & Mary Quarterly* 58 (October 2001): 915–76; Ford, *Deliver Us From Evil,* 207–37; Governor Thomas Bennett, "Message Providing Information on a Detachment of State Militia Sent to Apprehend Fugitive Slaves, 9 December 1822," SCDAH; John Sarvis, "Petition and Supporting Papers Asking Compensation for a Slave Executed For Attempting An Insurrection in Horry District, c. 1822," SCDAH; John B. Girardeau, "Petition and Supporting Papers Asking Reimbursement for Services Rendered During a Slave Insurrection, 1823," SCDAH; Tim Lockley and David Doddington, "Maroon and Slave Communities in South Carolina Before 1865," *The South Carolina Historical Magazine* 113, no. 2 (April 2012): 125–45.

10. Ford, *Deliver Us From Evil,* 207–37; Inhabitants of Edisto, "Petition Advocating Curbing Certain Rights of Free Blacks . . . , 1820," SCDAH; Inhabitants of Charleston, "Petition Advocating a Curtailment of Certain Rights Granted to Free Blacks . . . , 16 October 1820," SCDAH; Alan F. January, "The South Carolina Association: An Agency for Race Control in Antebellum Charleston," *The South Carolina Historical Magazine* 78, no. 3 (July 1977): 191–201, available from http://www.jstor.org/stable/27567452. The votes broke down along broadly geographic lines, with lowcountry lawmakers generally supporting the bills and upcountry lawmakers being more divided.

11. Henry William DeSaussure to Joel R. Poinsett, 6 July 1822, quoted in Freehling, *Prelude to Civil War,* 112; Ford, *Deliver Us From Evil,* 285; Carl Lawrence Paulus, *The Slaveholding Crisis: Fear of Insurrection and the Coming of the Civil War* (Baton Rouge, LA: Louisiana State

University Press, 2017), 12–20; Robert Pierce Forbes, *The Missouri Compromise and Its Aftermath: Slavery and the Meaning of America* (Chapel Hill, NC: University of North Carolina Press, 2007), 158–60.

12. William Johnson, *The Opinion of the Hon. William Johnson, Delivered on the 7th of August, 1823* (Charleston, SC: C. C. Sebring, 1823); Irwin F. Greenberg, "Justice William Johnson: South Carolina Unionist, 1823–1830," *Pennsylvania History: A Journal of Mid-Atlantic Studies* 36, no. 3 (July 1969): 307–34, available at http://www.jstor.org/stable/27771793.

13. Zeno and Caroliniensis, quoted in Thomas H. Cox, *Gibbons v. Ogden, Law, and Society in the Early Republic* (Athens, OH: Ohio University Press, 2009); Ford, *Deliver Us From Evil*, 287–89; Richard Campbell, "Patriotism, Poetry, and Personalities: The Politics of John L. Wilson and 'A Pasquinade of the Thirties,'" *The South Carolina Historical Magazine* 115, no. 1 (January 2014): 4–34, available at http://www.jstor.org/stable/24332770; Alan F. January, "The First Nullification: The Negro Seamen Acts Controversy in South Carolina, 1822–1860" (PhD diss., University of Iowa, 1976).

14. *Niles' Weekly Register*, 25 December 1824; *National Intelligencer*, 1 January 1825; Ford, *Origins of Southern Radicalism*, 116–19. As William W. Freehling notes, nationalists still held considerable power in the state legislature in the mid-1820s. In 1824, lawmakers selected a nationalist governor (Richard Manning) and a nationalist speaker of the house (John B. O'Neall), and two years later, they came within two votes (83 to 81) of sending nationalist Alfred Huger to the US Senate instead of Smith. See Freehling, *Prelude to Civil War*, 120.

15. *State Documents on Federal Relations: The States and the United States*, ed. Herman V. Ames (Philadelphia, PA: University of Pennsylvania Press, 1911); Theodore Dehon Jervey, *Robert Y. Hayne and His Times* (New York, NY: Macmillan Company, 1909), 185; Matthew Karp, *This Vast Southern Empire: Slaveholders at the Helm of American Foreign Policy* (Cambridge: Harvard University Press, 2016), 13–14; William J. Cooper, *The Lost Founding Father: John Quincy Adams and the Transformation of American Politics* (New York, NY: Liveright Publishing Corporation, 2017), 228–29. The states that endorsed the antislavery resolutions were Ohio, Pennsylvania, Vermont, New Jersey, Delaware, Illinois, Indiana, Connecticut, and Massachusetts.

16. Robert William Fogel, *Without Consent or Contract: The Rise and Fall of American Slavery* (New York, NY: W. W. Norton, 1989), 253; *Statutes at Large of South Carolina*, 230–43. A New Englander living in Cheraw observed his neighbors' intense anxiety, noting that the "least stir of a leaf . . . causes alarm." That August, rumors of a slave rebellion terrified the village, and militiamen patrolled Cheraw for weeks to maintain order. See William C. Gale to Miller and Brewster, 13 August 1827, William C. Gale Letter, South Caroliniana Library (SCL hereafter).

17. *South Carolina State Gazette and Columbia Advertiser*, 11 August 1827; *Columbia Telescope and South Carolina State Journal*, 14 September 1827; Thomas Cooper to Martin Van Buren, 31 July 1827, Martin Van Buren Papers, Library of Congress.

18. Varon, *Disunion!*, 7–8. See also Erika J. Pribanic-Smith, "Rhetoric of Fear," *Journalism History* 38, no. 3 (Fall 2012): 166–77.

19. Thomas Cooper, "'Value of the Union' Speech, July 2, 1827," *The Nullification Era: A Documentary Record*, ed. William W. Freehling (New York, NY: Harper Torchbooks, 1967), 20–25.

20. *Charleston Courier,* 14 July 1827.

21. James Hamilton, *An Eulogium of the Public Services and Character of Robert J. Turnbull* (Charleston, SC: A. E. Miller, 1834), 15; Freehling, *Prelude to Civil War,* 126; Robert J. Turnbull, *The Crisis, or Essays on the Usurpations of the Federal Government* (Charleston, SC: A. E. Miller, 1827), 14, 147–52.

22. *Charleston Courier,* 14 July 1827, 20 July 1827, 23 July 1827, and 30 July 1827.

23. *Charleston Courier,* 23 August 1827.

24. *Charleston Courier,* 15 September 1827 and 25 September 1827.

25. William K. Bolt, *Tariff Wars and the Politics of Jacksonian America* (Nashville, TN: Vanderbilt University Press, 2017), 82–90.

26. Tinkler, *James Hamilton of South Carolina,* 86–88; *Niles' Weekly Register,* 22 November 1828.

27. *Columbia Telescope and South Carolina State Journal,* 14 June 1828, 28 June 1828, and 6 September 1828; William C. Davis, *Rhett: The Turbulent Life and Times of a Fire-Eater* (Columbia, SC: University of South Carolina Press, 2001), 38–42; *Georgia Courier,* 21 August 1828; *Indiana Journal,* 25 September 1828; *Niles' Weekly Register,* 20 September 1828.

28. Thomas Cooper to David J. McCord, 16 July 1828, Thomas Cooper Papers, SCL; *Charleston Mercury,* 14 July 1828, 14 August 1828, and 22 August 1828; *Winyaw Intelligencer,* 9 October 1828; *Columbia Telescope,* 11 September 1828.

29. Daniel Havens Skinner to Isaac Skinner, 2 October 1828, Daniel Havens Skinner Letter, SCL; Richard I. Manning to [illegible] Cox, 1828, Papers of the Williams, Chesnut, and Manning Families, SCL; *Camden Journal,* 26 July 1828; *Mountaineer,* 19 July 1828 and 7 February 1829; *Charleston Courier,* 19 July 1828 and 27 August 1828; *South Carolina State Gazette and Columbia Advertiser,* 4 October 1828.

30. *Charleston Courier,* 3 January 1828 through 12 February 1828 and 10 June 1828 through 8 July 1828; Erika Jean Pribanic-Smith, "Sowing the Seeds of Disunion: South Carolina's Partisan Newspapers and the Nullification Crisis, 1828–1833" (PhD diss., University of Alabama, 2010), 31.

31. *Charleston Mercury,* 11 August 1828; *Greenville Republican,* 19 July 1828; *South Carolina State Gazette and Columbia Advertiser,* 4 October 1828; *Niles' Weekly Register,* 20 September 1828.

32. Thomas Hanson to Stephen D. Miller, 6 September 1828, Stephen Decatur Miller Papers, SCHS.

33. *Charleston Mercury,* 27 August 1828 and 28 August 1828.

34. *Augusta Chronicle,* 8 October 1828; Tinkler, *James Hamilton of South Carolina,* 96; William K. Bolt, "Founding Father and Rebellious Son: James Madison, John C. Calhoun, and the Use of Precedents," *American Nineteenth Century History* 5, no. 3 (Fall 2004): 1–27.

35. David J. McCord to Philip H. Nicklin, 16 October 1828, David J. McCord Letter, New York Historical Society (NYHS hereafter); *Charleston Mercury,* 10 October 1828, 15 October 1828, and 16 October 1828.

36. *Charleston Mercury,* 10 October 1828, 15 October 1828, and 16 October 1828; *Camden Journal,* 18 October 1828; Thomas Grimké to Alfred Huger, 1 December 1828, Grimké Family

Papers, Special Collections, College of Charleston Libraries (CC hereafter); Job Johnston to Stephen D. Miller, 20 August 1828, Stephen D. Miller Papers, SCHS. On the power of deferential politics, see William D. Martin to Lewis Ayer, 5 October 1826, Lewis M. Ayer Papers, SCL.

37. *Charleston Mercury*, 2 December 1828; Elliott to Anne Elliott, 29 November 1828, 6 December 1828, and 14 December 1828, Elliott and Gonzales Family Papers, Southern Historical Collection, University of North Carolina at Chapel Hill (SHC hereafter).

38. John C. Calhoun, "Rough Draft of What Is Called the South Carolina Exposition," in *Union and Liberty: The Political Philosophy of John C. Calhoun,* ed. Ross M. Lence (Indianapolis, IN: Liberty Fund, 1992), 311–65.

39. Tinkler, *James Hamilton of South Carolina,* 100; *South Carolina State Gazette and Columbia Advertiser,* 6 December 1828 and 27 December 1828. The strongest support for the convention came from Butler's Edgefield District and coastal St. Bartholomew's Parish, home of Robert Barnwell Smith. All six of Edgefield's representatives and all four of St. Bartholomew's voted in favor of the convention.

40. William Elliott to Anne Elliott, 24 November 1828, quoted in Tinkler, *James Hamilton of South Carolina,* 99.

41. George McDuffie to Unknown, 9 September 1828, George McDuffie Papers, SCL.

42. *South Carolina State Gazette and Columbia Advertiser,* 27 December 1828.

2. DEFINING CONVICTIONS

1. *Proceedings of the State Rights Celebration at Charleston, S.C., July 1, 1830* (Charleston, SC: A. E. Miller, 1830), 1–3.

2. *Proceedings of the State Rights Celebration,* 51–56.

3. *Proceedings of the State Rights Celebration,* 10–22.

4. *Proceedings of the State Rights Celebration,* 5–8, 49–50.

5. *Proceedings of the State Rights Celebration,* 5–8.

6. Henry D. Capers, *The Life and Times of C. G. Memminger* (Richmond, VA: Everett Waddey, 1893), 78.

7. Unknown to Unknown, 14 December 1829, Townes Family Papers, SCL; James Hamilton to John C. Calhoun, 10 May 1829, *The Papers of John C. Calhoun, Volume 10: 1825–1829,* ed. Clyde N. Wilson (Columbia, SC: University of South Carolina Press, 1977). Because of the structure of the antebellum election cycle, this was the second session of the 20th Congress, which had been elected in 1826. The full 21st Congress, elected in 1828, would not convene until December 1829.

8. Freehling, *Prelude to Civil War,* 62–63. For the petitions related to the Georgetown slave conspiracy, see Records of the General Assembly, 1829, SCDH.

9. *Columbia Telescope,* 2 January 1829; 11 September 1829; *Winyaw Intelligencer,* 5 August 1829; *Charleston Courier,* 28 November 1829; Warren R. Davis, quoted in Freehling, *Prelude to Civil War,* 176.

10. Freehling, *Prelude to Civil War,* 180; *Niles' Weekly Register,* 19 September 1829.

11. Thomas S. Grimké, *Speech of Thomas Smith Grimké, Delivered in the Senate of South*

Carolina in December 1828 (Charleston, SC: W. Riley, 1829); *Daily National Intelligencer,* 16 September 1829; James H. Smith to Frederick Fraser, 7 September 1829, Fraser Family Papers, SCHS.

12. *Mountaineer,* 19 December 1829 and 26 December 1829; Unknown to Unknown, 14 December 1829, Townes Family Papers, SCL; *Charleston Courier,* 9 December 1829.

13. John R. Van Atta, *Securing the West: Politics, Public Lands, and the Fate of the Old Republic, 1785–1850* (Baltimore, MD: Johns Hopkins University Press, 2014), 156–67; Jon Meacham, *American Lion: Andrew Jackson in the White House* (New York, NY: Random House, 2008), 126–27; Christopher Childers, *The Webster, Hayne Debate: Defining Nationhood in the Early American Republic* (Baltimore, MD: Johns Hopkins University Press, 2018); *Register of Debates,* Senate, 21st Cong., 2nd Sess., 31–41; *Speeches of Hayne and Webster in the United States Senate on the Resolution of Mr. Foot* (Boston, MA: A. T. Hotchkiss and W. P. Fetridge, 1853), 3–36.

14. *Register of Debates,* Senate, 21st Cong., 2nd Sess., 59–80.

15. Meacham, *American Lion,* 126; *Southern Times & State Gazette,* 25 February 1830; Harry L. Watson, *Liberty and Power: The Politics of Jacksonian America* (New York, NY: Hill and Wang, 1990), 120–21; Robert V. Remini, *The Life of Andrew Jackson* (New York, NY: Harper & Row, 1998), 195–97. Jackson intended to toast "Our federal Union" but inadvertently left out the word "federal." Hayne asked him to include the word in the published accounts of the dinner, and the president agreed.

16. *Newbern Spectator,* 22 May 1830; *Charleston Mercury,* 21 April 1830 and 24 April 1830; *Southern Times & State Gazette,* 3 May 1830.

17. Francis W. Pickens to James Henry Hammond, 8 March 1830 and 13 May 1830, in James Henry Hammond Papers, LOC; Clariosophic Literary Society Records, vol. 6, 1826–31 Minutes, South Carolina Digital Library; *Raleigh Weekly Register,* 1 April 1830; *Beaufort Gazette,* 28 January 1830; Isaac W. Hayne to James Henry Hammond, 29 June 1830, James Henry Hammond Papers, LOC.

18. *Charleston Courier,* 30 May 1831.

19. Ford, *Origins of Southern Radicalism,* 111–13.

20. Len Travers, *Celebrating the Fourth: Independence Day and the Rites of Nationalism in the Early Republic* (Amherst, MA: University of Massachusetts Press, 1997); A. V. Huff Jr., "The Eagle and the Vulture: Changing Attitudes Toward Nationalism in Fourth of July Orations Delivered in Charleston, 1778–1860," *South Atlantic Quarterly* 73 (1974): 10–22; Kimberly R. Kellison, "Men, Women, and the Marriage of the Union: Fourth of July Celebrations in Antebellum Georgia," *The Georgia Historical Quarterly* 8, no. 3 (Fall 2014): 129–54.

21. *Pendleton Messenger,* 7 July 1830; *Southern Times & State Gazette,* 5 July 1830; *Greenville Mountaineer,* 9 July 1830 and 30 July 1830.

22. *Pendleton Messenger,* 7 July 1830; *Greenville Mountaineer,* 9 July 1830 and 16 July 1830. In the 1830s, some writers still spelled Spartanburg as "Spartanburgh" and Orangeburg as "Orangeburgh." I use the simplified modern spelling throughout this book.

23. James H. Smith to Frederick Fraser, 6 August 1830, Fraser Family Papers, SCHS; *Greenville Mountaineer,* 16 July 1830; *Camden Journal,* 11 September 1830; *Charleston Courier,* 29 June 1830, 3 September 1830, and 8 October 1830.

24. *Edgefield Hive,* 26 February 1830; *Charleston Courier,* 17 May 1830, 16 June 1830, and 27 August 1830.

25. Thomas Grimké, *Speech of Thomas Grimké Delivered in the Senate of South Carolina in December 1828; Charleston Courier,* 12 August 1830 and 11 October 1830.

26. *Greenville Mountaineer,* 6 August 1830; *Southern Times & State Gazette,* 12 August 1830 and 26 August 1830; *Pendleton Messenger,* 18 August 1830.

27. *Charleston Courier,* 3 September 1830; *Pendleton Messenger,* 1 September 1830; *Camden Journal,* 28 August 1830; *Southern Times & State Gazette,* 2 August 1830, 16 August 1830, and 9 September 1830; *Edgefield Hive,* 3 September 1830; *Southern Times & State Gazette,* 2 September 1830; John S. Richardson, *The Argument of the Hon. J. S. Richardson in Reply to Chancellor Harper, and in Opposition to Nullification and Convention* (Columbia, SC: Times and Gazette Office, 1830).

28. Stephen Elliott to William Elliott, 27 July 1830, Elliott and Gonzales Family Papers, SHC; Joseph Johnson to Joel R. Poinsett, 17 July 1830, Papers of Joel R. Poinsett, HSP; James Hamilton to Stephen D. Miller, 9 August 1830, Stephen D. Miller Papers, SCHS; *Vermont Courier,* 18 September 1830; *Middlebury Free Press,* 16 September 1830; *Edgefield Hive,* 8 October 1830; *Southern Times & State Gazette,* 13 September 1830 and 16 September 1830. In 1829, Pinckney defeated Grimké 560 to 487. In 1830, Pringle won the election by a vote of 838 to 754.

29. Robert Mackay to George, 9 October 1830, Mackay Family Papers, SCL; *Niles' Weekly Register,* 9 October 1830; *Charleston Mercury,* 19 October 1830.

30. *Charleston Mercury,* 29 September 1830; *Southern Times,* 7 October 1830. In his speech at the "great state rights celebration" that fall, Governor Miller warned the crowd about the dangers of colonization. Virginia Congressman Charles Fenton Mercer had introduced a bill supporting the American Colonization Society, and Miller argued that without nullification the state would have "no security that the colonization bill will not be matured and sanctioned." See *Niles' Weekly Register,* 9 October 1830. These appeals resonated with at least some voters. One writer observed that the "probable insurrection of the slaves" had drawn the consequences of submission into "full relief." See Robert Mackay to George, 9 October 1830, Mackay Family Papers, SCL.

31. Tinkler, *James Hamilton of South Carolina,* 117–19; *Southern Times & State Gazette,* 29 July 1830; Maria Pinckney, *Quintessence of Long Speeches, Arranged as a Political Catechism* (Charleston, SC: A. E. Miller, 1830). Many Nullifiers cultivated a democratic tone, telling voters that "Government was constituted by and for you." Privately, however, they expressed a deep distrust of democracy. In a letter to Governor Stephen D. Miller, Hamilton insisted that voters expected their leaders to "think for them," and he assured the governor that "they will be prepared to *act* as their leaders *think.*" After the election, Hammond observed that universal white manhood suffrage had given many people "power which they are totally incompetent to exercise—if not absolutely unworthy of it." He urged the state to return to *viva voce* voting, in which community pressure could help ensure political orthodoxy. See James Hamilton to Stephen D. Miller, 9 August 1830, Stephen D. Miller Papers, SCHS; *Southern Times & State Gazette,* 14 October 1830.

32. George Washington, "Washington's Farewell Address," *The Avalon Project: Documents*

in Law, History and Diplomacy, Yale Law School, available at http://www.avalon.law.yale.edu; *Greenville Mountaineer,* 8 October 183, 17 October 1830, and 24 October 1830.

33. See Martyn Lyons, *Post-Revolutionary Europe, 1815–1856* (New York, NY: Palgrave Macmillan, 2006); Philip Mansel, *Paris Between Empires: Monarchy and Revolution, 1814–1852* (New York: St. Martin's Press, 2003).

34. *Southern Times,* 13 September 1830; *Charleston Mercury,* 11 September 1830 and 17 September 1830; *Fête Civique: Célébrée a Charleston, S.C. en Commémoration de la Glorieuse Révolution Française de 1830* (Charleston, SC: A. E. Miller, 1830); John Merriman, "European Revolutions of 1830," in *The Encyclopedia of Political Revolutions,* ed. Jack A. Goldstone (New York, NY: Routledge, 2014), 165–68; Elisabeth Jay, *British Writers and Paris: 1830–1875* (New York, NY: Oxford University Press, 2016), 11–13; Munro Price, *The Perilous Crown: France Between Revolutions, 1814–1848* (London, England: Pan Books, 2007), 187–93.

35. See Lang, *A Contest of Civilizations.*

36. *The Southern Times & State Gazette,* 13 September 1830, 16 September 1830, and 10 January 1831; *United States Telegraph,* 16 July 1831.

37. *Charleston Courier,* 1 July 1830, 17 September 1830, and 8 October 1830; *Southern Times & State Gazette,* 9 August 1830.

38. *Charleston Courier,* 8 October 1830, 11 October 1830, 12 October 1830. See Ryan Chamberlain, *Pistols, Politics and the Press: Dueling in 19th Century American Journalism* (Jefferson, NC: McFarland and Company, Inc., 2009).

39. Chauncey Samuel Boucher, *The Nullification Controversy in South Carolina* (Chicago, IL: University of Chicago Press, 1916), 101–3; *Raleigh Weekly Register,* 4 October 1830 and 14 October 1830. Union men averaged 1,261 votes, while Nullifiers averaged 1,245 votes.

40. *Charleston Mercury,* 22 October 1830; *Camden Journal,* 16 October 1830; *Greenville Mountaineer,* 1830; Joseph N. Whitner to James Henry Hammond, 22 July 1830, James Henry Hammond Papers, LOC; *Southern Times & State Gazette,* 14 October 1830 and 28 October 1830.

41. *South Carolina State Gazette and Columbia Advertiser,* 18 October 1828; *Southern Times & State Gazette,* 14 October 1830; *Greenville Mountaineer,* 15 October 1830.

42. *Greenville Mountaineer,* 3 December 1830 and 10 December 1830; John Ravenel to Anna E. Ravenel, 6 December 1830, John Ravenel Papers, SCL. Miller's election, in particular, demonstrated the complete breakdown of the old Smithite and Calhounite factions. Throughout the 1820s, Miller had been one of Smith's closest allies. When Smith came out against a convention, however, radical former Calhounites like Francis Pickens began encouraging Miller to run against Smith. As Pickens explained in June 1830, the combined support of the old Calhounite faction and "a part of his own party will elect him. Their party will then be divided, and we will have the power of the state in our own hands." Radical Smithites abandoned their former leader, and Miller eventually agreed to run against him. The general assembly elected Miller over Smith by a vote of 81 to 77, and Smith left the state the following year. See Freehling, *Prelude to Civil War,* 214–16.

43. Davis, *Rhett,* 56–57; *Southern Times & State Gazette,* 2 December 1830; Boucher, *The Nullification Controversy in South Carolina,* 104–6.

44. Daniel Huger, *Speech of the Honorable Daniel E. Huger, in the House of Representatives*

of South Carolina, December 1830 (Charleston, SC: W. Riley, 1831). Huger and Smith narrowly avoided a duel during the session. Huger accused Nullifiers of "flinching and concealing their intention [to nullify the tariff] and deceiving the people." Smith, enraged, pointed his finger at Huger and replied that he "scorned and despised the imputation." Huger believed Smith's action had crossed the line from political debate to personal attack, and he promptly challenged Smith to a duel. The Nullifier accepted, naming Governor Hamilton as his second. The other legislators, however, intervened and persuaded both men to back down and withdraw their public attacks. See Davis, *Rhett*, 58–59.

45. *The Debate in the South Carolina Legislature in December 1830,* 100–110.

46. *Southern Times & State Gazette* 23 December 1830; *Charleston Mercury*, 21 December 1830; David J. McCord to David Bailie Warden, 29 June 1831, David James McCord Papers, SCL; *Greenville Mountaineer,* 22 October 1830; *Camden Journal*, 23 October 1830; Daniel E. Huger to James Chesnut, 22 December 1830, Papers of the Williams, Chesnut, and Manning Families, SCL. William Drayton shared these apprehensions. He observed that many of the legislators who voted against a convention "were not against that measure, upon principle, only averse to it at this time." If Congress failed to lower the tariff, he predicted, these men would add their strength to the State Rights Party, giving them the two-thirds majority necessary to call a convention. See William Drayton to Joel R. Poinsett, 29 January 1831, Papers of Joel R. Poinsett, HSP.

3. CONTESTING MANHOOD

1. Benjamin F. Perry Diary, August 1832, Benjamin Franklin Perry Papers, SHC.

2. Benjamin F. Perry Diary, August 1832, Benjamin Franklin Perry Papers, SHC; James Hamilton to Waddy Thompson, 31 August 1832, James Hamilton Papers, SCL; Samuel A. Townes to George F. Townes, 23 August 1832, Townes Family Papers, SCL; James H. Hammond, Plantation Book, 16 August 1832, James Henry Hammond Papers, LOC; Patricia McNeely, "Dueling Editors: The Nullification Plot of 1832," *Words at War: The Civil War and American Journalism*, eds. David B. Sachsman, S. Kittrell Rushing, and Roy Morris Jr. (West Lafayette, IN: Purdue University Press, 2008), 30.

3. Julia M. Brown to Jonathan Ralph Flynt, 12 October 1832, Julia M. Brown Letter, SCL; *Greenville Mountaineer*, 28 April 1832.

4. James Hamilton Jr., to James H. Hammond, 8 January 1831 and 3 May 1831, in "Letters on the Nullification Movement in South Carolina, 1830–1834," *The American Historical Review* 6, no. 4 (July 1901), available at http://www.jstor.org/stable/1834178; James Hamilton to Stephen D. Miller, 9 August 1830, Stephen D. Miller Papers, SCHS; James Hamilton to Stephen D. Miller, 25 June 1831, James Hamilton Papers, SCL.

5. Stewart, "'A Great Talking and Eating Machine,'" 217; *Charleston Mercury*, 21 May 1831; George McDuffie, *Speech of the Hon. George McDuffie at a Public Dinner Given to Him by the Citizens of Charleston, May 19, 1831* (Charleston, SC: A. E. Miller, 1831).

6. Calhoun, "The Fort Hill Address: On the Relations of the States and Federal Government," in *Union and Liberty,* 367–400; John C. Calhoun to Samuel L Gouverneur, 8 August 1831, and

John C. Calhoun to Christopher Van Deventer, 5 August 1831, *Papers of John C. Calhoun, Volume 11: 1829–1832*, ed. Clyde N. Wilson (Columbia, SC: University of South Carolina Press, 1978).

7. *United States Telegraph*, 18 July 1831 and 20 July 1831; *Pendleton Messenger*, 6 July 1831; Harriott Pinckney to Charles Cotesworth Pinckney Jr., 1 August 1831, available at http:/www. sparedshared11.wordpress.com; *Camden Journal*, 9 July 1831 and 16 July 1831; *Camden and Lancaster Beacon*, 12 July 1831. A few guests at these public dinners resisted nullification. In Pendleton, William B. Martin toasted Henry Clay as a "friend to our Union, and firm in his integrity; may he never cease to rise." The crowd drank to the toast with empty glasses. In Edisto, a guest toasted William Drayton. While every other toast received at least six cheers—and some as many as fifteen—his received none.

8. *Camden Journal*, 9 July 1831; *United States Telegraph*, 16 July 1831; *Pendleton Messenger*, 6 July 1831; *Proceedings of the Celebration of the 4th July, 1831 at Charleston by the State Rights and Free Trade Party* (Charleston, SC: A. E. Miller, 1831). A Beaufort Nullifier urged the party to refrain from "joyance and festivity of all kinds" on July 4, arguing that "it should be a day, not of mutual congratulation, but of humiliation and regretful remembrance . . . Let it be a day, not of exultation, but of fasting, humiliation, and prayer." *Wyoming Herald* (Wilkes-Barre, PA), 27 July 1831.

9. James Hamilton to Stephen D. Miller, 19 July 1831, Stephen D. Miller Papers, SCHS; Records of the Free Trade and State Rights Association of the Parishes of St. Stephen's, St. John's Berkeley, and St. James Santee, 1831, SCHS; *United States Telegraph*, 14 September 1831; *Camden Republican and Lancaster Beacon*, 27 September 1831 and 15 November 1831; Henry H. Townes to George F. Townes, 4 August 1831, and 3 November 1831, Townes Family Papers, SCL.

10. Lucretia A. Townes to Eliza P. Blassingame, 5 December 1832, Townes Family Papers, SCL; *Southern Times & State Gazette*, 13 September 1830 and 16 September 1830; *Camden Journal*, 18 September 1830, 6 November 1830, and 1 January 1833; *Charleston Mercury*, 11 October 1830 and 14 October 1830; *State Rights and Free Trade Evening Post*, 4 October 1831. Both Constans Daniels and Aaron Willington were born in New England.

11. *Greenville Mountaineer*, 3 October 1832; *Southern Whig*, 9 August 1832; *Charleston Courier*, 4 October 1832; *Camden Journal*, 7 August 1830; *Charleston Courier*, 17 May 1830 and 30 May 1831.

12. *Charleston Courier*, 19 August 1831 and 5 September 1831; *Greenville Mountaineer*, 3 October 1832; *Southern Whig*, 9 August 1832.

13. *Charleston Courier*, 31 August 1831.

14. *Columbia Telescope*, 11 September 1832; *Charleston Courier*, 7 October 1830; *Winyaw Intelligencer*, 10 November 1832; *Greenville Mountaineer*, 25 June 1831.

15. James L. Petigru to William Elliott, 25 August 1831, James L. Petigru Papers, SCHS; *Camden Journal*, 20 August 1831; *Greenville Mountaineer*, 10 September 1831; William Smith, *Speech of the Hon. William Smith, Delivered on Monday, August 1, 1831* (Columbia, SC: Office of the Columbia Hive, 1832).

16. James L. Petigru to William Elliott, 25 August 1831, James L. Petigru Papers, SCHS; *Camden Journal*, 20 August 1831; *Greenville Mountaineer*, 10 September 1831; *Charleston Courier*, 14 March 1831.

17. *Greenville Mountaineer,* 10 September 1831; William Smith to Joel R. Poinsett, 24 July 1831, Joel Roberts Poinsett Papers, HSP.

18. Patrick H. Breen, *The Land Shall Be Deluged in Blood: A New History of the Nat Turner Revolt* (New York, NY: Oxford University Press, 2016); Samuel A Townes to brother, 8 October 1831, Townes Family Papers, SCL; Cader Hughes, "Petition and Supporting Paper Asking Compensation for Supplying Food to The Militia Company, 22 November 1831," SCDAH; Robert A. Cunningham, "Petition for Compensation for His Slave, Ned, 22 November 1831," SCDAH; Benjamin Holt et al, "Petition and Supporting Paper Asking Compensation for Feeding a Volunteer Company, 24 November 1831," SCDAH; John G. Vernon, "Petition Asking for Funds to Repair a Field Piece and Carriage, 1832," SCDAH; Samuel C. Jackson Diary, 17 November 1832, Samuel C. Jackson Papers, SCL.

19. Moses Taggart, "Chairman, On Behalf of the Commissioners of Public Buildings for Abbeville, c. 1830–1835," SCDAH; James Hamilton, "Message No. 2," 6 December 1831, SCDAH.

20. *Columbia Hive,* 11 February 1832; *Charleston Courier,* 10 November 1831 and 20 December 1831.

21. *National Gazette* (Philadelphia, PA), 13 September 1831; William C. Bee to Frederick C. Fraser, 14 September 1831, Frederick Fraser Papers, DU; *Charlotte Journal,* 9 November 1831; *Newbern Sentinel,* 21 September 1831; *Greenville Mountaineer,* 24 September 1831. In 1830, Pringle won the election 838 to 754. In 1831, Pinckney triumphed by a vote of 1,040 to 932.

22. Jacob F. Schirmer Diary, 6 September 1831, Schirmer Family Journals and Registers, SCHS; James L. Petigru to William Elliott, 7 September 1831, James L. Petigru Papers, SCHS; Jane H. Pease and William H. Pease, "The Economics and Politics of Charleston's Nullification Crisis," *The Journal of Southern History* 47, no. 3 (August 1981): 355.

23. James L. Petigru to William Elliott, 7 September 1831, James L. Petigru Papers, SCHS; *Greenville Mountaineer,* 17 September 1831 and 3 December 1831; *Camden Journal,* 24 September 1831.

24. *Charleston Mercury,* 24 February 1832 and 25 February 1832; John C. Schulz to Maria B Schulz, 24 February 1832, "Some Letters from John Christopher Schulz, 1829–1883," *The South Carolina Historical Magazine* 56, no. 1 (January 1955): 1–7. Pendleton, the lone exception, had "not deemed it expedient to form an Association" because of the "unanimity" of its people in support of nullification. On a more practical level, the Nullifiers resolved to increase their political activity in the coming months. They resolved to publish two pamphlets each month to "explain and inculcate nullification," planning to distribute 10,000 copies of each issue throughout the state. Reflecting the growing sophistication of their party machinery, they detailed the exact number of pamphlets to send to each district. Local associations would help raise the $4,000 necessary for production by drawing money from their members." Although Hamilton had helped consciously construct the party's political machinery, he described the State Rights Associations as a spontaneous outburst of republican principle. The organizations, he insisted, had "suddenly . . . risen up throughout our land like camp fires" to resist the "vast central power" of federal tyranny.

25. Thomas Grimké, *Letter to the Honorable John C. Calhoun, Robert Y. Hayne, George McDuffie, and James Hamilton* (Charleston, SC: James S. Burges, 1832); Jacob F. Schirmer

Diary, 22 February 1832, Schirmer Family Journals and Registers, SCHS; *Charleston Courier,* 24 February 1832; Schulz, 24 February 1832 letter, "Some Letters," 1–7, also available at http://www.jstor.org/stable/27565981; Merrill G. Christopherson, "A Rhetorical Study of Hugh Swinton Legaré: South Carolina Unionist" (PhD diss., University of Florida, 1954).

26. *Register of Debates in Congress,* 22nd Cong., 1st Sess., 5 June and 7 June 1832; William Drayton to Joel R. Poinsett, 20 December 1830, Joel Roberts Poinsett Papers, HSP.

27. *Greenville Mountaineer,* 7 April 1832 and 15 September 1832; *Camden Journal,* 21 July 1832; *Southern Whig,* 29 September 1832; *Newbern Spectator,* 13 July 1832; *Southern Sentinel,* 4 August 1832; *Columbia Telescope,* 5 June 1832; Freehling, *Prelude to Civil War,* 248–49. Robert Y. Hayne, Stephen D. Miller, George McDuffie, Warren R. Davis, John M. Felder, John K. Griffin, William T. Nuckolls, and Robert W. Barnwell all signed the "Address to the People of South Carolina." The Union Party congressmen—Drayton, Blair, and Mitchell—did not.

28. *Columbia Telescope,* 11 September 1832; Turnbull, *An Oration Delivered in the City of Charleston; Pendleton Messenger,* 11 July 1832.

29. *Camden Journal,* 1 September 1832, reprinted from *Southern Times & State Gazette.*

30. Turnbull, *An Oration Delivered in the City of Charleston; Pendleton Messenger,* 11 July 1832; *Camden Republican and Lancaster Beacon,* 11 July 1832; *Charleston Mercury,* 4 July 1832 and 11 July 1832. At the Independence Day dinners in Pendleton and Anderson, for example, roughly one-fourth of the toasts explicitly endorsed nullification.

31. *State Rights and Free Trade Almanac for the Year of Our Lord 1832* (Charleston, SC: A. E. Miller, 1831).

32. John Chesnut to James Chesnut, 13 January 1833, Papers of the Williams, Chesnut, and Manning Papers, SCL; *Columbia Hive,* 21 July 1832 and 28 July 1832; *Carolina Watchman,* 4 August 1832; *Greenville Mountaineer,* 12 May 1832; *Charleston Courier,* 30 May 1831 and 22 August 1832; *Columbia Telescope,* 11 September 1832; *Camden Journal,* 7 August 1830.

33. James L. Petigru to William Elliott, 7 August 1832, 4 September 1832, 28 September 1832, and 3 October 1832, James L. Petigru Papers, SCHS; Chapman Levy to William Elliott, 27 August 1832, Elliott and Gonzales Family Papers, SHC. Newspaper circulation increased dramatically during the nullification crisis. The pronullification *Abbeville Whig and Southern Nullifier*'s list of subscribers grew from about 200 in September 1831 to 425 in December 1831 and to 600 by June 1832. The Union Party's *Greenville Mountain*'s circulation increased from about 250 in July 1832 to 400 by that December. The impact of these newspapers was far greater than their circulation numbers, as subscribers shared them with family and friends, read them out loud, and debated their ideas. Editors, furthermore, shared excerpts from other newspapers across the state and country. South Carolina's white population was well-read and highly politicized. In one coastal village, all but three of the forty white families subscribed to at least one newspaper. The average family in the village subscribed to three newspapers and one journal, and one family subscribed to ten. See Samuel A. Townes to brother, 13 September 1831 and 11 December 1831; Samuel A. Townes to George F. Townes, 14 June 1832, SCL; Village Census, 1832, Thomas P. Ravenel Papers, SCHS.

34. Capers, *The Life and Times of C. G. Memminger,* 40–42.

35. Capers, *The Life and Times of C. G. Memminger,* 45–48. Until 1831, both parties in

South Carolina had supported Jackson and laid claim to his image. Nullifiers initially called themselves the "State Rights and Jackson Party," while Union men organized "Jackson and Anti-Nullification meetings." The tensions between Jackson and Calhoun prompted Charleston Nullifiers to change their name to the State Rights and Free Trade Party in May 1831, but many still insisted the president was on their side. After July 4, however, Nullifiers denounced the president, and he became a symbol of the Union Party. See John Knox to James N. Knox, John Knox Letter, SCL; David J. McCord to Stephen D. Miller, 11 December 1831, David James McCord Papers, SCL.

36. Ellen to Harriet Davis, 15 September 1832, Davis Family Papers, Furman University Special Collections and Archives; Julia M. Brown to Jonathan Ralph Flynt, 12 October 1832, Julia M. Brown Letter, SCL; *Pittsburgh Weekly Gazette,* 17 August 1832; Lillian Adele Kibler, *Benjamin F. Perry: South Carolina Unionist* (Durham, NC: Duke University Press, 1946); Benjamin F. Perry Diary, August 1832, B.F. Perry Papers, SHC; Bertram Wyatt-Brown, *Honor and Violence in the Old South* (New York, NY: Oxford University Press, 1986).

37. Eliza Hemphill to William Hemphill, 22 August 1832, Hemphill Family Papers, DU; Robert E. Yates, 9 May 1832, Stephen D. Miller Papers, SCHS; *Greenville Mountaineer,* 28 April 1832; *Columbia Hive,* 5 May 1832; Timothy S. Huebner, *The Southern Judicial Tradition: State Judges and Sectional Distinctiveness, 1790–1890* (Athens, GA: University of Georgia Press, 1999), 100–101.

38. *Southern Patriot,* 10 October 1832. Shachte unequivocally stated his belief that "I was assaulted because I was a Union man."

39. *Camden Journal,* 12 March 1831, reprinted from *The Georgetown Union;* Samuel D. McGill, *Narrative of Reminiscences in Williamsburg County* (Columbia, SC: Bryan Printing Co., 1897), 69–74.

40. Ellen to Harriet Davis, 15 September 1832, Davis Family Papers, Furman University Special Collections and Archives; John N. Barillon to John Seibels, 29 August 1832, Seibels Family Papers, SCL; *Charleston Observer,* 8 September 1832; William H. Pease and Jane H. Pease, *James Louis Petigru: Southern Conservative, Southern Dissenter* (Columbia, SC: University of South Carolina Press, 2002), 50–52. As one writer explained, both parties kept "open houses," which were "large four story brick houses in the centre of the city, in which were provided refreshments of all kinds, free to all persons." The parties kept these houses open all Saturday night "whilst haranguing &c were carried on without regard to the Sabbath." See *North Carolina Free Press,* 18 September 1832.

41. James L. Petigru to William Elliott, 20 September 1832, James L. Petigru Papers, SCHS; James H. Smith to William Elliott, 26 September 1832, Elliott and Gonzales Family Papers, SHC; *Greenville Mountaineer,* 22 September 1832; *Southern Whig,* 29 September 1832; Boucher, *Nullification Controversy in South Carolina,* 200–203; *Fayetteville Weekly Observer,* 18 September 1832; *Vicksburg Whig,* 10 October 1832; Paul H. Bergeron, "Tennessee's Response to the Nullification Crisis," *The Journal of Southern History* 39, no. 1 (February 1973): 23–44. The Union Party convention elected Revolutionary War veteran Thomas Taylor as its president, symbolically linking their struggle to preserve the Union with the legacy of the War for Independence.

42. Abraham Moise, quoted in Capers, *The Life and Times of C. G. Memminger,* 78; Hugh S.

Legaré to Mary S. Legaré, 4 July 1833, *The Writings of Hugh Swinton Legaré,* vol. 1; Thomas S. Grimké, *To the People of the State of South Carolina* (Charleston, SC: J. S. Burges, 1832).

43. *Southern Patriot,* 8 September 1832.

44. *Cheraw Republican,* 13 October 1832; James L. Petigru to Hugh Legaré, 29 October 1832, James L Petigru Papers, SCL; Unknown to Edward Rutledge, 10 October 1832, and H. P. Holbrook to Edward Rutledge, 18 October 1832, Rutledge Family Papers, SCL. A "street battle" broke out in Charleston between Edward Frost, the Nullifiers' leading candidate, and a cooper who belonged to the Union Party. When Frost struck the cooper—"a great sturdy ox of a man"—he retaliated by knocking Frost to the ground. In a fight in Cheraw, one man fell and hit his head on the pavement, dying several hours later. See *Camden Journal,* 20 October 1832.

45. *Pendleton Messenger,* 10 October 1832.

46. *Columbia Hive,* 13 October 1832; Unknown to Jon, 17 October 1832, Henry William DeSaussure Papers, SCHS; James Hamilton to Patrick Noble, 9 October 1832, James Hamilton Papers, SCL; James R. Ervin to Philip Phillips, 26 October 1832, Philip Phillips Family Papers, LOC; *Greenville Mountaineer,* 3 November 1832; Freehling, *Prelude to Civil War,* 260. Hamilton was so confident of success that he drafted the proclamation before the election began.

47. *Greenville Mountaineer,* 13 October 1832, 20 October 1832, 27 October 1832, and 3 November 1832; *Camden Journal,* 20 October 1832; *Southern Patriot,* 11 October 1832; Edward McCrady, Richard Yeadon, and John Phillips to Joshua Teague, 2 November 1832, "Letters on the Nullification Movement in South Carolina, 1830–1834"; Richard G. Arnold to Zachariah Allen, 8 November 1832, Richard G Arnold Letter, SCL; *Southern Patriot,* 25 October 1832; Daniele Huger, quoted in Freehling, *Prelude to Civil War,* 261. The Union Party also objected to the convention's system of representation. Each district received delegates equal to the number of its state legislators. Because house representation was based on total population—not just white population—Union men claimed the convention made "our very slaves elements in the composition of the sovereignty of our State."

48. *The Greenville Mountaineer,* 13 October 1832 and 27 October 1832; *The Southern Patriot,* 8 October 1832.

49. *The Greenville Mountaineer,* 17 November 1832; John Chesnut to Ellen Chesnut, 20 November 1832, John Chesnut Letter, James Chesnut Papers, SCHS. The districts were Greenville, Spartanburg, Clarendon, Kershaw, Darlington, Lancaster, Chesterfield, and Horry. Horry was an exception in the nullification-era polarization. Although it was located in the lowcountry, it remained staunchly Unionist. Geographically, its soil was too poor to support the massive plantations that dominated much of the state, and it was cut off from the other districts by the swamps of the Lumber and Pee Dee Rivers. See Catherine H. Lewis, *Horry County, South Carolina, 1730–1993* (Columbia, SC: University of South Carolina Press, 1998), 27.

50. Pierce M. Butler to James H. Hammond, 22 November 1832 and 23 November 1832, James Henry Hammond Papers, LOC.

51. "Journal of the Convention of the People of South Carolina, assembled at Columbia, November 19, 1832," in *State Papers on Nullification* (Boston, MA: Dutton and Wentworth, 1834).

52. "An Ordinance to Nullify certain of Congress of the United States," in *State Papers on Nullification*; James Hamilton, "Governor's Message," 27 November 1832, SCDAH.

53. Davis, *Rhett,* 69; James Hamilton, "Governor's Message," 27 November 1832, SCDAH; *Greenville Mountaineer,* 24 March 1832.

4. IMAGINING DISUNION

1. Joel R. Poinsett to Andrew Jackson, 25 November 1832, Andrew Jackson Papers, LOC; Joel R. Poinsett, *Address of the Washington Society to the People of South Carolina* (Charleston, SC: J. R. Burges, 1832), 2. See also Joshua Cain, "'We Will Strike at the Head and Demolish the Monster': The Impact of Joel R. Poinsett's Correspondence on President Andrew Jackson during the Nullification Crisis, 1832–1833," *Proceedings of the South Carolina Historical Association* (2011): 13–26.

2. William Gilmore Simms to James Lawson, 25 November 1832, *The Letters of William Gilmore Simms, Volume 1: 1830–1844,* ed. Mary C. Simms Oliphant, Alfred Taylor Odell, and T. C. Duncan Eaves (Columbia, SC: University of South Carolina Press, 1952); Mitchell King to William Drayton, 15 January 1833, Drayton Family Papers, HSP; Caroline Howard Gilman to A. M. White, 15 January 1833, Caroline Howard Gilman Papers, SCHS; Charles Fraser to Hugh Legaré, 30 January 1833, Charles Fraser Papers, SCL; *Greenville Mountaineer,* 6 April 1833. On the role of fear and rumor in antebellum politics, see Mark Wahlgren Summers, *A Dangerous Stir: Fear, Paranoia, and the Making of Reconstruction* (Chapel Hill, NC: University of North Carolina Press, 2009), 7–22. As early as 1916, Chauncey Boucher recognized that the nullification crisis "missed being civil war by a narrow margin," and William Freehling also acknowledged the prospect of war. More recent scholars (including Ford, McCurry, and Sinha), however, either neglect to discuss the nullification winter or describe it only in passing. Sinha, for example, writes that an "atmosphere of impending civil war pervaded the state" but devotes only three pages to the tensions, uncertainties, and military preparations that defined the winter. See Boucher, *The Nullification Controversy,* vii; Sinha, *The Counterrevolution of Slavery,* 52–54.

3. *Camden Republican and Lancaster Beacon,* 5 March 1833; *Charleston Mercury,* 13 February 1833 and 14 February 1833; *Greenville Mountaineer,* 24 March 1832.

4. *Edgefield Hive,* 3 September 1830; William Gilmore Simms to James Lawson, 19 January 1833, *The Letters of William Gilmore Simms, Vol. 1: 1830–1844;* Joel R. Poinsett to James Campbell, 20 November 1833, Papers of Joel Roberts Poinsett, HSP.

5. James Hamilton, "Governor's Message," 27 November 1832, SCDAH; James Hamilton, "To the Senate and House of Representatives," 8 December 1832, SCDAH.

6. *Acts and Resolutions of the General Assembly of the State of South Carolina, Passed in December 1832* (Columbia, SC: Miller & Bran, 1833).

7. Freehling, *Prelude to Civil War,* 264; Robert Y. Hayne, "Inaugural Address," *Southern Orators: Speeches and Orations,* ed. Joseph Moore McConnell (New York, NY: Macmillan Company, 1910), 64–71. In 1832, South Carolina's legislators still chose the state's presidential electors, and they refused to support either Andrew Jackson or Henry Clay. Instead, they gave the state's electoral votes to Virginia governor John Floyd, who sympathized with nullification.

8. James H. Hammond to Robert Y. Hayne, 8 January 1833, "Letters on the Nullification Movement"; Robert Y. Hayne, "Message Regarding the Mobilization of Volunteers During the

Nullification Crisis," SCDAH. An agent offered to purchase 125,000 pounds of gunpowder from the Du Pont Company in Delaware for $24,000. E. I. Du Pont responded that, "[t]he destination of this powder being obvious, we think it right to decline furnishing any part of the above order" (Du Pont, quoted in B. G. Du Pont, *E. I. Du Pont de Nemours and Company: A History, 1802–1902* [Boston, MA: Riverside Press, 1920], 57). Hamilton and other Nullifiers crossed the Savannah River to Augusta in late December with plans to capture weapons from the city's federal arsenal. News leaked out, however, and the United States soldiers carefully guarded the arsenal, forcing the Nullifiers to abandon their plan. See Tinkler, *James Hamilton of South Carolina*, 139.

9. Robert Y. Hayne to Francis W. Pickens, 26 December 1832, "Letters on the Nullification Movement"; Robert Y. Hayne, Circular, January 1833, The Papers of James Henry Hammond, LOC.

10. *Pendleton Messenger*, 9 February 1833; *Charleston Mercury*, 5 January 1833. After the Pendleton militia muster, a Unionist observer noted that these gendered appeals were a "favorite theme" among Nullifiers. In this instance, however, they failed to resonate with the crowd, and most men chose not to volunteer. As the observer explained, "there is another source from whence our firesides are in danger." Union men feared that Hayne would try to compel them to fight against the federal government—dragging them "from their firesides to aid in a cause" they condemned.

11. William C. Preston to Stephen D. Miller, 24 December 1832 and 17 December 1832, Stephen D. Miller Papers, SCHS; *Charleston Mercury*, 3 January 1833, 5 January 1833, 8 January 1833, 14 January 1833, and 29 January 1833; Henry H. Townes to George F. Townes, 10 February, 1832, Townes Family Papers, SCL.

12. James H. Hammond to Robert Y. Hayne, 7 February 1833, "Letters on the Nullification Movement"; *Abbeville Whig and Southern Nullifier*, 24 January 1833; Tandy Walker to George F. Townes, 23 February, 1833, Townes Family Papers, SCL.

13. William H. Pease and Jane H. Pease, *The Web of Progress: Private Values and Public Styles in Boston and Charleston, 1828–1843* (New York, NY: Oxford University Press, 1985), 78; Mary Gallant, "Recollections of a Charleston Childhood, 1822–1836," *South Carolina Historical Magazine* 98, no. 1 (January 1997): 56–74; Henry Allen Tupper, quoted in George Braxton Taylor, *Virginia Baptist Ministers*, Fifth Series (Lynchburg, VA: J. P. Bell Company, 1915), 14; Ellennor Arnold Pen Practice Verses, SCL.

14. Jon Grinspan, *The Virgin Vote: How Young Americans Made Democracy Social, Politics Personal, and Voting Popular in the Nineteenth Century* (Chapel Hill, NC: University of North Carolina Press, 2016), 8, 61; *Charleston Mercury*, 2 February 1833. Students at the state medical college organized meetings and insisted that South Carolina was fighting for the "great cause" of states' rights and constitutional liberty. Debating societies at South Carolina College discussed the merits of slavery, partisanship, nullification, and secession. They decided in favor of nullification and agreed that the Union would one day collapse like the "Republicks of antiquity" (*Charleston Mercury*, 2 February 1833); Clariosophic Literary Society Records, vol. 6, 1826–31, SCL.

15. Robert Y. Hayne to Francis W. Pickens, 7 February 1833 and 12 February 1833, "Letters on the Nullification Movement"; James H. Hammond to William E. Hayne, 24 February 1833, "Letters on the Nullification Movement."

16. James H. Hammond to William E. Hayne, 7 February 1833, "Letters on the Nullification Movement"; James H. Hammond to Robert Y. Hayne, 7 February 1833, "Letters on the Nullification Movement." When one officer requested $40 to pay regimental musicians, Hayne refused, writing that spending money on *"Music,* when we want every cent for *Arms* is out of the question."

17. Samuel Townes to George Townes, 13 January 1833, and Henry H. Townes to George Townes, Townes Family Papers, SCL; James L. Clark to Stephen D. Miller, 19 January 1833, and John L. Miller to Stephen D. Miller, 10 January 1833, Papers of the Williams, Chesnut, and Manning Families, SCL. Writing to a third brother, Henry Townes articulated the duties of martial manhood in the crisis. He encouraged George to "seek eagerly military command," writing that the brothers had been "among the foremost in talking" and now needed to be "foremost in fighting."

18. James H. Hammond to Robert Y. Hayne, 20 December 1832, "Letters on the Nullification Movement"; J. Canty to Stephen D. Miller, 4 January 1833, Papers of the Williams, Chesnut, and Manning Families, SCL; *Columbia Telescope,* 26 March 1833; A. and Sarah McClurken to John A. Cooper, 18 February 1833, Papers of the Cooper-McClurken-Nisbet Families, SCL; John W. Burbidge to Rosina Mix, 28 January 1833, Rosina Mix Papers, SHC.

19. Hayne, "Message Regarding the Mobilization of Volunteers," SCDAH; Robert Y. Hayne to Francis W. Pickens, 11 January 1833, "Letters on the Nullification Movement"; *Southern Times and State Gazette,* 11 January 1833; Henry H. Townes to George Townes, 10 February 1833, Townes Family Papers, SCL.

20. Rebecca Motte Rutledge to Edward Rutledge, 30 January 1833, Rutledge Family Papers, SCL; *Greenville Mountaineer,* 24 March 1832; Lucretia A. Townes to Eliza P. Blassingame, 5 December 1832, Townes Family Papers, SCL.

21. Samuel Townes to George Townes, 13 January 1833, Townes Family Papers, SCL; *Charleston Mercury,* 1 January 1833 and 5 January 1833; James Hamilton, "To the Senate and House of Representatives," 8 December 1832, SCDAH.

22. Andrew Jackson to Levi Woodbury, 1 September 1832, Andrew Jackson Papers, LOC; Andrew Jackson to Andrew J. Donelson, 17 September 1832, Andrew Jackson Papers, LOC; Andrew Jackson to George Breathitt, 7 November 1832, Andrew Jackson Papers, LOC; Joel R. Poinsett to Andrew Jackson, 24 November 1832, Andrew Jackson Papers, LOC.

23. Andrew Jackson to Joel R. Poinsett, 2 December 1832, Andrew Jackson Papers, LOC; Alexander Macomb to J. F. Heileman, 29 October 1832, in "Military Orders," *Niles' Weekly Register,* 23 February 1833; US Bureau of the Census, "Armed Forces and Veterans: Military Personnel on Active Duty: 1789–1957," *Historical Statistics of the United States: Colonial Times to 1957* (Washington, DC: GPO, 1960), 737; "Report of the Major General for 1831, accompanying the Report of the Secretary of War for 1831," *Congressional Serial Set,* 22nd Congress, 1st sess.; US Returns from Military Posts, 1806–1916, Charleston Harbor, September 1832 and January 1833, available at http://www.ancestry.com; Louis McLane to James R. Pringle, 6 November 1832, quoted in Gautham Gao, *National Duties: Custom Houses and the Making of the American State* (Chicago, IL: University of Chicago Press, 2016), 199.

24. Andrew Jackson to Joel R. Poinsett, 7 November 1832, Andrew Jackson Papers, LOC;

Andrew Jackson to John Coffee, 14 December 1832, Andrew Jackson Papers, LOC; Andrew Jackson to Martin Van Buren, 15 December 1832, Andrew Jackson Papers, LOC; Andrew Jackson to Joel R. Poinsett, 24 January 1833, Papers of Joel Roberts Poinsett, HSP; Andrew Jackson to Amos Kendall, 7 October 1844, Amos Kendall Letters, DU. In his letter to Kendall in 1844, Jackson observed that readers would "not find any notice of this in my official papers," because he destroyed the tenders after the crisis ended. During the nullification winter, he placed the number of volunteers at 200,000; in 1844, he remembered it as 150,000.

25. "President Jackson's Proclamation Regarding Nullification," 10 December 1832, *The Avalon Project: Documents in Law, History and Diplomacy,* Yale Law School, available at http://www.avalon.law.yale.edu.

26. Joel R. Poinsett to Andrew Jackson, 16 January 1833, Andrew Jackson Papers, LOC; *Charleston Courier,* 12 January 1833; Richard Manning to James Chesnut, 15 January 1832, John Chesnut Papers, SCHS; *Southern Patriot,* 8 October 1832. William Gilmore Simms confessed that he considered himself "now rather a visitor in the state than a citizen." See William Gilmore Simms to James Lawson, 25 November 1832, *The Letters of William Gilmore Simms, Volume 1: 1830–1844.*

27. Walter B. Edgar, *South Carolina: A History* (Columbia, SC: University of South Carolina Press, 1998), 276. *Arkansas Times and Advocate,* 9 October 1833; *Newbern Spectator,* 8 March 1833; John C. Nisbet to John A. Cooper, 17 March 1832, Papers of the Cooper-McClurken-Nisbet Families, SCL; James Hemphill to Andrew Murrett, 24 December 1833, Hemphill Family Papers, DU; J. Carter to William Drayton, 25 December 1832, Drayton Family Papers, HSP; Joel R. Poinsett to Andrew Jackson, 29 November 1832, Andrew Jackson Papers, LOC; William Gilmore Simms to James Lawson, 27 November 1833, *The Letters of William Gilmore Simms, Volume 1: 1830–1844.*

28. John Ravenel to Anna Elizabeth Ravenel, 6 December 1830, John Ravenel Papers, SCL; Timothy Green to John W. Mitchell, 4 December 1832 and 15 December 1832, John Wroughton Mitchell Papers, SHC.

29. Daniel E. Huger, *Speech of the Honorable Daniel E. Huger,* 40; *Speeches Delivered in the Convention of the State of South Carolina, Held in Columbia, in March 1833* (Charleston, SC: E. J. Van Brunt, 1833); Daniel Huger to William Drayton, 17 December 1832, Drayton Family Papers, HSP; *The Globe,* 9 March 1833; *Charleston Courier,* 28 February 1833. Appealing to moderate manhood, Huger insisted that the honor of the state was "not that of a duellist." It "demands nothing rash," instead requiring South Carolinians to act with "reason, judgment and prudence." Huger accepted the title of submission man, observing that it "has been the pride of my life, to submit to the laws of my country."

30. Samuel C. Jackson to William True, 14 December 1832, Samuel C. Jackson Papers, SCL; Joel R. Poinsett to Andrew Jackson, 17 December 1832, Andrew Jackson Papers, LOC; James O'Hanlon to Andrew Jackson, 20 December 1832, Andrew Jackson Papers, LOC; *Greenville Mountaineer,* 29 December 1832.

31. *Greenville Mountaineer,* 19 January 1833 and 9 February 1833; Andrew Jackson to Joel R. Poinsett, 2 December 1833, Andrew Jackson Papers, LOC; Joel R. Poinsett to Andrew Jackson, 22 February 1833, Andrew Jackson Papers, LOC. In February, Poinsett estimated the

Union Societies' strength at 8,400, including 1,000 men in Greenville, 1,500 in Spartanburg, 800 in York, 750 in Chester, 500 in Cheraw, 700 in Lancaster, 487 in Horry, 300 in Chesterfield, 450 in Marion, 1,457 in Charleston, and a "very respectable force" in the "minority districts" dominated by Nullifiers. The specific numbers he listed produce a total of 7,944. Newspaper records, however, reveal about 300 Union Society members in Edgefield, 150 in Colleton, 262 in Abbeville, and between 200 and 400 in Pendleton. Another writer reported Chester's total at 900 rather than 750. Darlington, Kershaw, Union, Williamsburg, St. Luke's, and other districts and parishes also held Union Party meetings during the nullification winter, so the number of Union Society members was likely even higher. Enrollment statistics reveal that some districts were deeply divided. In York District, for example, 43 percent of military-age white men joined the Nullifiers' volunteer force while 37 percent enrolled in Union Societies. Most districts, however, clearly mobilized behind one party or the other. See *Charleston Courier* issues for January and February 1833.

32. *Greenville Mountaineer,* 12 January 1833, 9 February 1833, and 16 February 1833; *Charleston Courier,* 17 January 1833.

33. *Charleston Courier,* 8 January 1833, 12 February 1833, 15 February 1833, and 28 February 1833; *Greenville Mountaineer,* 2 March 1833. On the contested meanings of liberty poles in the early republic, see Shira Lurie, "Politics at the Poles: Liberty Poles and the Popular Struggle for the New Republic" (PhD diss., University of Virginia, 2019).

34. William Gilmore Simms to James Lawson, 25 November 1832 and 19 January 1833, *The Letters of William Gilmore Simms, Volume 1: 1830–1844*; Jonathan Mickle to Thomas Shivers, 11 February 1833, Joel Roberts Poinsett Papers, HSP; Joel R. Poinsett to Andrew Jackson, 16 January 1833 and 27 January 1833, Andrew Jackson Papers, LOC.

35. *Southern Times,* 8 February 1830; Hugh S. Legaré to I. E. Holmes, 2 October 1832, *The Writings of Hugh Swinton Legaré; Southern Whig,* 15 March 1832; *Charleston Courier,* 12 August 1832.

36. *Charleston Courier,* 26 January 1833; *Greenville Mountaineer,* 26 January 1833; *The Debate in the South Carolina Legislature in December 1830,* 107; *Southern Whig,* 9 February 1832.

37. *Greenville Mountaineer,* 3 October 1832; Thomas Grimké, *Speech of Thomas Grimké, One of the Senators from St. Philip's and St. Michael's, Delivered in the Senate of South Carolina, in December 1828* (Charleston, SC: W. Riley, 1829), 97; William Gilmore Simms to James Lawson, 25 November 1832, *The Letters of William Gilmore Simms, Volume 1*: 1830–1844; Thomas S. Grimké, *To the People of the State of South Carolina, December 1, 1832,* 12.

38. Moses Benbow to Stephen D. Miller, 15 September 1830, Stephen Decatur Miller Papers, SCHS; David J. McCord to David B. Warden, 29 June 1831, David James McCord Papers, SCL; William Elliott, *Address to the People of St. Helena Parish* (Charleston, SC: William Estill, 1832), 13; Poinsett, *Address of the Washington Society,* 2.

39. Elliott, *Address to the People of St. Helena Parish,* 14; *Southern Patriot,* 17 November 1832; Poinsett, *Address of the Washington Society,* 3.

40. John Fenwick, quoted in Sarah Rayser Ragonese, "A Drayton Leads th'Embattled Line: Colonel William Drayton and the South Carolina Nullification Controversy" (MA thesis, Temple University, 2000), 61; *The Debate in the South Carolina Legislature in December 1830,*

101; *Speeches of the Hon. Robert Y. Hayne, and the Hon. Daniel Webster, Jan. 21 and 26, 1830* (Boston, MA: Carter and Hendee, 1830), 25; Hugh Legaré to Isaac Holmes, 8 April 1833, *The Writings of Hugh Swinton Legaré*; Samuel C. Jackson to William True, 17 November 1832, Samuel C. Jackson Papers, SCL; Jonathan Mickle to Thomas Shivers, 11 February 1833, Joel Roberts Poinsett Papers, HSP.

41. Andrew Jackson to Maunsel White, 22 December 1832, Andrew Jackson Papers, LOC; *Southern Whig*, 29 March 1832; *Charleston Observer*, 9 August 1832; William Drayton to Joel R. Poinsett, 20 December 1830, Joel Roberts Poinsett Papers, HSP; *Camden Journal*, 6 November 1830 and 29 September 1832; *Columbia Hive*, 18 February 1832.

42. *Camden Journal*, 6 November 1830 and 29 September 1832; *Columbia Hive*, 18 February 1832; Thomas Grimké, *Letter to the Honorable John C. Calhoun, Robert Y. Hayne, George McDuffie, and James Hamilton*; Robert E. Yates to Stephen D. Miller, 9 May 1832, Stephen Decatur Miller Papers, SCHS; *Columbia Telescope*, 3 April 1829.

43. *Greenville Mountaineer*, 3 January 1835; *Columbia Hive*, 24 March 1832; Samuel Cram Jackson to Elizabeth Jackson, 22 January 1833, Samuel C. Jackson Papers, SCL.

44. Unknown to James Chesnut, 15 January 1832, Papers of the Williams, Chesnut, and Manning Families, SCL; Caroline Howard Gilman to A. M. White, 15 January 1833, Caroline Howard Gilman Papers, SCHS; *Charleston Courier*, 22 February 1833; *Southern Whig*, 15 September 1832.

45. *Greenville Mountaineer*, 23 February 1833; Thomas Grimké, *Speech of Thomas Grimké*, 97; *Charleston Courier*, 27 February 1833.

46. Joel R. Poinsett to Andrew Jackson, 27 January 1833, Andrew Jackson Papers, LOC.

47. Hugh S. Legaré to Mary Legaré, 27 December 1832, in Shirley Carter Hughson, "Excerpts from the Correspondence of Hugh Swinton Legaré," SCHS; James Buchanan to Andrew Jackson, 29 May 1833, *The Works of James Buchanan, Volume 2: 1830–1836*, ed. John Bassett Moore (Philadelphia, PA: J. B. Lippincott Company, 1908); *National Gazette*, 24 October 1832.

48. *State Papers on Nullification*, 219–25, 229–31, 289–92.

49. *State Papers on Nullification*, 222–23, 237–39, 277–80. Among these proposals were amendments to define the powers delegated to the federal government, determine the "power of coercion by the General Government," settle the principle of protectionism, establish an equal system of taxation, decide the "jurisdiction and process" of the Supreme Court, create a "tribunal of last resort" that could adjudicate disputes between the federal government and the states, determine the constitutionality of internal improvement appropriations, secure the election of the president and vice president "to the people," limit presidents to one term, and settle the "rights of the Indians."

50. John Floyd, *The Life and Diary of John Floyd*, ed. Charles H. Ambler (Richmond, VA: Richmond Press, 1918), 204–6; *State Papers on Nullification*, 195–97, 332–33.

51. Hayne, "Message Regarding the Mobilization of Volunteers," SCDAH; James L. Petigru to Hugh Legaré, 6 February 1833, James Louis Petigru Papers, SCL; *Charleston Courier*, 26 January 1833.

52. *Evening Post* (New York, NY), 30 January 1833.

53. Samuel C. Jackson Diary, 1 February 1833, SHC; Mary Chesnut to James Chesnut Jr., 3

February 1833, Papers of the Williams, Chesnut, and Manning Families, SCL; *Greenville Mountaineer,* 9 February 1833; Jasper Adams to Sewall Harding, 16 January 1833 [postscript dated 6 February 1833], Jasper Adams Papers, SCL.

54. *Camden Journal,* 9 February 1833; *Charleston Mercury,* 12 February 1833; *New York Spectator,* 13 February 1833.

55. Richard E. Ellis, *The Union at Risk: Jacksonian Democracy, States' Rights and the Nullification Crisis* (New York, NY: Oxford University Press, 1987), 98–101; Merrill D. Peterson, *Olive Branch and Sword: The Compromise of 1833* (Baton Rouge, LA: Louisiana State University Press, 1982), 68–69; John C. Calhoun, *Register of Debates,* Senate, 22nd Cong., 2nd sess., 477–78.

56. Henry Townes to George Townes, 10 February 1833, Townes Family Papers, SCL; *Charleston Mercury,* 28 January 1833; Clay, quoted in Merrill D. Peterson, *The Great Triumvirate: Webster, Clay, and Calhoun* (New York, NY: Oxford University Press, 1987), 230–31. The House passed the tariff by a vote of 119 to 85 and the Force Bill by a vote of 149 to 48. The Senate voted 29 to 16 in favor of the tariff and 31 to 1 in support of the Force Bill. Several Southern senators, however, abstained from the latter vote. John Tyler cast the lone dissenting vote in the Senate.

57. *Speeches Delivered in the Convention of the State of South Carolina, Held in Columbia, in March 1833; Southern Times & State Gazette,* 22 March 1833; *Pendleton Messenger,* 31 July 1833; *Sumter Gazette and Constitutional Advocate,* 20 April 1833; Hamilton, *An Eulogium.*

58. *Speeches Delivered in the Convention of the State of South Carolina;* Davis, *Rhett,* 75.

59. Freehling, *Prelude to Civil War,* 296; Davis, *Rhett,* 74–75; *Columbia Telescope,* 26 March 1833; *Pendleton Messenger,* 17 July 1833; *Niles' Weekly Register,* 20 April 1833; John C. Calhoun to Christopher Van Deventer, 24 March 1833, *The Papers of John C. Calhoun, Volume 12: 1833–1835,* ed. Clyde N. Wilson (Columbia, SC: University of South Carolina Press, 1979).

60. McInnis, *The Politics of Taste,* 80; *Camden Journal,* 6 April 1833; *Niles' Weekly Register,* 20 April 1833.

61. *Charleston Mercury,* 3 April 1833.

62. William Blanding to James Blanding, 24 March 1833, William Blanding Papers, SCL; Benjamin Perry to Joel R. Poinsett, 24 March 1833, Joel Roberts Poinsett Papers, HSP; J. Mauldin Lesesne, "The Nullification Controversy in an Up-Country District," *The Proceedings of the South Carolina Historical Association,* ed. Robert L. Meriwether and Arney R. Childs (Columbia, SC: South Carolina Historical Association, 1939), 22; Jacob M. Bailey to William M Bailey, March 1833, Miscellaneous Manuscripts, Charleston Library Society, on microform at SCHS; Levin M. Powell, quoted in Howard H. Wehmann, "Noise, Novelties, and Nullifiers: A US Navy Officer's Impressions of the Nullification Controversy," in *South Carolina Historical Magazine* 76, no. 1 (January 1975): 21–24.

63. William Blanding to James Blanding, 24 March 1833, William Blanding Papers, SCL; Benjamin Perry to Joel R. Poinsett, 24 March 1833, Joel Roberts Poinsett Papers, HSP; James L. Petigru to William Elliott, 15 April 1833, James L. Petigru Papers, SCHS; Joel R. Poinsett to Daniel Webster, *The Papers of Daniel Webster, Correspondence, Volume 3: 1830–1834,* ed. Charles M. Wiltse (Hanover, NH: University Press of New England, 1977); *Camden Journal,* 4 May 1833.

5. SWEARING ALLEGIANCE

1. *Greenville Mountaineer,* 4 October 1834; *Pendleton Messenger,* 5 February 1834.

2. *Charleston Courier,* 9 March 1833; *Greenville Mountaineer,* 4 October 1834.

3. *National Gazette,* 29 April 1833; *Niles' Weekly Register,* 13 April 1833; *Charleston Courier,* 13 March 1833 and 22 August 1833.

4. Mitchell King to Hugh Legaré, 5 May 1833, in Shirley Carter Hughson, "Excerpts from the Correspondence of Hugh Swinton Legaré," SCHS; *Columbia Telescope,* 26 March 1833 and 2 April 1833; *Pendleton Messenger,* 10 April 1833.

5. John Edwards to Richard Crallé, 29 May 1833, Richard K. Crallé Papers, CU; George William Featherstonhaugh, *Excursions Through the Slave States* (New York, NY: Harper & Brothers, 1844), 157.

6. Joel R. Poinsett to Daniel Webster, 25 March 1833, *The Papers of Daniel Webster: Correspondence, Volume 3: 1830–1834,* ed. Charles M. Wiltse (Hanover, NH: University Press of New England, 1977); *National Banner and Daily Advertiser* (Nashville, TN), 24 April 1833; *Charleston Courier,* 16 March 1833; *Charleston Mercury,* 22 March 1833.

7. *Charleston Mercury,* 17 June 1833 and 20 June 1833; *Pendleton Messenger,* 3 July 1833 and 10 July 1833; *Camden Republican and Lancaster Beacon,* 25 June 1833; *Columbia Telescope,* 6 August 1833; Hamilton, *An Eulogium; Examiner,* 10 June 1835; McInnis, *The Politics of Taste,* 78.

8. *Columbia Telescope,* 9 July 1833 and 16 July 1833; *Charleston Mercury,* 12 July 1833 and 16 July 1833.

9. See issues of *The Charleston Courier* for July 1833, especially 4 July 1833, 17 July 1833, 25 July 1833.

10. *Charleston Courier,* 4 July 1833 and 24 July 1833; *Greenville Mountaineer,* 2 March 1833.

11. "At the period of the Revolution of the Acordada," Union Party Circular, William Drayton Papers, SCL.

12. "At the period of the Revolution of the Acordada," Union Party Circular, William Drayton Papers, SCL; *Brattleboro Messenger* (Brattleboro, VT), 1 June 1833; *Niles' Weekly Register,* 11 May 1833; *North Carolina Constitutionalist and Peoples' Advocate* (Raleigh, NC), 28 May 1833.

13. *Charleston Courier,* 12 July 1833 and 26 August 1833.

14. *Charleston Courier,* 17 August 1833, 20 August 1833, and 4 September 1833. Among Nullifiers, party discipline remained strong, despite the lower turnout. In September 1832, the party's municipal candidates all received between 1,102 and 1,116 votes. In September 1833, they received between 904 and 937 votes (with the exception of three candidates who appeared on both parties' tickets). The Independent Ticket's party discipline was reasonably strong as well, as most of its candidates received between 586 and 600 votes. Of its twelve candidates, at least seven were Union men and four were Nullifiers (the party allegiance of one candidate—George Hervey—could not be determined). Editors calculated that only seventy-nine of the Independent Ticket's voters were former Nullifiers; while the exact number cannot be determined, the ticket clearly drew most of its strength from Union men.

15. *Charleston Courier,* 5 September 1833, 7 September 1833, and 14 September 1833. Election returns are drawn primarily from *The Charleston Mercury* and *The Charleston Courier* for

September 1833. In the 7th Congressional District, composed of Spartanburg, Union, Chester, and York, Nullifier William K. Clowney defeated Union man Thomas Williams by a vote of 4,564 to 4,339. In the 8th Congressional District—Pendleton and Greenville—Nullifier Warren R. Davis defeated Joseph Grisham 2,938 to 2,869. Analysis of voter turnout is drawn from a comparison of fourteen districts and parishes with contested elections for both 1832 and 1833: Marion, Darlington, Horry, Spartanburg, Union, Chester, York, Edgefield, Abbeville, Pendleton, Greenville, St. Luke's Parish, St. George Dorchester, and St. Helena Parish. For these fourteen sites, Nullifier turnout fell from 12,377 to 11,931, while Union Party turnout declined from 10,199 to 10,021.

16. *Niles' Weekly Register,* 6 April 1833; Kibler, *Benjamin F. Perry,* 155.

17. *Southern Times & State Gazette,* 6 December 1833; *Charleston Mercury,* 5 December 1833.

18. Hayne, "Message Regarding the Mobilization of Volunteers During the Nullification Crisis," SCDAH.

19. *Columbia Telescope,* 10 December 1833 and 17 December 1833.

20. *The Globe,* 31 December 1833.

21. Unknown to William R. Hemphill, 5 January 1834, Hemphill Family Papers, DU; James Hemphill to Unknown, 24 December 1833, Hemphill Family Papers, DU; *Charleston Courier,* 15 January 1834.

22. Unknown to William R. Hemphill, 5 January 1834, Hemphill Family Papers, DU; John C. Nisbet to John A. Cooper, 17 January 1834, Papers of the Cooper-McClurken-Nisbet Families, SCL; James Edward Henry to Samuel F. Patterson, 31 January 1834, Samuel Finley Patterson Papers, DU.

23. *Charleston Courier,* 15 January 1834, 17 January 1834, and 24 January 1834.

24. *Charleston Courier,* 23 January 1834; *Camden Journal,* 1 March 1834 and 15 March 1834.

25. George McDuffie to Waddy Thompson, 24 January 1834, Waddy Thompson Papers, LOC; Henry H. Townes to George F. Townes, Townes Family Papers, SCL; *Charleston Mercury,* 18 February 1834.

26. Freehling, *Prelude to Civil War,* 315–16; James L. Petigru to William Drayton, 26 March 1834, in James Petigru Carson, *Life, Letters and Speeches of James Louis Petigru: The Union Man of South Carolina* (Washington, DC: W. H. Lowdermilk & Co., 1920); *Charleston Courier,* 23 January 1834; James Edward Henry to Samuel F. Patterson, 31 January 1834, Samuel Finley Patterson Papers, DU.

27. Kibler, *Benjamin F. Perry,* 162–63; *Charleston Courier,* 18 February 1834.

28. *Charleston Courier,* 12 February 1834.

29. George F. Townes to John A. Townes, 3 April 1834, Townes Family Papers, SCL; Daniel Huger to Philip Phillips, 20 April 1834, Philip Phillips Family Papers, LOC; *Charleston Mercury,* 31 March 1834; James L. Petigru to Hugh S. Legaré, 24 April 1834, in Carson, *Life, Letters and Speeches of James Louis Petigru.*

30. *Charleston Courier,* 1 April 1834 and 4 April 1834; *Charlotte Journal,* 19 April 1834.

31. *Charleston Courier,* 4 April 1834; Elias S. Davis to Robert Leckie, 26 March 1834, Elias S. Davis Letter, SCL; Joel Poinsett to Daniel Webster, 17 March 1834, *The Papers of Daniel Webster: Correspondence, Volume 3: 1830–1834.*

32. Freehling, *Prelude to Civil War*, 316–17.

33. *Columbia Telescope*, 11 October 1834; *Charleston Courier*, 11 September 1834.

34. David M. Potter, "The Historian's Use of Nationalism and Vice Versa," *The American Historical Review* 67, no. 4 (July 1962): 931; *Greenville Mountaineer*, 12 July 1834; *Charleston Courier*, 9 March 1833 and 12 July 1833.

35. Pease and Pease, *James Louis Petigru*, 58–62; Davis, *Rhett*, 81–86; Boucher, *The Nullification Controversy*, 336; Robert Y. Hayne to Francis W. Pickens, 10 June 1834, "Letters on the Nullification Movement." Harper drafted a searing dissent challenging federal authority and arguing that state officers had a duty to carry out *"every* act of the sovereign authority of the State."

36. Daniel Huger to Philip Phillips, 20 April 1834, Philip Phillips Family Papers, LOC; John P. Richardson to Philip Phillips, 25 April 1834, Philip Phillips Family Papers, LOC; John P. Richardson to Philip Phillips, 18 May 1834, Philip Phillips Family Papers, LOC.

37. *Camden Journal*, 19 April 1834; *Charleston Courier*, 12 April 1834, 21 April 1834, and 23 April 1834; *Greenville Mountaineer*, 12 July 1834; William Lowndes Yancey, quoted in Eric H. Walther, *William Lowndes Yancey and the Coming of the Civil War* (Chapel Hill, NC: University of North Carolina Press, 2006), 28–30.

38. *Greenville Mountaineer*, 28 June 1834, 12 July 1834, 19 July 1834, and 4 October 1834.

39. Petitions circulated in Greenville, Spartanburg, Pendleton, Kershaw, Lancaster, Union, York, Edgefield, Abbeville, Orangeburg, Charleston, Christ Church, St. Luke's Parish, Orange Parish, Prince George Winyaw, and St. George's Dorchester. See "Inhabitants of Abbeville, Kershaw, Lancaster, Greenville, Pendleton, and Union Districts, Petition Protesting against the Proposed Amendment to the State Constitution," SCDAH; "Inhabitants of Spartanburg District, Petition Opposing the Test Oath and Protesting its Being Included in the Constitution of the State," SCDAH; "Inhabitants of Edgefield District, Petition Protesting the Proposed Alteration of the State Constitution," SCDAH; Clarendon Resolutions, 2 August 1834, republished in *The Edgefield Advertiser*, 24 September 1840; *Greenville Mountaineer*, 4 October 1834.

40. Samuel MacCalla, quoted in James Albert Woodburn, "The Scotch-Irish Presbyterians in Monroe County, Indiana," *Indiana Historical Society Publications* (Indianapolis, IN: Bobbs-Merrill Company, 1895), 452n; Pease and Pease, *Web of Progress*, 81; James L. Petigru to Hugh S. Legaré, 26 October 1834, *Life, Letters and Speeches*, 162–64.

41. James L. Petigru to Hugh S. Legaré, 26 October 1834, *Life, Letters and Speeches*; *Greenville Mountaineer*, 4 October 1834. For election results, see *Charleston Courier* issues for October 1834.

42. *Southern Patriot*, 25 October 1834; James L. Petigru to Hugh S. Legaré, 26 October 1834, *Life, Letters and Speeches*, 162–64; *Greenville Mountaineer*, 25 October 1834, 15 November 1834, and 22 November 1834.

43. *Greenville Mountaineer*, 6 December 1834.

44. *Greenville Mountaineer*, 13 December 1834.

45. James L. Petigru to Hugh S. Legaré, 29 November 1834 and December 15, 1834, *Life, Letters and Speeches*.

46. James L. Petigru to Hugh S. Legaré, December 15, 1834, *Life, Letters and Speeches*.

47. *Greenville Mountaineer,* 20 December 1834; Pease and Pease, *James Louis Petigru,* 65–66; Ford, *Origins of Southern Radicalism,* 151–52.

48. Abram Blanding to Henry DeSaussure, 18 December 1834, DeSaussure Family Papers, SCHS; *Charleston Mercury,* 15 December 1834, 19 December 1834, 23 December 1834, and 6 January 1835; *Greenville Mountaineer,* 20 December 1834.

49. *Greenville Mountaineer,* 14 February 1835.

50. *Greenville Mountaineer,* 24 January 1835.

51. *Greenville Mountaineer,* 1 August 1835, 22 August 1835, and 19 September 1835.

52. *Greenville Mountaineer,* 29 August 1835 and 12 September 1835.

53. *Greenville Mountaineer,* 1 August 1835.

54. *Charleston Mercury,* 2 September 1834, 2 September 1835, and 8 September 1835; *Greenville Mountaineer,* 12 September 1834.

55. John C. Nisbet to John A. Cooper, 6 November 1835, and Samuel Nisbet to John A. Cooper, 18 September 1835, Papers of the Cooper-McClurken-Nisbet Families, SCL; *Charleston Courier,* 10 August 1835.

6. FORGING CONSENSUS

1. *Southern Sentinel,* 4 August 1832; *Pendleton Messenger,* 1 September 1830; *Southern Times & State Gazette,* 7 October 1830; *The Debate in the South Carolina Legislature in December 1830,* 202.

2. Grimké, *Speech of Thomas Grimké Delivered in the Senate of South Carolina in December 1828; Columbia Hive,* 21 April 1832.

3. *Evening Post,* 12 August 1835. On the "Slave Power Conspiracy," see Leonard L. Richards, *The Slave Power: The Free North and Southern Domination, 1780–1860* (Baton Rouge, LA: Louisiana State University Press, 2000).

4. [Edwin C. Holland], *A Refutation of the Calumnies Circulated Against the Southern & Western States, Respecting the Institution and Existence of Slavery Among Them* (Charleston, SC: A. E. Miller, 1822), 56; *Columbia Telescope,* 17 September 1833, 15 October 1833, and 24 December 1833; Stephen Miller, quoted in Freehling, *Prelude to Civil War,* 81; James Henry Hammond, *Remarks of Mr. Hammond of South Carolina, on the Question of Receiving Petitions for the Abolition of Slavery in the District of Columbia* (Washington, DC: Duff Green, 1836), 11. For a discussion of this idea of "herrenvolk democracy," see George M. Frederickson, *The Black Image in the White Mind: The Debate on Afro-American Character and Destiny, 1817–1914* (New York, NY: Harper and Row, 1971).

5. *Mountaineer,* 21 February 1829; Benjamin Perry to Daniel Webster, 14 May 1833, *The Papers of Daniel Webster*; Julia M. Brown to Jonathan R. Flynt, Julia M. Brown Letter, SCL; Pease and Pease, *James Louis Petigru,* 30–31, 134–39; David W. Dangerfield, "Hard Rows to Hoe: Free Black Farmers in Antebellum South Carolina" (PhD diss., University of South Carolina, 2014), 64–65; Lyon G. Tyler, "James Louis Petigru: Freedom's Champion in a Slave Society," *The South Carolina Historical Magazine* 83, no. 4 (October 1982): 272–86.

6. Mark Perry, *Lift Up Thy Voice: The Grimké Family's Journey from Slaveholders to Civil*

Rights Leaders (New York, NY: Penguin Books, 2001), 111; Catherine H. Birney, *The Grimké Sisters: Sarah and Angelina Grimké, the First American Women Advocates of Abolition and Woman's Rights* (Boston, MA: Lee and Shepard, 1885), 110; Ebenezer Cooper to John A. Cooper, 6 March 1832, Papers of the Cooper-McClurken-Nisbet Families, SCL; Michael A. Broadstone, *History of Greene County, Ohio: Its People, Industries and Institutions, Volume 1* (Indianapolis, IN: B. F. Bowen & Company, Inc., 1918), 504–5; Samuel Brown Wylie, *Memoir of Alexander McLeod, D.D.* (New York, NY: Charles Scribner, 1855), 504–5; Joseph S. Moore, *Founding Sins: How a Group of Antislavery Radicals Fought to Put Christ into the Constitution* (New York, NY: Oxford University Press, 2016), 90–116.

7. *Camden Journal,* 4 September 1830; *Mountaineer,* 21 February 1829; Benjamin Perry to Daniel Webster, 14 May 1833, *The Papers of Daniel Webster;* Julia M. Brown to Jonathan R. Flynt, Julia M. Brown Letter, SCL; Joseph Kelly, *America's Longest Siege: Charleston, Slavery, and the Slow March Toward Civil War* (New York, NY: Overlook Press, 2013),196–97; Pease and Pease, *James Louis Petigru,* 30–31, 134–39.

8. *Camden Journal,* 4 September 1830, 5 March 1831, 1 October 1831, and 4 May 1833; *Charleston Courier,* 22 July 1833; Benjamin Perry to Daniel Webster, 14 May 1833, *The Papers of Daniel Webster.*

9. Henry L. Pinckney, *An Oration Delivered in the Independent, or Congregational Church, Charleston, Before the State Rights & Free Trade Party* (Charleston, SC: A. E. Miller, 1833), 41–43; Pierce M. Butler to James Henry Hammond, 10 July 1835, James Henry Hammond Papers, LOC.

10. *Camden Journal,* 4 May 1833 and 1 June 1833; Benjamin Perry to Daniel Webster, 14 May 1833, *The Papers of Daniel Webster.* Pegues took over as editor of *The Camden Journal* after Daniels resigned.

11. *Charleston Courier,* 4 July 1833, 19 July 1833, 22 July 1833, and 5 August 1833.

12. Sinha, *The Slave's Cause,* 249; Michael A. Schoeppner, *Moral Contagion: Black Atlantic Sailors, Citizenship, and Diplomacy in Antebellum America* (New York, NY: Cambridge University Press, 2019), 98; Bertram Wyatt-Brown, *Lewis Tappan and the Evangelical War against Slavery* (Cleveland, OH: The Press of Case Western Reserve University, 1969), 145.

13. Bertram Wyatt-Brown, "The Abolitionists' Postal Campaign of 1835," *The Journal of Negro History* 50, no. 4 (October 1965): 227–29; Ford, *Deliver Us From Evil,* 481; Alfred Huger to Samuel L. Gouverneur, 1 August 1835, in "Postmaster Huger and the Incendiary Publications," ed. Frank Otto Gatell, *The South Carolina Historical Magazine* 64, no. 4 (October 1963): 193–201; Susan Wyly-Jones, "The 1835 Anti-Abolition Meetings in the South: A New Look at the Controversy over the Abolition Postal Campaign," *Civil War History* 47, no. 4 (December 2001): 289–309.

14. Alfred Huger to Samuel L. Gouverneur, 1 August 1835, and Samuel L. Gouverneur to Alfred Huger, 8 August 1835, "Alfred Huger and the Incendiary Publications."

15. *Charleston Courier,* 4 August 1835; Alfred Huger to Samuel L. Gouverneur, 15 August 1835 and 22 August 1835, "Postmaster Huger and the Incendiary Publications"; *National Gazette,* 12 August 1835; *Charleston Southern Patriot,* 4 August 1835; Jennifer Rose Mercieca, "The Culture of Honor: How Slaveholders Responded to the Abolitionist Mail Crisis of 1835," *Rhetoric & Public Affairs* 10, no. 1 (Spring 2007): 51–76.

16. *National Gazette,* 12 August 1835.

17. *Proceedings of the Citizens of Charleston on the Incendiary Machinations Now in Progress Against the Peace and Welfare of the Southern States* (Charleston, SC: A. E. Miller, 1835).

18. See *The Charleston Mercury, The Charleston Courier,* and *The Southern Patriot* for August and September 1835.

19. *Charleston Mercury,* 11 September 1835, 12 September 1835, and 18 September 1835; Susan Wyly-Jones, "The 1835 Anti-Abolition Meetings in the South: A New Look at the Controversy Over the Abolition Postal Campaign," *Civil War History* 47, no. 4 (December 2001): 305–6.

20. *Evening Post,* 12 August 1835.

21. *Charleston Mercury,* 20 August 1835 and 5 September 1835; *Charleston Courier,* 7 August 1835, 28 August 1835, and 16 September 1835; Pierce M. Butler to A. C. Preston, 7 January 1835, Pierce Mason Butler Papers, SCL.

22. *Southern Patriot,* 21 August 1835; *Charleston Courier,* 22 August 1835 and 25 August 1835; Michael D. Thompson, *Working on the Dock of the Bay: Labor and Enterprise in an Antebellum Southern Port* (Columbia, SC: University of South Carolina Press, 2015). Hammond remarked that abolitionists "can be silenced in but one way—*Terror—death.* The nonslaveholding states must pass laws denying protection to them." James Henry Hammond to Mordecai Manuel Noah, 19 August 1835, James Henry Hammond Papers, LOC.

23. *Charleston Mercury,* 14 September 1835; Robert I. Gage to James M. Gage, 31 August 1835, James M. Gage Papers, SHC.

24. *Camden Journal,* 22 August 1835; *Charleston Courier,* 25 August 1835; *Greenville Mountaineer,* 22 August 1835.

25. *Charleston Mercury,* 21 August 1835, 12 September 1835, 16 September 1835, 27 November 1835; *Greenville Mountaineer,* 12 September 1835 and 19 September 1835; Henry H. Townes to George F. Townes, 26 September 1835, Townes Family Papers, SCL. For a discussion of centrism and antipartisanship in the antebellum and Civil War eras, see Mark Voss-Hubbard, *Beyond Party: Cultures of Antipartisanship in Northern Politics before the Civil War* (Baltimore, MD: Johns Hopkins University Press, 2002); Glenn C. Altschuler and Stuart M. Blumin, *Rude Republic: Americans and Their Politics in the Nineteenth Century* (Princeton, NJ: Princeton University Press, 2001); Adam I. P. Smith, *The Stormy Present: Conservatism and the Problem of Slavery in Northern Politics, 1846–1865* (Chapel Hill, NC: University of North Carolina Press, 2017); Smith, *No Party Now;* Jack Furniss, "States of the Union: The Rise and Fall of the Political Center in the Civil War North" (PhD diss., University of Virginia, 2018).

26. *Camden Journal,* 8 August 1835; *Greenville Mountaineer,* 8 August 1835 and 22 August 1835; *Charleston Courier,* 12 August 1835. Figure calculated by compiling membership lists of vigilance committees and committees on resolutions from the state's newspapers and searching for each man in the records of party meetings for the years 1830–34.

27. *Charleston Mercury,* 24 September 1835, 28 September 1835, and 13 October 1835; *Greenville Mountaineer,* 15 August 1835, 22 August 1835, and 12 September 1835; Benjamin Perry Diary, 8 August 1835, SHC.

28. *Charleston Mercury,* 11 September 1835.

29. *Charleston Mercury,* 16 September 1835.

30. Petition from the Pennsylvania Society for Promoting the Abolition of Slavery, National Archives Catalog, available at http://www.catalog.archives.gov/id/306388; Freehling, *Road to Disunion*, 308–11; Ford, *Deliver Us From Evil*, 500–501; David A. Moss, *Democracy: A Case Study* (Cambridge, MA: Belknap Press of Harvard University Press, 2017), 253; *Register of Debates in Congress*, House of Representatives, 24th Cong., 1st Sess., 1966–68; Drew Gilpin Faust, *James Henry Hammond and the Old South: A Design for Mastery* (Baton Rouge, LA: Louisiana State University Press, 1982), 168–80. Many petitioners favored limited and gradual measures, acknowledging that Congress had no power to abolish slavery in the states. Southern radicals, however, ignored these distinctions and accused all Northerners who sympathized with the AASS of promoting immediate abolition.

31. *Register of Debates*, House of Representatives, 24th Cong., 1st Sess., 1975–76, 1979–80, 2039–40.

32. Francis W. Pickens, quoted in Freehling, *Road to Disunion*, 311–12; John B. Edmunds Jr., *Francis W. Pickens and the Politics of Destruction* (Chapel Hill, NC: University of North Carolina Press, 2009), 42–43.

33. Cooper, *The Lost Founding Father*, 328–31; Freehling, *Road to Disunion*, 322–28.

34. Freehling, *Road to Disunion*, 328–30; Ford, *Deliver Us From Evil*, 501–3.

35. *Charleston Mercury*, 23 February 1836 and 25 March 1836.

36. *Charleston Mercury*, 25 February 1836, 27 February 1836, 18 March 1836, and 29 March 1836; Thomas Harrison to James Henry Hammond, 16 February 1836, James Henry Hammond Papers, LOC; John B. Bowers to James Henry Hammond, 17 February 1836, James Henry Hammond Papers, LOC.

37. *Charleston Mercury*, 4 January 1836, 25 February 1836, 1 March 1836, and 18 March 1836.

38. Robert Y. Hayne to James Henry Hammond, 14 January 1836, James Henry Hammond Papers, LOC; Pierce M. Butler to James Henry Hammond, 30 December 1835, James Henry Hammond Papers, LOC; Thomas Harrison to James Henry Hammond, 16 February 1836, James Henry Hammond Papers, LOC.

39. Henry J. Nott to James Henry Hammond, 8 March 1836, James Henry Hammond Papers, LOC; James Davis to James Henry Hammond, 2 April 1836, James Henry Hammond Papers, LOC.

40. Thomas Cooper to James Henry Hammond, 8 January 1836, James Henry Hammond Papers, LOC.

41. Thomas Cooper to Martin Van Buren, 14 March 1837, in Ernest M. Lander Jr., ed., "Dr. Cooper's Views in Retirement," *The South Carolina Historical Magazine* 54, no. 4 (October 1953): 173–84; Thomas Cooper to Langdon Cheves, 2 March 1837, Louisa S. McCord Family Papers, SCHS.

42. J. Adams to James Henry Hammond, 29 March 1836, James Henry Hammond Papers, LOC; Thomas S. Twiss to James Henry Hammond, 19 February 1836, James Henry Hammond Papers, LOC; Thomas Stark to James Henry Hammond, 14 April 1836, James Henry Hammond Papers, LOC; Beverley Tucker to James Henry Hammond, 17 February 1836, James Henry Hammond Papers, LOC; George McDuffie to James Henry Hammond, 11 March 1836, James Henry Hammond Papers, LOC; Freehling, *Road to Disunion*, 316–17.

43. *Charleston Courier,* 19 February 1836 and 23 September 1836; *Camden Journal,* 11 June 1836. In February 1836, Columbia editor Edward Johnston informed Hammond that *The Charleston Mercury, Winyaw Intelligencer, The Columbia Times,* and *The Pendleton Messenger* (all Nullifier papers) "will take ground warmly with us," while *The Southern Patriot, The Greenville Mountaineer, The Camden Journal, The Columbia Hive,* and *The Charleston Courier* (all Union Party papers) were "Against us." See Edward W. Johnston to James Henry Hammond, 20 February 1836, James Henry Hammond Papers, LOC.

44. J. B. Lamar to James Henry Hammond, 27 February 1836, James Henry Hammond Papers, LOC; John Knox to James Henry Hammond, 24 March 1836, James Henry Hammond Papers, LOC; Edward W. Johnston to James Henry Hammond, 28 February 1836 and 24 March 1836, James Henry Hammond Papers, LOC.

45. Alfred Huger to Joel R. Poinsett, 27 August 1836, Joel Roberts Poinsett Papers, HSP; *Charleston Courier,* 23 September 1836, 26 September 1836.

46. Joel R. Poinsett to James Campbell, 25 August 1836, Joel Roberts Poinsett Papers, HSP; *Charleston Courier,* 26 September 1836.

47. *Southern Patriot,* 19 September 1836, 24 September 1836, and 30 September 1836; Alfred Huger to Joel R. Poinsett, 27 August 1836, Joel Roberts Poinsett Papers, HSP; Joel R. Poinsett to James Campbell, 10 September 1836, Joel Roberts Poinsett Papers, HSP.

48. *Charleston Courier,* 23 September 1836, 26 September 1836;

49. *Charleston Courier,* 17 September 1836, 24 September 1836; Joel R. Poinsett to the Editor of *Georgetown Union,* 13 August 1836, Joel Roberts Poinsett Papers, HSP.

50. *Charleston Courier,* 23 September 1836; *Charleston Mercury,* 22 September 1836, 24 September 1836, 27 September 1836, 1 October 1836, and 3 October 1836.

51. *Charleston Courier,* 10 October 1836.

52. *Charleston Courier,* 24 September 1836, 4 October 1836, and 10 October 1836; Jacob F. Schirmer Journal, 11 October 1836, Schirmer Family Journals and Registers, SCHS; James L. Petigru to Hugh S. Legaré, 6 September 1836, Pease Research Collection, SCHS.

53. *Charleston Courier,* 15 October 1836; *Charleston Mercury,* 15 October 1836.

54. Daniel E. Huger to James Chesnut, 23 August 1836, Papers of the Williams, Chesnut, and Manning Families, SCL; James Chesnut, Sen., to James Chesnut, Jr., 5 August 1836, John Chesnut Papers, SCHS.

55. *Cheraw Republican,* 1 November 1836; *New York Evening Post,* 4 November 1836; *Charleston Courier,* 16 September 1836. For election results, see *Charleston Mercury* and *Charleston Courier* for October 1836.

56. *Pendleton Messenger,* 17 April 1835; Edward W. Johnston to James Henry Hammond, 9 March 1836, James Henry Hammond Papers, LOC.

57. *Greenville Mountaineer,* 22 August 1835; *Charleston Courier,* 12 August 1835.

58. John C. Calhoun to James Edward Calhoun, 23 September 1835, *The Papers of John C. Calhoun, Volume 12: 1833–1835,* ed. Clyde N. Wilson (Columbia, SC: University of South Carolina Press, 1979); *Anderson Intelligencer,* 18 October 1860. On South Carolina in the later antebellum era, see Robert Barnwell, *Love of Order: South Carolina's First Secession Crisis* (Chapel Hill, NC: University of North Carolina Press, 1982); Steven A. Channing, *Crisis of Fear: Secession*

in South Carolina (New York, NY: Simon and Schuster, 1970); Ford, *Origins of Southern Radicalism*; McCurry, *Masters of Small Worlds*; Harold S. Schultz, *Nationalism and Sectionalism in South Carolina, 1852–1860* (Durham, NC: Duke University Press, 1950).

EPILOGUE

1. *Charleston Mercury,* 21 December 1860; David Detzer, *Allegiance: Fort Sumter, Charleston, and the Beginning of the Civil War* (New York, NY: Harcourt, 2001), 90–91. See also Lawrence T. McDonnell, *Performing Disunion: The Coming of the Civil War in Charleston, South Carolina* (New York, NY: Cambridge University Press, 2018) and Channing, *A Crisis of Fear.*

2. "Declaration of the Immediate Causes Which Induce and Justify the Secession of South Carolina from the Federal Union," *The Avalon Project: Documents in Law, History and Diplomacy,* Yale Law School, available at http://www.avalon.law.yale.edu; J. David Hacker, "A Census-Based Count of the Civil War Dead," *Civil War History* 57, no. 4 (December 2011): 307–48. For an account of the secession winter and the thwarted efforts at compromise, see Russell McClintock, *Lincoln and the Decision for War: The Northern Response to Secession* (Chapel Hill, NC: University of North Carolina Press, 2008); Daniel W. Crofts, *Lincoln and the Politics of Slavery: The Other Thirteenth Amendment and the Struggle to Save the Union* (Chapel Hill, NC: University of North Carolina Press, 2016).

3. *Cecil Whig,* 19 January 1861; *St. Louis Globe-Democrat,* 15 January 1861; *Oregon Statesman,* 14 January 1861 and 18 March 1861.

4. McClintock, *Lincoln and the Decision for War,* 127; *Cecil Whig,* 19 January 1861; *Evansville Daily Journal,* 7 January 1861; *Evening Star,* 9 January 1861; *New York Times,* 8 January 1861; *Journal of the House of Representatives of the Commonwealth of Pennsylvania of the Session Begun at Harrisburg on the First Day of January, A.D. 1861* (Harrisburg, PA: A. Boyd Hamilton, 1861), 56.

5. Winfield Scott to William C. Preston, 14 December 1832, in *The Nullification Era: A Documentary Era,* ed. William W. Freehling (New York, NY: Harper Torchbooks, 1967), 175–77; *Wheeling Daily Intelligencer,* 23 November 1860; *Daily Evening Express,* 9 January 1861; McClintock, *Lincoln and the Decision for War,* 127; *Wyandot Pioneer,* 3 January 1861; *Republican Banner,* 27 February 1861.

6. *Cleveland Daily Leader,* 12 January 1861; *Centre Democrat,* 13 December 1860; *Wisconsin State Journal,* 5 March 1861; Francis P. Blair Sr., to Montgomery Blair, 12 March 1861, Blair Family Papers, LOC; Montgomery Blair to Abraham Lincoln, 15 March 1861, Abraham Lincoln Papers, LOC.

7. Charles B. Dew, *Apostles of Disunion: Southern Secession Commissioners and the Causes of the Civil War* (Charlottesville, VA: University of Virginia Press, 2001); *Southern Enterprise,* 22 November 1860; *Charleston Mercury,* 12 September 1860. See also Lauren N. Haumesser, "Party of Patriarchy: Democratic Gender Politics and the Coming of the Civil War" (PhD diss., University of Virginia, 2018).

8. *Yorkville Enquirer,* 20 December 1860, 10 January 1861, and 5 December 1861; *Camden*

Journal, 30 April 1861; *Charleston Mercury,* 23 October 1860; *Charleston Courier,* 15 December 1860. Robert Barnwell Smith changed his surname to Rhett in 1837.

9. *Yorkville Enquirer,* 21 March 1861; *Charleston Mercury,* 12 November 1860 and 20 November 1860; *Athens Post,* 23 November 1860; Walther, *The Fire-Eaters,* 158; *Lancaster News,* 31 October 1860; *Charleston Courier,* 2 May 1861.

10. *Yorkville Enquirer,* 20 December 1860 and 10 January 1861; *Charleston Courier,* 15 December 1860; John S. Palmer to James J. Palmer, 16 November 1860, in *A World Turned Upside Down: The Palmers of South Santee, 1818–1881,* ed. Louis P. Towles (Columbia, SC: University of South Carolina Press, 1996), 273.

11. *The Debate in the South Carolina Legislature in December 1830,* 100–110; *Columbia Hive,* 28 April 1832.

12. See Freehling, *Road to Disunion,* vol. 1.

13. *Anderson Intelligencer,* 18 October 1860.

14. William J. Cooper, *We Have the War Upon Us: The Onset of the Civil War, November 1860–April 1861* (New York, NY: Vintage Books, 2012), 25; Alfred Huger to William Porcher Miles, 1 June 1860, William Porcher Miles Papers, SHC; Alfred Huger to Sally Baxter Hampton, 9 December 1860, Sally Baxter Hampton Papers, SCL; Lillian Adele Kibler, "Unionist Sentiment in South Carolina in 1860," *The Journal of Southern History* 4, no. 3 (August 1938): 361–62; James L. Petigru to Alfred Huger, 5 September 1860, in *Life, Letters and Speeches of James Louis Petigru,* 356; *Daily Evening Express,* 19 March 1861; Clement Eaton, *History of the Southern Confederacy* (New York, NY: Collier Books, 1961), 19; James Petigru, quoted in Kelly, *America's Longest Siege.*

15. *New York Tribune,* 11 December 1860; David Golightly Harris, 24 November 1860, 5 January 1861, and 9 January 1861, *Piedmont Farmer: The Journals of David Golightly Harris, 1855–1870,* ed. Philip N. Racine (Knoxville, TN: University of Tennessee Press, 1990); Ford, *Origins of Southern Radicalism,* 369; Benjamin Perry, quoted in Archie Vernon Huff Jr., *Greenville: The History of the City and County in the South Carolina Piedmont* (Columbia, SC: University of South Carolina Press, 1995), 135. In Horry District, another Unionist stronghold during the nullification crisis, 1,074 men voted for the secession ticket and only 28 men voted against it. *Charleston Courier,* 10 December 1860.

16. Andrew Jackson to Joel R. Poinsett, 7 November 1832, Andrew Jackson Papers, LOC; Stephen A. Hurlbut to Abraham Lincoln, 27 March 1861, Abraham Lincoln Papers, LOC. Stephen Hurlbut's father Martin Luther Hurlbut was a staunch Union man during the nullification crisis. He published a pamphlet refuting the radical doctrine and wrote to James Madison asking him to clarify the constitutional questions involved in the crisis. See Jeffrey Norman Lash, *A Politician Turned General: The Civil War Career of Stephen Augustus Hurlbut* (Kent, OH: Kent State University Press, 2003), 9–10.

Bibliography

PRIMARY SOURCES

Manuscript and Archival Sources

Alabama

W. S. Hoole Special Collections Library, University of Alabama
    Manly Family Papers

New York

New York Historical Society
    David James McCord Letter to Philip H. Nicklin, 16 October 1828
    William C. Preston Letter to R. H. Wilde, ca. 1832

North Carolina

David M. Rubenstein Rare Book & Manuscript Library, Duke University
    Benson-Thompson Family Papers
    Iveson L. Brookes Papers
    Armistead A. Burt Papers
    Frederick Fraser Papers
    Hemphill Family Papers
    Amos Kendall Letters
    George McDuffie Papers
    New England Man's Travel Diary, 1831
    Samuel Finley Patterson Papers
    Ebenezer Pettigrew Papers
    Joseph Starke Sims Papers
    Francis Wilkinson Pickens Papers
    George M. Witherspoon Papers
Southern Historical Collection, University of North Carolina at Chapel Hill
    Francis Everett Barnard Papers
    Iveson L. Brookes Papers

Brumby and Smith Family Papers
Dickson Family Papers
Elliott and Gonzales Family Papers
John Berkley Grimball Diaries
James T. Harrison Papers
Hughes Family Papers
Samuel C. Jackson Diary
Mitchell King Papers
C. G. Memminger Papers
William Porcher Miles Papers
Milligan Family Papers
John Wroughton Mitchell Papers
Rosina Mix Papers
Benjamin Franklin Perry Papers
Pettigrew Family Papers
Robert Barnwell Rhett Papers
William Royall Letter
Springs Family Papers
Isaac Tompkins Letters

Pennsylvania

Historical Society of Pennsylvania
Butler Family Papers
Drayton Family Papers
Gilpin Family Papers
Joel Roberts Poinsett Papers
Stevens-Cogdell-Sanders-Venning Collection

South Carolina

Clemson University Special Collections and Archives
John C. Calhoun Papers
Thomas Green Clemson Papers
Richard K. Crallé Papers
Holmes Collection
Benjamin Ryan Tillman Papers
College of Charleston Special Collections
Barnwell Family Papers

John Berkley Grimball Diary
Blamyer, Wigfall, and Deas Family Collection
Cohen, Emanuel, Moses, and Seixas Family Papers
Drayton Family Papers
Grimké Family Papers
Isaac W. Hayne Papers
Heyward and Ferguson Family Papers
Lazarus and Hirsch Family Papers
Joseph Lyons Diary
Nathaniel Russell Middleton Papers
Samuel Prioleau Papers
Temple Sinai Records
Washington Light Infantry Records, 1820–1936
Wilkinson and Keith Family Papers
Furman University Special Collections and Archives
John H. Dargan Family Papers
Davis Family Papers
James C. Furman Papers
William Bullein Johnson Papers
South Caroliniana Library
Jasper Adams Papers
Margaret E. Adams Papers
Papers of the Adger, Smyth, and Flynn Families
Letterbook of Orsamus D. Allen
Robert F. W. Allston Papers
Ellennor Arnold Pen Practice Verses
Richard G. Arnold Letter
Asylum Plantation Journal
Lewis M. Ayer Papers
Peter Samuel Bacot Papers
Robert Woodward Barnwell Papers
William Blanding Papers
Alexander Bowie Letter
William Boykin Letter
Julia M. Brown Letter
Pierce Mason Butler Papers
Cantey Family Papers
William H. Chapman Papers
Langdon Cheves Papers

William Choice Letter

John Milton Clapp Papers

Clariosophic Literary Society Records

Papers of the Cooper, McClurken, and Nisbet Families

Thomas Cooper Papers

C. F. Daniels Papers

Elias Davis Letter

James Sutherland Deas Papers

William Drayton Papers

William Christopher Dukes Commonplace Books

"Election Song: Hurra! Say the Nullies the traitors and bullies"

John Christopher Faber Papers

John Fox Papers

Charles Fraser Papers

William C. Gale Letter

Papers of the Gaston, Strait, Wylie, and Baskin Families

John King Griffin Letter

Thomas Smith Grimké Papers

James Hamilton Papers

Hampton Family Papers

Sally Baxter Hampton Papers

Robert Young Hayne Papers

Samuel C. Jackson Papers

Timothy W. Johnson Papers

Jones, Watts, and Davis Family Papers

Papers of the Kincaid and Anderson Families

John Knox Letter

Joseph W. Lesesne Papers

Papers of the Lide, Coker, and Stout Families

Sarah Bond Lowndes Letter

Mackay Family Papers

David James McCord Papers

McCutchen Family Papers

William Anderson McDowell Papers

George McDuffie Papers

John Blount Miller Papers

Smith Mowry Papers

Noble Family Papers

"Nullification: A Patriotick Ballad"

John Belton O'Neall Papers

James Louis Petigru Papers

John S. Pressly Letter

Rutledge Family Papers

Seibels Family Papers

Simpson, Young, Dean and Coleman Family Papers

Daniel Havens Skinner Letter

Alexander Ross Taylor Papers

Benjamin Franklin Taylor Papers

John Taylor Papers

John W. Taylor Letter

P. B. Tomlinson Letter

Townes Family Papers

Beaufort Taylor Watts Papers

"Union Meeting at Waterloo, Laurens District, 1834 February 12," broadside

William May Wightman Papers

Williams, Chesnut, and Manning Family Papers

David Rogerson Williams Papers

John Lyde Wilson Papers

Witherspoon Family Papers

James Faucett Woods Papers

South Carolina Department of Archives and History

    Legislative Papers: Governors' Messages

    Legislative Papers: Petitions to the General Assembly

South Carolina Historical Society

    James Butler Campbell Papers

    James Petigru Carson Papers

    James Chesnut Papers

    John Chesnut Papers

    Henry William DeSaussure Papers

    Fraser Family Papers

    Caroline Howard Gilman Papers

    Anne King Gregorie, "Papers Relating to Thomas Sumter," ca. 1930

    Shirley Carter Hughson, "Excerpts from the Correspondence of Hugh Swinton Legaré," 1893

    Randell Hunt, "Journal of a Traveller," 1832

    Journal of the Whig Association, 1833–861

    Macbeth Family Papers

    Joseph Manigault Papers

McCord Family Papers
Louisa S. McCord Family Papers
Miscellaneous Manuscripts, Charleston Library Society
Stephen Decatur Miller Papers
Pease Research Collection
James Louis Petigru Papers
Read Family Papers
Records of the Free Trade and State Rights Association of the Parishes of St. Stephen's, St. John's Berkeley, and St. James Santee, 1831
Schirmer Family Journals and Registers
State Rights and Union Party Ticket
Elias Vanderhorst Papers
Daniel Cannon Webb Plantation Journals
Langdon Cheves West Papers
Winfield Scott Letter

Virginia

Albert and Shirley Small Special Collections Library, University of Virginia
Jacob Whitman Bailey Letter to William M. Bailey, 11 April 1833
David James McCord Letters to Stephen Decatur Miller
Littleton Tazewell Letters
Virginia Historical Society
Cocke Family Papers
Crump Family Papers
Peachy Gilmer Papers
William Hammet Papers
Jesse Burton Harrison Papers
Lee Family Papers

Washington, DC

Library of Congress
Blair Family Papers
Warren R. Davis Letter
David G. Farragut Papers
James Henry Hammond Papers
Andrew Jackson Papers

Abraham Lincoln Papers
James Madison Papers
Philip Phillips Family Papers
Waddy Thompson Papers
Martin Van Buren Papers

Newspapers

Arkansas

Arkansas Times and Advocate

Georgia

Augusta Chronicle
Georgia Courier
Macon Telegraph

Indiana

Evansville Daily Journal
Indiana Journal

Kentucky

Louisville Public Advertiser

Maryland

Cecil Whig
Niles' Weekly Register

Massachusetts

Liberator

Mississippi

Natchez Weekly Democrat
Vicksburg Whig

Bibliography

Missouri

   St. Louis Globe-Democrat

New York

   Evening Post
   New York Spectator
   New York Times
   New York Tribune

North Carolina

   Carolina Watchman
   Charlotte Journal
   Fayetteville Weekly Observer
   Newbern Sentinel
   Newbern Spectator
   North Carolina Constitutionalist and Peoples' Advocate
   North Carolina Free Press
   People's Press
   Raleigh Weekly Register

Ohio

   Wyandot Pioneer

Oregon

   Oregon Statesman

Pennsylvania

   Aurora & Pennsylvania Gazette
   Centre Democrat
   Daily Evening Express
   National Gazette
   Pittsburgh Weekly Gazette
   Wyoming Herald

South Carolina

Abbeville Whig and Southern Nullifier
Aiken Telegraph
Anderson Intelligencer
Beaufort Gazette
Camden Journal
Camden and Lancaster Beacon
Camden Republican and Lancaster Beacon
Charleston Courier
Charleston Mercury
Charleston Observer
Cheraw Republican
Columbia Hive
Columbia Telescope
Edgefield Advertiser
Edgefield Carolinian
Edgefield Hive
Georgetown Union
Greenville Mountaineer
Greenville Republican
Irishman and Southern Democrat
Keowee Courier
Mountaineer
Pee Dee Gazette
Pendleton Messenger
South Carolina State Gazette and Columbia Advertiser
Southern Enterprise
Southern Patriot
Southern Sentinel
Southern Times & State Gazette
Southern Whig
State Rights and Free Trade Evening Post
Sumter Gazette and Constitutional Advocate
Winyaw Intelligencer
Yorkville Enquirer
Yorkville Pioneer and South Carolina Whig

Bibliography

Tennessee

   Athens Post
   National Banner and Daily Advertiser
   Republican Banner

Vermont

   Brattleboro Messenger
   Burlington Times
   Middlebury Free Press
   Vermont Courier
   Vermont Republican and American Journal

Washington, DC

   Evening Star
   Globe
   National Intelligencer
   United States Telegraph

West Virginia

   Wheeling Daily Intelligencer

Wisconsin

   Wisconsin State Journal

Published Primary Sources

Acts and Resolutions of the General Assembly of the State of South Carolina, Passed in December 1830. Columbia, SC: S. J. McMorris, 1831.

Acts and Resolutions of the General Assembly of the State of South Carolina, Passed in December 1831. Columbia, SC: A. Landrum, 1832.

Acts and Resolutions of the General Assembly of the State of South Carolina, Passed in December 1832. Columbia, SC: Miller & Bran, 1833.

Address by the Free Trade and State Rights Association to the People of South Carolina. Columbia: Office of the Telescope and Times, 1832.

Address to the People of Chester District, Assembled to Discuss the Question of Nullification. Charleston, SC: n.p., 1832.

Allston, Washington. *The Correspondence of Washington Allston.* Edited by Nathalia Wright. Lexington, KY: University Press of Kentucky, 2014.

An Appeal to the People on the Question What Shall We Do Next? Columbia, SC: Office of the Telescope, 1832.

Annals of the Congress of the United States. 16th Congress (1819–21).

Broadus, John Albert. *Memoir of James Petigru Boyce.* New York, NY: A. C. Armstrong and Son, 1893.

Bulfinch, S. G. *The Benefits and Dangers Belonging to Seasons of Public Excitement: A Discourse, Delivered in the Unitarian Church at Charleston, S.C. on the Day of Humiliation and Prayer, January 31, 1833.* Charleston, SC: J. S. Burges, 1833.

Buchanan, James. *The Works of James Buchanan: Volume 2: 1830–1836.* Edited by John Bassett Moore. Philadelphia, PA: J. B. Lippincott Company, 1908.

The Calhoun Doctrine, or State Nullification Discussed. Charleston, SC: Office of The Irishman, 1831.

Calhoun, John C. *Important Correspondence on the Subject of State Interposition Between his Excellency Gov. Hamilton, and Hon. J. C. Calhoun.* Columbia, SC: Office of the Telescope and Times, 1832.

——. *The Papers of John C. Calhoun, Volume 10: 1825–1829.* Edited by Clyde N. Wilson. Columbia, SC: University of South Carolina Press, 1977.

——. *The Papers of John C. Calhoun, Volume 11: 1829–1832.* Edited by Clyde N. Wilson. Columbia, SC: University of South Carolina Press, 1978.

——. *The Papers of John C. Calhoun, Volume 12: 1833–1835.* Edited by Clyde N. Wilson. Columbia, SC: University of South Carolina Press, 1979.

——. *Speech of the Hon. J. C. Calhoun of South Carolina, on the Abolition Petitions, Delivered on Wednesday, March 9, 1836.* Washington, DC: Duff Green, 1836.

——. *Union and Liberty: The Political Philosophy of John C. Calhoun.* Edited by Ross M. Lence. Indianapolis, IN: Liberty Fund, 1992.

Carey, Mathew. *The Crisis: An Appeal to the Good Sense of the Nation.* Philadelphia, PA: William F. Geddes, 1832.

A Catechism on the Tariff, for the Use of Plain People of Common Sense. Charleston, SC: E. J. Van Brunt, 1831.

Cater, Richard B. *A Discourse Delivered in the Presbyterian Church at Pendleton Village, on the 31st January, 1833.* Pendleton, SC: F. W. Symmes, 1833.

Chesnut, Mary Boykin Miller. *Mary Chesnut's Civil War.* Edited by C. Vann Woodward. New Haven, CT: Yale University Press, 1981.

Cocke, Charles. *Speech of Charles Cocke Delivered in the Senate of Virginia, in Committee of the Whole, on the State of the Relations Between the U. States and*

S. Carolina on Thursday, January 24, 1833. Richmond, VA: Thomas White, 1833.

The Crisis, or Nullification Unmasked by an Exposition. Charleston: n.p, n.d.

Dialogue Between a Merchant and a Planter. Columbia, SC: Office of the Telescope and Times, 1832.

The Debate in the South Carolina Legislature in December 1830 on the Reports of the Committees of Both Houses in Favor of Convention. Columbia, SC: S. J. McMorris, 1831.

"Declaration of the Immediate Causes Which Induce and Justify the Secession of South Carolina from the Federal Union." 24 December 1860. *The Avalon Project: Documents in Law, History and Diplomacy*. Yale Law School. Last modified 2008. http://www.avalon.law.yale.edu/19th_century/csa_scarsec.asp.

Elliott, William. *Address to the People of St. Helena Parish*. Charleston, SC: William Estill, 1832.

Featherstonhaugh, George William. *Excursions Through the Slave States*. New York, NY: Harper & Brothers, 1844.

Féte Civique: Célébrée a Charleston, S. C. en Commémoration de la Glorieuse Révolution Française de 1830. Charleston, SC: A. E. Miller, 1830.

Floyd, John. *The Life and Diary of John Floyd*. Edited by Charles H. Ambler. Richmond, VA: Richmond Press, Inc., 1918.

Freehling, William W., ed. *The Nullification Era: A Documentary Record*. New York, NY: Harper Torchbooks, 1967.

Gallant, Mary. "Recollections of a Charleston Childhood, 1822–1836." *South Carolina Historical Magazine* 98, no. 1 (January 1997): 56–74.

Goulding, Thomas. *A Fast Day Sermon for Thursday, January 31st, 1833, Columbia, SC*. Columbia, SC: Telescope Office, 1833.

Greeley, Horace. *Life of Col. Fremont*. New York, NY: Greeley and McElrath, 1856.

Grimké, Thomas S. *Letter to the Honorable John C. Calhoun, Robert Y. Hayne, George McDuffie, and James Hamilton*. Charleston, SC: James S. Burges, 1832.

———. *To the People of the State of South Carolina, December 1, 1832*. Charleston, SC: J. S. Burges, 1832.

———. *Speech of Thomas Grimké Delivered in the Senate of South Carolina in December 1828*. Charleston, SC: W. Riley, 1829.

———. *Speech of Thomas Grimké, one of the Senators from St. Philip's and St. Michael's, Delivered in the Senate of South Carolina, in December 1828*. Charleston, SC: W. Riley, 1829.

Hamilton, James. *An Eulogium on the Public Services and Character of Robert J. Turnbull*. Charleston, SC: A. E. Miller, 1834.

Hammond, James Henry. *Remarks of Mr. Hammond of South Carolina, on the*

Question of Receiving Petitions for the Abolition in the District of Columbia, Delivered in the House of Representatives, February 1, 1836. Washington, DC: Duff Green, 1836.

Harris, David Golightly. *Piedmont Farmer: The Journals of David Golightly Harris, 1855–1870.* Edited by Philip N. Racine. Knoxville, TN: University of Tennessee Press, 1990.

Hayne, Robert Y. "Inaugural Address." *Southern Orators: Speeches and Orations.* Edited by Joseph Moore McConnell. New York, NY: Macmillan Company, 1910.

Historical Statistics of the United States: Colonial Times to 1957. Washington, DC: Government Printing Office, 1960.

[Holland, Edwin C.]. *A Refutation of the Calumnies Circulated Against the Southern & Western States, Respecting the Institutions and Existence of Slavery Among Them.* Charleston, SC: A. E. Miller, 1822.

Huger, Daniel E. *Speech of the Honorable Daniel E. Huger, in the House of Representatives of South Carolina, December 1830.* Charleston, SC: W. Riley, 1831.

Jackson, Andrew. "December 8, 1829: First Annual Message to Congress." Presidential Speeches: Andrew Jackson Presidency. Miller Center. Last modified 2019. http://www.millercenter.org/the-presidency/presidential-speeches/december-8-1829-first-annual-message-congress.

——. "December 6, 1830: Second Annual Message to Congress." Presidential Speeches: Andrew Jackson Presidency. Miller Center. Last modified 2019. http://www.millercenter.org/the-presidency/presidential-speeches/december-6-1830-second-annual-message-congress.

——. "May 27, 1830: Veto Message Regarding Funding of Infrastructure Development." Presidential Speeches: Andrew Jackson Presidency. Miller Center. Last modified 2019. http://millercenter.org/the-presidency/presidential-speeches/may-27-1830-veto-message-regarding-funding-infrastructure.

——. *The Papers of Andrew Jackson, Volume 7: 1829.* Edited by Daniel Feller et al. Knoxville, TN: University of Tennessee Press, 2007.

——. *The Papers of Andrew Jackson, Volume 8: 1830.* Edited by Daniel Feller, Thomas Coens, and Laura-Eve Moss. Knoxville, TN: University of Tennessee Press, 2010.

——. *The Papers of Andrew Jackson, Volume 9: 1831.* Edited by Daniel Feller et al. Knoxville, TN: University of Tennessee Press, 2013.

——. *The Papers of Andrew Jackson, Volume 10: 1832.* Edited by Daniel Feller, Thomas Coens, and Laura-Eve Moss. Knoxville, TN: University of Tennessee Press, 2016.

——. "President Jackson's Proclamation Regarding Nullification." 10 December

1832. *The Avalon Project: Documents in Law, History and Diplomacy.* Yale Law School. Last modified 2008. http://www.avalon.law.yal.edu/19th_century/jack01.asp.

Johnson, William. *The Opinion of the Hon. William Johnson, Delivered on the 7th of August, 1823.* Charleston, SC: C. C. Sebring, 1823.

Johnston, Algernon Sidney. *Memoirs of a Nullifier, Written by Himself.* Columbia, SC: Office of the Telescope, 1832.

The Journal of the Free Trade Convention Held in Philadelphia from September 30 to October 7, 1831. Philadelphia, PA: T. W. Ustick, 1831.

Journal of the House of Representatives of the Commonwealth of Pennsylvania of the Session Begun at Harrisburg on the First Day of January, A.D. 1861. Harrisburg, PA: A. Boyd Hamilton, 1861.

Lander, Ernest M., Jr., ed. "Columbia in the Doldrums, 1836." *The South Carolina Historical Magazine* 62, no. 4 (October 1961): 200–202.

———, ed. "Dr. Cooper's Views in Retirement." *The South Carolina Historical Magazine* 54, no. 4 (October 1953): 173–84.

[Legaré, Hugh S.] *The Writings of Hugh Swinton Legaré, Late Attorney General.* Two volumes. Charleston, SC: Burges & James, 1846.

"Letters on the Nullification Movement in South Carolina, 1830–1834." *The American Historical Review* 6, no. 4 (July 1901): 736–65. Available at http://www.jstor.org/stable/1834178.

———. *The American Historical Review* 7, no. 1 (October 1901): 92–119.

Lubbock, Francis. *Six Decades in Texas, or Memoirs of Francis Richard Lubbock.* Edited by C. W. Raines. Austin, TX: Ben C. Jones & Co., 1900.

Madison, James. *Selected Writings of James Madison.* Edited by Ralph Ketcham. Indianapolis: IN: Hackett Publishing Company, 2006.

McDuffie, George. *Speech of the Hon. George McDuffie at a Public Dinner Given to Him by the Citizens of Charleston, May 19, 1831.* Charleston, SC: A. E. Miller, 1831.

McGill, Samuel D. *Narrative of Reminiscences in Williamsburg County.* Columbia, SC: Bryan Printing Co., 1897.

Middleton, Henry. *Prospects of Disunion.* Charleston, SC: James S. Burges, 1833.

Pickens, Francis W. "Five Letters from Francis W. Pickens to Patrick Noble, 1835–1836." Edited by Alice Noble Waring. *The South Carolina Historical Magazine* 54, no. 2 (April 1953): 75–82.

Pinckney, Harriott. Letter of Harriott Pinckney to Charles Cotesworth Pinckney, Jun. *Spared & Shared 11: Saving History One Letter at a Time.* Last modified 2016. http://www.sparedshared11.wordpress.com/2016/01/02/1831-harriott-pinckney-to-charles-cotesworth-pinckney-jun.

Pinckney, Henry. *An Oration Delivered in the Independent, or Congregational Church, Charleston, Before the State Rights & Free Trade Party.* Charleston, SC: A. E. Miller, 1833.

Pinckney, Maria. *Quintessence of Long Speeches Arranged as a Political Catechism.* Charleston, SC: A. E. Miller, 1830.

Poinsett, Joel R. *Address of the Washington Society to the People of South Carolina.* Charleston, SC: J. R. Burges, 1832.

Proceedings of the Celebration of the 4th July, 1831 at Charleston by the State Rights and Free Trade Party. Charleston, SC: A. E. Miller, 1831.

Proceedings of the Citizens of Charleston on the Incendiary Machinations Now in Progress Against the Peace and Welfare of the Southern States. Charleston, SC: A. E. Miller, 1835.

Proceedings of the State Rights Celebration at Charleston, S.C., July 1, 1830. Charleston, SC: A. E. Miller, 1830.

Register of Debates in Congress. 19th Congress–24th Congress (1825–37).

Returns from Military Posts, 1806–1916. Records of the Adjutant General's Office, 1780s–1917. Record Group 94. National Archives. Accessed through http://www.ancestry.com.

Richardson, John S. *The Argument of the Hon. J. S. Richardson in Reply to Chancellor Harper, and in Opposition to Nullification and Convention.* Columbia, SC: Times and Gazette Office, 1830.

Schulz, John Christopher. "Some Letters from John Christopher Schulz, 1829–1883." *The South Carolina Historical Magazine* 56, no. 1 (January 1955): 1–7.

Scott, Winfield. *Memoirs of Lieut.-General Winfield Scott.* Edited by Timothy D. Johnson. Knoxville, TN: University of Tennessee Press, 2015.

Simms, William Gilmore Simms. *The Letters of William Gilmore Simms, Volume 1: 1830–1844.* Edited by Mary C. Simms Oliphant, Alfred Taylor Odell, and T. C. Duncan Eaves. Columbia, SC: University of South Carolina Press, 1952.

Smith, William. *Speech of the Hon. William Smith, Delivered on Monday, August 1, 1831.* Columbia, SC: Office of the Columbia Hive, 1832.

Speeches Delivered in the Convention of the State of South Carolina, Held in Columbia, in March 1833. Charleston, SC: E. J. Van Brunt, 1833.

Speeches of Hayne and Webster in the United States Senate on the Resolution of Mr. Foot. Boston, MA: A. T. Hotchkiss and W. P. Fetridge, 1853.

Speeches of the Hon. Robert Y. Hayne, and the Hon. Daniel Webster, Jan. 21 and 26, 1830. Boston, MA: Carter and Hendee, 1830.

State Documents on Federal Relations: The States and the United States. Edited by Herman V. Ames. Philadelphia, PA: University of Pennsylvania Press, 1911.

State Papers on Nullification. Boston, MA: Dutton and Wentworth, 1834.

State Rights and Free Trade Almanac for the Year of Our Lord 1832. Charleston, SC: A. E. Miller, 1831.

Statutes at Large of South Carolina: Volume 1. Edited by Thomas Cooper. Columbia, SC: A. S. Johnston, 1836.

Tazewell, Littleton Waller. *Gov. Tazewell's Review of President Jackson's Proclamation of the 10th of December 1832.* Norfolk, VA: J. D. Ghiselin, 1888.

Turnbull, Robert J. *The Crisis, or Essays on the Usurpations of the Federal Government.* Charleston, SC: A. E. Miller, 1827.

——. *An Oration Delivered in the City of Charleston Before the State Rights and Free Trade Party.* Charleston, SC: A. E. Miller, 1832.

Washington, George. "Washington's Farewell Address." 1796. *The Avalon Project: Documents in Law, History, and Diplomacy.* Yale Law School. Last modified 2008. http://www.avalon.law.yale.edu/18th_century/washing.asp.

Webster, Daniel. *The Papers of Daniel Webster: Correspondence, Volume 3: 1830–1834.* Edited by Charles Wiltse. Hanover, NH: University Press of New England, 1977.

Wylie, Samuel Brown. *Memoir of Alexander McLeod, D.D.* New York, NY: Charles Scribner, 1855.

SECONDARY SOURCES

Books, Book Chapters, and Articles

Allgor, Catherine. *Parlor Politics: In Which the Ladies of Washington Help Build a City and a Government.* Charlottesville, VA: University of Virginia Press, 2000.

Anderson, Lawrence M. *Federalism, Secession, and the American State: Divided, We Secede.* New York, NY: Routledge, 2014.

Andrew, Rod, Jr. *Wade Hampton: Confederate Warrior to Southern Redeemer.* Chapel Hill, NC: University of North Carolina Press, 2008.

Appleby, Joyce. *Inheriting the Revolution: The First Generation of Americans.* Cambridge, MA: Belknap Press of Harvard University Press, 2000.

Altschuler, Glenn C., and Stuart M. Blumin. *Rude Republic: Americans and Their Politics in the Nineteenth Century.* Princeton, NJ: Princeton University Press, 2000.

Baker, Jean. *Affairs of Party: The Political Culture of Northern Democrats in the Mid-Nineteenth Century.* New York, NY: Fordham University Press, 1998.

Banner, James M., Jr. "The Problem of South Carolina." *The Hofstadter Aegis: A Memorial.* Edited by Stanley Elkins and Eric McKitrick. New York, NY: Knopf, 1974.

Barnwell, John. *Love of Order: South Carolina's First Secession Crisis.* Chapel Hill, NC: University of North Carolina Press, 1982.

Belohlavek, John M. *Broken Glass: Caleb Cushing and the Shattering of the Union.* Kent, OH: Kent State University Press, 2005.

Bergeron, Paul H. "Tennessee's Response to the Nullification Crisis." *The Journal of Southern History* 39, no 1 (February 1973): 23–44.

Birney, Catherine H. *The Grimké Sisters: Sarah and Angelina Grimké, the First American Women Advocates of Abolition and Woman's Rights.* Boston, MA: Lee and Shepard, 1855.

Bolt, William K. "Founding Father and Rebellious Son: James Madison, John C. Calhoun, and the Use of Precedents. *American Nineteenth Century History* 5, no. 3 (Fall 2004): 1–27.

——. *Tariff Wars and the Politics of Jacksonian America.* Nashville, TN: Vanderbilt University Press, 2017.

Bond, Bradley G. *Political Culture in the Nineteenth Century South: Mississippi, 1830–1900.* Baton Rouge, LA: Louisiana State University Press, 1995.

Bonner, Robert E. *Mastering America: Southern Slaveholders and the Crisis of American Nationhood.* New York, NY: Cambridge University Press, 2009.

Boucher, Chauncey Samuel. *The Nullification Controversy in South Carolina.* Chicago, IL: University of Chicago Press, 1916.

Bourke, Paul, and Donald DeBats. *Washington County: Politics and Community in Antebellum America.* Baltimore, MD: Johns Hopkins University Press, 1995.

Bowman, Shearer Davis. *At the Precipice: Americans North and South During the Secession Crisis.* Chapel Hill, NC: University of North Carolina Press, 2010.

Breen, Patrick H. *The Land Shall Be Deluged in Blood: A New History of the Nat Turner Revolt.* New York, NY: Oxford University Press, 2016.

Broadstone, Michael A. *History of Greene County, Ohio: Its People, Industries and Institutions, Vol. 1.* Indianapolis, IN: B. F. Bowen & Company, Inc., 1918.

Cain, Joshua. "'We Will Strike at the Head and Demolish the Monster': The Impact of Joel R. Poinsett's Correspondence on President Andrew Jackson during the Nullification Crisis, 1832–1833." *Proceedings of the South Carolina Historical Association* (2011): 13–26.

Campbell, Richard. "Patriotism, Poetry, and Personalities: The Politics of John L. Wilson and the Pasquinade of the Thirties." *The South Carolina Historical Magazine* 115, no 1 (January 2014): 4–34.

Capers, Henry D. *The Life and Times of C. G. Memminger.* Richmond, VA: Everett Waddey Co., 1893.

Carey, Anthony Gene. *Parties, Slavery, and the Union in Antebellum Georgia.* Athens, GA: University of Georgia Press, 1997.

Carmichael, Peter S. *The Last Generation: Young Virginians in Peace, War, and Reunion.* Chapel Hill, NC: University of North Carolina Press, 2005.

Carney, Charity R. *Ministers and Masters: Methodism, Manhood, and Honor in the Old South.* Baton Rouge, LA: Louisiana State University Press, 2011.

Carson, James Petigru. *Life, Letters and Speeches of James Louis Petigru: The Union Man of South Carolina.* Washington, DC: W. H. Lowdermilk & Co., 1920.

Cauthen, Charles Edward. *South Carolina Goes to War, 1860–1865.* Chapel Hill, NC: University of North Carolina Press, 1950.

Chamberlain, Ryan. *Pistols, Politics and the Press: Dueling in 19th Century American Journalism.* Jefferson, NC: McFarland and Company, Inc., 2009.

Channing, Steven A. *Crisis of Fear: Secession in South Carolina.* New York, NY: Simon and Schuster, 1970.

Chapman, John A. *History of Edgefield County, From the Earliest Settlements to 1897.* Newberry, SC: Elbert H. Aull, 1897.

Childers, Christopher. *The Webster-Hayne Debate: Defining Nationhood in the Early American Republic.* Baltimore, MD: Johns Hopkins University Press, 2018.

Clark, H. Lee, Jr. *Calhoun and Popular Rule: The Political Theory of the Disquisition and Discourse.* Columbia, MO: University of Missouri Press, 2001.

Clavin, Matthew J. *Toussaint Louverture and the American Civil War: The Promise and Peril of a Second Haitian Revolution.* Philadelphia, PA: University of Pennsylvania Press, 2010.

Cogan, Neil H. *Union & States' Rights: A History and Interpretation of Interposition, Nullification, and Secession, 150 Years After Sumter.* Akron, OH: University of Akron Press, 2014.

Cole, Donald B. *Martin Van Buren and the American Political System.* Princeton, NJ: Princeton University Press, 1984.

Conlin, Michael F. *One Nation Divided by Slavery: Remembering the American Revolution While Marching toward the Civil War.* Kent, OH: Kent State University Press, 2015.

Cooper, William J. *Liberty and Slavery: Southern Politics to 1860.* New York, NY: Alfred A. Knopf, 1983.

———. *The Lost Founding Father: John Quincy Adams and the Transformation of American Politics.* New York, NY: Liveright Publishing Corporation, 2017.

———. *The South and the Politics of Slavery, 1828–1856.* Baton Rouge, LA: Louisiana State University Press, 1978.

———. *We Have the War Upon Us: The Onset of the Civil War, November 1860–April 1861.* New York, NY: Vintage Books, 2012.

Cox, Thomas H. *Gibbons v. Ogden, Law, and Society in the Early Republic.* Athens, OH: Ohio University Press, 2009.

Crofts, Daniel W. *Lincoln and the Politics of Slavery: The Other Thirteenth Amend-*

ment and the Struggle to Save the Union. Chapel Hill, NC: University of North
   Carolina Press, 2016.

——. *Reluctant Confederates: Upper South Unionists in the Secession Crisis.* Chapel Hill, NC: University of North Carolina Press, 1989.

Dabbs, James McBride. *Pee Dee Panorama.* Columbia, SC: University of South
   Carolina Press, 1951.

Dallas, James Maxwell. *Historic Greenvale: "Old Greenville Church."* Abbeville, SC:
   Banner Publishing Co., 1925.

David, James Corbett. "The Politics of Emasculation: The Caning of Charles
   Sumner and Elite Ideologies of Manhood in the Mid-Nineteenth-Century
   United States." *Gender & History* 19, no. 2 (2007): 324–45.

Davidson, Chalmers Gaston. The Last Foray: The South Carolina Planters of
   1860: A Sociological Study. Columbia, SC: University of South Carolina Press,
   1971.

Davis, William C. *Rhett: The Turbulent Life and Times of a Fire-Eater.* Columbia,
   SC: University of South Carolina Press. 2001.

Degler, Carl Neumann. *The Other South: Southern Dissenters in the Nineteenth
   Century.* New York, NY: Harper & Row, 1974.

Detzer, David. *Allegiance: Fort Sumter, Charleston, and the Beginning of the Civil
   War.* New York, NY: Harcourt, Inc., 2001.

Dew, Charles B. *Apostles of Disunion: Southern Secession Commissioners and the
   Causes of the Civil War.* Charlottesville, VA: University of Virginia Press, 2001.

Dickey, Christopher. *Our Man in Charleston: Britain's Secret Agent in the Civil
   War South.* New York, NY: Broadway Books, 2015.

Dorn, Charles. *For the Common Good: A New History of Higher Education in America.* Ithaca, NY: Cornell University Press, 2017.

Du Pont, B. G. *E. I. Du Pont de Nemours and Company: A History, 1802–1902.* Boston, MA: Riverside Press, 1920.

Durham, David I. *A Southern Moderate in Radical Times: Henry Washington Hilliard, 1808–1892.* Baton Rouge, LA: Louisiana State University Press, 2008.

Earle, Jonathan H. *Jacksonian Antislavery & the Politics of Free Soil, 1824–1854.*
   Chapel Hill, NC: University of North Carolina Press, 2004.

Eaton, Clement. *History of the Southern Confederacy.* New York, NY: Collier
   Books, 1961.

Edgar, Walter B. *South Carolina: A History.* Columbia, SC: University of South
   Carolina, 1998.

Edmunds, John B., Jr. *Francis W. Pickens and the Politics of Destruction.* Chapel
   Hill, NC: University of North Carolina Press, 1986.

Edwards, Laura F. *The People and Their Peace: Legal Culture and the Transforma-*

tion of Inequality in the Post-Revolutionary South. Chapel Hill, NC: University of North Carolina Press, 2009.

Eisenhower, John S. D. *Agent of Destiny: The Life and Times of General Winfield Scott.* Norman, OK: University of Oklahoma Press, 1997.

Elder, Robert. *Calhoun: American Heretic.* New York, NY: Basic Books, 2021.

Ellis, Richard E. *The Union at Risk: Jacksonian Democracy, States' Rights and the Nullification Crisis.* New York, NY: Oxford University Press, 1987.

Ericson, David F. "The Nullification Crisis, American Republicanism, and the Force Bill Debate." *The Journal of Southern History* 61, no. 2 (May 1995): 249–70.

Eustace, Nicole. *1812: War and the Passions of Patriotism.* Philadelphia, PA: University of Pennsylvania Press, 2012.

Faust, Drew Gilpin. *James Henry Hammond and the Old South: A Design for Mastery.* Baton Rouge, LA: Louisiana State University Press, 1982.

Fehrenbacher, Don E. *The Slaveholding Republic: An Account of the United States Government's Relations to Slavery.* Completed and Edited by Ward M. McAfee. New York, NY: Oxford University Press, 2001.

Field, Corinne T. *The Struggle for Equal Adulthood: Gender, Race, Age, and the Fight for Citizenship in Antebellum America.* Chapel Hill, NC: University of North Carolina Press, 2014.

Fitz, Caitlin. *Our Sister Republics: The United States in an Age of American Revolutions.* New York, NY: Liveright Publishing Corporation, 2016.

Fleche, Andrew M. *The Revolution of 1861: The American Civil War in the Age of Nationalist Conflict.* Chapel Hill, NC: University of North Carolina Press, 2012.

Floyd, Viola C. *Lancaster County Tours.* Lancaster, SC: Lancaster County Historical Commission, 1956.

Fogel, Robert William. *Without Consent or Contract: The Rise and Fall of American Slavery.* New York, NY: W. W. Norton, 1989.

Forbes, Robert Pierce. *The Missouri Compromise and Its Aftermath.* Chapel Hill, NC: University of North Carolina Press, 2007.

Ford, Lacy K. *Deliver Us From Evil: The Slavery Question in the Old South.* New York, NY: Oxford University Press, 2009.

———. "James Louis Petigru: The Last South Carolina Federalist." *Intellectual Life in Antebellum Charleston.* Edited by Michael O'Brien and David Moltke-Hansen. Knoxville, TN: University of Tennessee Press, 1986.

———. *Origins of Southern Radicalism: The South Carolina Upcountry, 1800–1860.* New York, NY: Oxford University Press, 1988.

Ford, Peter A. "An American In Paris: Charles S. Storrow and the 1830 Revolution." *Proceedings of the Massachusetts Historical Society* 104 (1992): 21–42.

Formisano, Ronald P. *The Transformation of Political Culture: Massachusetts Parties, 1790–1840s*. New York, NY: Oxford University Press, 1983.

Frederickson, George M. *The Black Image in the White Mind: The Debate on Afro-American Character and Destiny, 1817–1914*. New York, NY: Harper and Row, 1971.

Freehling, William W. *Prelude to Civil War: The Nullification Controversy in South Carolina, 1816–1836*. New York, NY: Oxford University Press, 1965.

———. *The Reintegration of American History: Slavery and the Civil War*. New York, NY: Oxford University Press, 1994.

———. *The Road to Disunion: Secessionists at Bay, 1776–1854*. Two volumes. New York, NY: Oxford University Press, 1990.

———. *The South vs. The South: How Anti-Confederate Southerners Shaped the Course of the Civil War*. New York, NY: Oxford University Press, 2001.

Freeman, Joanne B. *The Field of Blood: Violence in Congress and the Road to Civil War*. New York, NY: Farrar, Straus and Giroux, 2018.

Friend, Craig Thompson, and Lorri Glover, eds. *Southern Manhood: Perspectives on Masculinity in the Old South*. Athens, GA: University of Georgia Press, 2004.

Gallagher, Gary W. *The Confederate War: How Popular Will, Nationalism, and Military Strategy Could Not Stave Off Defeat*. Cambridge, MA: Harvard University Press, 1997.

———. *The Union War*. Cambridge, MA: Harvard University Press, 2011.

Gambrell, Herbert P. "Three Letters on the Revolution of 1830." *The Journal of Modern History* 1, no. 4 (December 1929): 594–606.

Gao, Gautham. *National Duties; Custom Houses and the Making of the American State*. Chicago, IL: University of Chicago Press, 2016.

Gatell, Frank Otto. "Postmaster Huger and the Incendiary Publications." *The South Carolina Historical Magazine* 64, no. 4 (October 1963): 193–201.

Ginsberg, Benjamin. *Moses of South Carolina: A Jewish Scalawag During Radical Reconstruction*. Baltimore, MD: Johns Hopkins University Press, 2010.

Goldstone, Jack A., ed. *The Encyclopedia of Political Revolutions*. New York, NY: Routledge, 2014.

Gosse, Van. *The First Reconstruction: Black Politics in America from the Revolution to the Civil War*. Chapel Hill, NC: University of North Carolina Press, 2021.

Graham, Cole Blease, Jr. *The South Carolina State Constitution*. New York, NY: Oxford University Press, 2011.

Grayson, William J. *Witness to Sorrow: The Antebellum Biography of William J. Grayson*. Edited by Richard J. Calhoun. Columbia, SC: University of South Carolina Press, 1990.

Green, Jennifer R. *Military Education and the Emerging Middle Class in the Old South*. New York, NY: Cambridge University Press, 2008.

Greenberg, Amy S. *Manifest Manhood and the Antebellum American Empire*. New York, NY: Cambridge University Press, 2005.

Greenberg, Irwin F. "Justice William Johnson: South Carolina Unionist, 1823–1830." *Pennsylvania History: A Journal of Mid-Atlantic Studies* 36, no. 3 (July 1969): 307–34.

Greenberg, Kenneth S. *Honor & Slavery: Lies, Duels, Noses, Masks, Dressing as a Woman, Gifts, Strangers, Humanitarianism, Death, Slave Rebellions, The Proslavery Argument, Baseball, Hunting, Gambling in the Old South*. Princeton, NJ: Princeton University Press, 1996.

Grimsted, David. *American Mobbing, 1828–1861: Toward Civil War*. New York, NY: Oxford University Press, 1998.

Grinspan, Jon. *The Virgin Vote: How Young Americans Made Democracy Social, Politics Personal, and Voting Popular in the Nineteenth Century*. Chapel Hill, NC: University of North Carolina Press, 2016.

Hacker, J. David. "A Census-Based Count of the Civil War Dead." *Civil War History* 57, no. 4 (December 2011): 307–48.

Hahn, Steven. *A Nation Without Borders: The United States and Its World in an Age of Civil Wars, 1830–1910*. New York, NY: Penguin Books, 2016.

Hart, Emma. *Building Charleston: Town and Society in the Eighteenth-Century British Atlantic World*. Columbia, SC: University of South Carolina Press, 2010.

Hofstadter, Richard. *The Idea of a Party System: The Rise of Legitimate Opposition in the United States, 1780–1840*. Berkeley, CA: University of California Press, 1969.

Holden, Charles J. *In the Great Maelstrom: Conservatives in Post-Civil War South Carolina*. Columbia, SC: University of South Carolina, 2002.

Holt, Michael F. *Political Parties and American Political Development from the Age of Jackson to the Age of Lincoln*. Baton Rouge, LA: Louisiana State University Press, 1992.

———. *The Rise and Fall of the American Whig Party: Jacksonian Politics and the Onset of the Civil War*. New York, NY: Oxford University Press, 1999.

Houston, David Franklin. *A Critical Study of Nullification in South Carolina*. New York, NY: Longmans, Green, and Co., 1896.

Howe, Daniel Walker. *The Political Culture of the American Whigs*. Chicago, IL: University of Chicago Press, 1979.

———. *What Hath God Wrought: The Transformation of America, 1815–1848*. New York, NY: Oxford University Press, 2007.

Howe, George. *History of the Presbyterian Church in South Carolina.* Vol. II. Columbia, SC: W. J. Duffie, 1883.

Huebner, Timothy S. *The Southern Judicial Tradition: State Judges and Sectional Distinctiveness, 1790–1890.* Athens, GA: University of Georgia Press, 1999.

Huff, Archie Vernon V., Jr. "The Eagle and the Vulture: Changing Attitudes Toward Nationalism in Fourth of July Orations Delivered in Charleston, 1778–1860." *South Atlantic Quarterly* 73 (1974): 10–22.

———. *Greenville: The History of the City and County in the South Carolina Piedmont.* Columbia, SC: University of South Carolina Press, 1995.

Hunt, Alfred N. *Haiti's Influence on Antebellum America: Slumbering Volcano in the Caribbean.* Baton Rouge, LA: Louisiana State University Press, 1988.

Huston, James L. "Virtue Besieged: Virtue, Equality and the General Welfare in the Tariff Debates of the 1820s." *Journal of the Early Republic* 14, no. 4 (Winter 1994): 523–47.

Irons, Charles F. *The Origins of Proslavery Christianity: White and Black Evangelicals in Colonial and Antebellum Virginia.* Chapel Hill, NC: University of North Carolina Press, 2008.

January, Alan F. "The South Carolina Association: An Agency for Race Control in Antebellum Charleston." *The South Carolina Historical Magazine* 78, no. 3 (July 1977): 191–201.

Jay, Elisabeth. *British Writers and Paris: 1830–1875.* New York, NY: Oxford University Press, 2016.

Jervey, Theodore Dehon. *Robert Y. Hayne and His Times.* New York, NY: Macmillan Company, 1909.

Johnson, Michael P. "Denmark Vesey and His Co-Conspirators." *William & Mary Quarterly* 58 (October 2001): 915–76.

———. *Toward a Patriarchal Republic: The Secession of Georgia.* Baton Rouge, LA: Louisiana State University Press, 1977.

Johnson, Ronald Angelo. *Diplomacy in Black and White: John Adams, Toussaint Louverture, and Their Atlantic World Alliance.* Athens, GA: University of Georgia Press, 2014.

Jones, Lewis Pinckney. "William Elliott, South Carolina Non-Conformist." *Journal of Southern History* 17, no. 3 (August 1951): 361–81.

Karp, Matthew. *This Vast Southern Empire: Slaveholders at the Helm of American Foreign Policy.* Cambridge, MA: Harvard University Press, 2016.

Kellison, Kimberly R. "Men, Women, and the Marriage of the Union: Fourth of July Celebrations in Antebellum Georgia." *The Georgia Historical Quarterly* 8, no. 3 (Fall 2014): 129–54.

Kelly, Joseph. *America's Longest Siege: Charleston, Slavery, and the Slow March Toward Civil War.* New York, NY: Overlook Press, 2013.

Kibler, James Everett, Jr. *The Poetry of William Gilmore Simms: An Introduction and Bibliography.* Spartanburg, SC: The Reprint Company, 1979.

Kibler, Lillian Adele. *Benjamin F. Perry: South Carolina Unionist.* Durham, NC: Duke University Press, 1946.

——. "Unionist Sentiment in South Carolina in 1860." *The Journal of Southern History* 4, no. 3 (August 1938): 346–66.

King, Alvy L. *Louis T. Wigfall: Southern Fire-eater.* Baton Rouge, LA: Louisiana State University Press, 1970.

Klein, Rachel N. *Unification of a Slave State: The Rise of the Planter Class in the South Carolina Backcountry, 1760–1808.* Chapel Hill, NC: University of North Carolina Press, 1990.

Lang, Andrew F. *A Contest of Civilizations: Exposing the Crisis of American Exceptionalism in the Civil War Era.* Chapel Hill, NC: University of North Carolina Press, 2021.

Latner, Richard B. "The Nullification Crisis and Republican Subversion." *The Journal of Southern History* 43, no 1 (February 1977): 19–38.

Lerner, Gerda. *The Grimké Sisters from South Carolina: Pioneers for Women's Rights and Abolition.* New York, NY: Oxford University Press, 1998.

Lesesne, J. Mauldin. "The Nullification Controversy in an Up-Country District." *The Proceedings of the South Carolina Historical Association.* Edited by Robert L. Meriwether and Arney R. Childs. Columbia, SC: South Carolina Historical Association, 1939.

Lewis, Catherine H. *Horry County, South Carolina, 1730–1993.* Columbia, SC: University of South Carolina Press, 1998.

Lewis, Charles. *David Glasgow Farragut: Admiral in the Making.* Annapolis, MD: Naval Institute Press, 1941.

Link, William A. *Roots of Secession: Slavery and Politics in Antebellum Virginia.* Chapel Hill, NC: University of North Carolina Press, 2003.

Lockley, Tim, and David Doddington. "Maroon and Slave Communities in South Carolina Before 1865." *The South Carolina Historical Magazine* 113, no. 2 (April 2012): 125–45.

Loveland, Anne C. *Emblem of Liberty: The Image of Lafayette in the American Mind.* Baton Rouge, LA: Louisiana State University Press, 1971.

Lyons, Martyn. *Post-Revolutionary Europe, 1815–1856.* New York, NY: Palgrave Macmillan, 2006.

McCandless, Peter. "The Political Evolution of John Bachman: From New York

Yankee to South Carolina Secessionist." *The South Carolina Historical Magazine* 108, no. 1 (January 2007): 6–31.

McClintock, Russell. *Lincoln and the Decision for War: The Northern Response to Secession.* Chapel Hill, NC: University of North Carolina Press, 2008.

McCormick, Richard P. *The Second American Party System: Party Formation in the Jacksonian Era.* New York, NY: W. W. Norton & Company, 1966.

McCurry, Stephanie. *Confederate Reckoning: Power and Politics in the Civil War South.* Cambridge, MA: Harvard University Press, 2010.

——. *Masters of Small Worlds: Yeoman Households, Gender Relations, & the Political Culture of the Antebellum South Carolina Low Country.* New York, NY: Oxford University Press, 1995.

McDonnell, Lawrence T. *Performing Disunion: The Coming of the Civil War in Charleston, South Carolina.* New York, NY: Cambridge University Press, 2018

McInnis, Maurie D. *The Politics of Taste in Antebellum Charleston.* Chapel Hill, NC: University of North Carolina Press, 2005.

McNeely, Patricia. "Dueling Editors: The Nullification Plot of 1832." In *Words at War: The Civil War and American Journalism,* edited by David B. Sachsman, S. Kittrell, and Roy Morris Jr., 25–36. West Lafayette, IN: Purdue University Press, 2008.

Maier, Pauline. "The Road Not Taken: Nullification, John C. Calhoun, and the Revolutionary Tradition in South Carolina." *The South Carolina Historical Magazine* 82, no 1 (January 1981). 1–19.

Mansel, Philip. *Paris Between Empires: Monarchy and Revolution, 1814–1852.* New York, NY: St. Martin's Press, 2003.

Marszalek, John F. *The Petticoat Affair: Manners, Mutiny, and Sex in Andrew Jackson's White House.* New York, NY: The Free Press, 1997.

Mason, Matthew. *Apostle of Union: A Political Biography of Edward Everett.* Chapel Hill, NC: University of North Carolina Press, 2016.

Masur, Louis P. *1831: Year of Eclipse.* New York, NY: Hill and Wang, 2001.

Meacham, Jon. *American Lion: Andrew Jackson in the White House.* New York, NY: Random House, 2008.

Merchant, Holt. *South Carolina Fire-Eater: The Life of Laurence Massillon Keitt, 1824–1864.* Columbia, SC: University of South Carolina Press, 2014.

Mercieca, Jennifer Rose. "The Culture of Honor: How Slaveholders Responded to the Abolitionist Mail Crisis of 1835." *Rhetoric & Public Affairs* 10, no. 1 (Spring 2007): 51–76.

Moore, Joseph S. *Founding Sins: How a Group of Antislavery Radicals Fought to Put Christ into the Constitution.* New York, NY: Oxford University Press, 2016.

Morris, J. Brent. "We Are Verily Guilty Concerning Our Brother": The Abolitionist Transformation of Planter William Henry Brisbane." *The South Carolina
Historical Magazine* 111, no. 3/4 (July–October 2010): 118–50.

Moss, David A. *Democracy: A Case Study*. Cambridge, MA: Belknap Press of Harvard University Press.

Nicoletti, Cynthia. "Roundtable IV Comment." Paper presented at the Power, Violence, and Inequality Collective Fellows Mini-Conference, April 2019.

O'Brien, Michael. *A Character of Hugh Legaré*. Knoxville, TN: University of Tennessee Press, 1985.

———. *Conjectures of Order: Intellectual Life and the American South, 1810–1860*.
Volume 1. Chapel Hill, NC: University of North Carolina Press, 2004.

———. *Conjectures of Order: Intellectual Life and the American South, 1810–1860*.
Volume 2. Chapel Hill, NC: University of North Carolina Press, 2004.

Ochenkowski, J. P. "The Origins of Nullification in South Carolina." *The South
Carolina Historical Society* 83, no. 2 (April 1982): 121–53.

Oertel, Kristen Tegtmeier. *Bleeding Borders: Race, Gender, and Violence in
Pre-Civil War Kansas*. Baton Rouge, LA: Louisiana State University Press,
2009.

Olwell, Robert. *Masters, Slaves, and Subjects: The Culture of Power in the South
Carolina Lowcountry, 1740–1790*. Ithaca, NY: Cornell University Press, 1998.

Osterweis, Rollin G. *Romanticism and Nationalism in the Old South*. Baton Rouge,
LA: Louisiana State University Press, 1967.

Paulus, Carl Lawrence. *The Slaveholding Crisis: Fear of Insurrection and the Coming of the Civil War*. Baton Rouge, LA: Louisiana State University Press, 2017.

Park, Benjamin E. *American Nationalisms: Imagining Union in the Age of Revolutions, 1783–1833*. New York, NY: Cambridge University Press, 2018.

———. "The Angel of Nullification: Imagining Disunion in an Era Before Secession."
Journal of the Earl Republic 37, no. 3 (Fall 2017): 507–36.

Peart, Daniel. *Era of Experimentation: American Political Practices in the Early
Republic*. Charlottesville, VA: University of Virginia Press, 2014.

Pease, William H., and Jane H. Pease. "The Economics and Politics of Charleston's
Nullification Crisis. *The Journal of Southern History* 47, no. 3 (August 1981):
335–62.

———. *A Family of Women: The Carolina Petigrus in Peace and War*. Chapel Hill,
NC: University of North Carolina Press, 1999.

———. *James Louis Petigru: Southern Conservative, Southern Dissenter*. Athens,
GA: University of Georgia Press, 1995.

———. *The Web of Progress: Private Values and Public Styles in Boston and Charleston, 1828–1843*. Athens, GA: University of Georgia Press, 1991.

Perry, Mark. *Lift Up Thy Voice: The Grimké Family's Journal from Slaveholders to Civil Rights Leaders.* New York, NY: Penguin Books, 2001.

Pessen, Edward. *Jacksonian America: Society, Personality, and Politics.* Homewood, IL: Dorsey Press, 1969.

Peterson, Merrill D. *The Great Triumvirate: Webster, Clay, and Calhoun.* New York, NY: Oxford University Press, 1987.

———. *Olive Branch and Sword: The Compromise of 1833.* Baton Rouge, LA: Louisiana State University Press, 1982.

Phillips, Jason. *Looming Civil War: How Nineteenth-Century Americans Imagined the Future.* New York, NY: Oxford University Press, 2018.

Pohjankoski, Pekka. "Federal Coercion and National Constitutional Identity in the United States." *American Journal of Legal History* 56, no. 3 (September 2016): 326–58.

Polasky, Janet. *Revolutions without Borders: The Call to Liberty in the Atlantic World.* New Haven, CT: Yale University Press, 2015.

Poole, W. Scott. *Never Surrender: Confederate Memory and Conservatism in the South Carolina Upcountry.* Athens, GA: University of Georgia Press, 2004.

Pope, Thomas H. *The History of Newberry, County, South Carolina.* Volume 1. Columbia, SC: University of South Carolina, 1973.

Potter, David M. "The Civil War in the History of the Modern World: A Comparative View." In *The South and the Sectional Conflict,* 287–99. Baton Rouge, LA: Louisiana State University Press, 1968.

———. "The Historian's Use of Nationalism and Vice Versa." *The American Historical Review* 67, no. 4 (July 1962): 924–50.

Pribanic-Smith, Erika J. "Conflict in South Carolina's Partisan Press of 1829." *American Journalism* 30 (no. 3): 365–92.

———. "Rhetoric of Fear." *Journalism History* 38, no. 3 (Fall 2012): 166–77.

———. "South Carolina's Rhetorical Civil War: Nullification and Local Partisanship in the Press, 1831–1833." *Media History Monographs* 17, no. 2 (2014): 1–32.

Price, Munro. *The Perilous Crown: France Between Revolutions, 1814–1848.* London, England: Pan Books, 2007.

Quigley, Paul. *Shifting Grounds: Nationalism & the American South, 1848–1865.* New York, NY: Oxford University Press, 2012.

Quintana, Ryan A. *Making a Slave State: Political Development in Early South Carolina.* Chapel Hill, NC: University of North Carolina Press, 2018.

———. "Planners, Planters, and Slaves: Producing the State in Early National South Carolina." *The Journal of Southern History* 81, no. 1 (February 2015): 79–116.

Rable, George C. *God's Almost Chosen Peoples: A Religious History of the American Civil War.* Chapel Hill, NC: University of North Carolina Press, 2010.

Ratcliffe, Donald J. "The Nullification Crisis, Southern Discontents, and the American Political Process." *American Nineteenth Century History* 1, no. 2 (Summer 2000): 1–30.

Remini, Robert V. *Andrew Jackson and the Course of American Democracy, 1833–1845*. New York, NY: Harper & Row, 1984.

———. *Andrew Jackson and the Course of American Empire, 1767–1821*. Baltimore, MD: Johns Hopkins University Press, 1977.

———. *At the Edge of the Precipice: Henry Clay and the Compromise that Saved the Union*. New York, NY: Basic Books, 2010.

———. *The Life of Andrew Jackson*. New York, NY: Harper & Row, 1998.

Reynolds, David S. *Waking Giant: America in the Age of Jackson*. New York, NY: Harper Perennial, 2008.

Reznikoff, Charles. *The Jews of Charleston: A History of an American Jewish Community*. Philadelphia, PA: Jewish Publication Society of America, 1950.

Richards, Leonard L. *The Slave Power: The Free North and Southern Domination, 1780–1860*. Baton Rouge, LA: Louisiana State University Press, 2000.

Roberts, Timothy Mason. *Distant Revolutions: 1848 and the Challenge to American Exceptionalism*. Charlottesville, VA: University of Virginia Press, 2009.

Robinson, Michael D. *A Union Indivisible: Secession and the Politics of Slavery in the Border South*. Chapel Hill, NC: University of North Carolina Press, 2017.

Rogers, George C., Jr. *The History of Georgetown County, South Carolina*. Columbia, SC: University of South Carolina Press, 1970.

———. "South Carolina Federalists and the Origins of the Nullification Movement." *South Carolina Historical Magazine* 101, no. 1 (January 2000): 53–67.

Rowland, Lawrence S, Alexander Moore, and George C. Rogers Jr. *The History of Beaufort County, South Carolina*. Volume 1. Columbia, SC: University of South Carolina Press, 1996.

Rubio, Philip F. "'Though He Had a White Face, He was a Negro in Heart': Examining the White Men Convicted of Supporting the Denmark Vesey Slave Insurrection Conspiracy." *The South Carolina Historical Magazine* 113, no. 1 (January 2012): 50–67.

Rugemer, Edward Bartlett. *The Problem of Emancipation: The Caribbean Roots of the American Civil War*. Baton Rouge, LA: Louisiana State University Press, 2008.

Scarborough, William K. "Propagandists for Secession: Edmund Ruffin of Virginia and Robert Barnwell Rhett of South Carolina." *South Carolina Historical Magazine* 112, nos. 3–4 (July–October 2011): 126–38.

Schlesinger, Arthur M., Jr. *The Age of Jackson*. Boston, MA: Little, Brown and Company, 1945.

Schoeppner, Michael A. *Moral Contagion: Black Atlantic Sailors, Citizenship, and Diplomacy in Antebellum America.* New York, NY: Cambridge University Press, 2019.

Schultz, Harold S. *Nationalism and Sectionalism in South Carolina, 1852–1860: A Study of the Movement for Southern Independence.* Durham, NC: Duke University Press, 1950.

Selinger, Jeffrey S. *Embracing Dissent: Political Violence and Party Development in the United States.* Philadelphia, PA: University of Pennsylvania Press, 2016.

Sheehan-Dean, Aaron. *Why Confederates Fought: Family & Nation in Civil War Virginia.* Chapel Hill, NC: University of North Carolina Press, 2007.

Sibley, Marilyn McAdams. "James Hamilton, Jr., vs. Sam Houston: Repercussions of the Nullification Controversy." *The Southwestern Historical Quarterly* 89, no. 2 (October 1985): 165–80.

Silbey, Joel H. *The American Political Nation, 1838–1893.* Stanford, CA: Stanford University Press, 1991.

——. *The Partisan Imperative: The Dynamics of American Politics Before the Civil War.* New York, NY: Oxford University Press, 1985.

Sinha, Manisha. *The Counterrevolution of Slavery: Politics and Ideology in Antebellum South Carolina.* Chapel Hill, NC: University of North Carolina Press, 2000.

——. *The Slave's Cause: A History of Abolition.* New Haven, CT: Yale University Press, 2016.

Smith, Adam I. P. *No Party Now: Politics in the Civil War North.* New York, NY: Oxford University Press, 2006.

——. *The Stormy Present: Conservatism and the Problem of Slavery in Northern Politics, 1846–1865.* Chapel Hill, NC: University of North Carolina Press, 2017.

Snay, Mitchell. *Gospel of Disunion: Religion and Separatism in the Antebellum South.* New York, NY: Cambridge University Press, 1993.

Stampp, Kenneth M. *The Peculiar Institution: Slavery in the Antebellum South.* New York, NY: Vintage Books, 1956.

Stewart, James Brewer. "'A Great Talking and Eating Machine': Patriarchy, Mobilization and the Dynamics of Nullification in South Carolina." *Civil War History* 27, no. 3 (September 1991): 197–220.

Sugrue, Michael. "South Carolina College and the Origins of Secession." *Slavery & Abolition* 39, no. 2 (June 2018): 280–89.

Summers, Mark Wahlgren. *A Dangerous Stir: Fear, Paranoia, and the Making of Reconstruction.* Chapel Hill, NC: University of North Carolina Press, 2009.

Symonds, Craig L. *Joseph E. Johnston: A Civil War Biography.* New York, NY: W. W. Norton, 1992.

Taylor, Alan. *The Internal Enemy: Slavery and War in Virginia, 1772–1832.* New York, NY: W. W. Norton & Company, 2013.

Taylor, George Braxton. *Virginia Baptist Ministers: Fifth Series.* Lynchburg, VA: J. P. Bell Company, 1915.

Thompson, Michael D. *Working on the Dock of the Bay: Labor and Enterprise in an Antebellum Southern Port.* Columbia, SC: University of South Carolina Press, 2015.

Thornton, J. Mills, III. *Politics and Power in a Slave Society: Alabama, 1800–1860.* Baton Rouge, LA: Louisiana State University Press, 1978.

Tinkler, Robert. *James Hamilton of South Carolina.* Baton Rouge, LA: Louisiana State University Press, 2004.

Tise, Larry E. *Proslavery: A History of the Defense of Slavery in America, 1701–1840.* Athens, GA: University of Georgia Press, 1987.

Towles, Louis P., ed. *A World Turned Upside Down: The Palmers of South Santee, 1818–1881.* Columbia, SC: University of South Carolina Press, 1996.

Travers, Len. *Celebrating the Fourth: Independence Day and the Rites of Nationalism in the Early Republic.* Amherst, MA: University of Massachusetts Press, 1997.

Tucker, Ann L. *Newest Born of Nations: European Nationalist Movements and the Making of the Confederacy.* Charlottesville, VA: University of Virginia Press, 2020.

Tyler, Lyon G. "James Louis Petigru: Freedom's Champion in a Slave Society." *The South Carolina Historical Magazine* 83, no. 4 (October 1982): 272–86.

Vajda, Zoltan. "Complicated Sympathies: John C. Calhoun's Sentimental Union and the South." *The South Carolina Historical Magazine* 114, no. 3 (July 2013): 210–30.

Van Atta, John R. *Securing the West: Politics, Public Lands, and the Fate of the Old Republic, 1785–1850.* Baltimore, MD: Johns Hopkins University Press, 2014.

Varon, Elizabeth. *Armies of Deliverance: A New History of the Civil War.* New York, NY: Oxford University Press, 2019.

———. *Disunion! The Coming of the American Civil War, 1789–1859.* Chapel Hill, NC: University of North Carolina Press, 2008.

———. "Disunion! The Coming of the American Civil War, 1789–1859." Paper presented at the Library of Virginia, December 2008.

———. *We Mean To Be Counted: White Women and Politics in Antebellum Virginia.* Chapel Hill, NC: University of North Carolina Press, 1998.

Voss-Hubbard, Mark. *Beyond Party: Cultures of Antipartisanship in Northern Politics before the Civil War.* Baltimore, MD: Johns Hopkins University Press, 2002.

Waldstreicher, David. *In the Midst of Perpetual Fetes: The Making of American Nationalism, 1776–1820.* Chapel Hill, NC: University of North Carolina Press, 1997.

Walther, Eric H. *The Fire-Eaters.* Baton Rouge, LA: Louisiana State University Press, 1992.

———. *William Lowndes Yancey and the Coming of the Civil War.* Chapel Hill, NC: University of North Carolina Press, 2006.

Watkins, William J., Jr. *Reclaiming the American Revolution: The Kentucky and Virginia Resolutions and Their Legacy.* New York, NY: Palgrave Macmillan, 2008.

Watson, Harry L. *Jacksonian Politics and Community Conflict: The Emergence of the Second Party System in Cumberland County, North Carolina.* Baton Rouge, LA: Louisiana State University Press, 1981.

———. *Liberty and Power: The Politics of Jacksonian America.* New York, NY: Hill and Wang, 1990.

Watson, Margaret. *Greenwood County Sketches: Old Roads and Early Families.* Greenwood, SC: Attic Press, Inc., 1970.

Wehmann, Howard H. "Noise, Novelties, and Nullifiers: A US Navy Officer's Impressions of the Nullification Controversy." *South Carolina Historical Magazine* 76, no. 1 (January 1975): 21–24.

Weir, Robert M. "'The Harmony We Were Famous For': An Interpretation of Pre-Revolutionary South Carolina Politics." *The William and Mary Quarterly* 26, no. 4 (October 1969): 473–501.

West, Stephen A. "Minute Men, Yeomen, and the Mobilization for Secession in the South Carolina Upcountry." *The Journal of Southern History* 71, no. 1 (February 2005): 75–104.

Wilentz, Sean. *No Property in Man: Slavery and Antislavery at the Nation's Founding.* Cambridge, MA: Harvard University Press, 2018.

———. *The Rise of American Democracy: Jefferson to Lincoln.* New York, NY: W. W. Norton & Company, 2005.

Williams, Timothy J. *Intellectual Manhood: University, Self, and Society in the Antebellum South.* Chapel Hill, NC: University of North Carolina Press, 2015.

Wilson, Major L. "'Liberty and Union': An Analysis of Three Concepts Involved in the Nullification Controversy." *The Journal of Southern History* 33, no. 3 (August 1967): 331–55.

Winik, Jay. *The Great Upheaval: America and the Birth of the Modern World, 1788–1800.* New York, NY: Harper Perennial, 2007.

Wood, Gordon S. *Empire of Liberty: A History of the Early Republic.* New York, NY: Oxford University Press, 2009.

Woodburn, James Albert. "The Scotch-Irish Presbyterians in Monroe County, Indiana." *Indiana Historical Society Publications.* Indianapolis, IN: Bobbs-Merrill Company, 1895.

Woods, James M. *Rebellion and Realignment: Arkansas's Road to Secession.* Fayetteville, AR: University of Arkansas Press, 1987.

Woods, Michael E. *Emotional and Sectional Conflict in the Antebellum United States.* New York, NY: Cambridge University Press, 2014.

Wright, Carroll D. *The History of the Growth of the United States Census, Prepared for the Senate Committee on the Census.* Washington, DC: Government Printing Office, 1900.

Wyatt-Brown, Bertram. "The Abolitionists' Postal Campaign of 1835." *The Journal of Negro History* 50, no. 4 (October 1965): 227–38.

——. *Honor and Violence in the Old South.* New York, NY: Oxford University Press, 1986.

——. *Lewis Tappan and the Evangelical War Against Slavery.* Cleveland, OH: Press of Case Western Reserve University, 1969.

Wyly-Jones, Susan. "The 1835 Anti-Abolition Meetings in the South: A New Look at the Controversy Over the Abolition Postal Campaign." *Civil War History* 47, no. 4 (December 2001): 289–309.

Young, Jeffrey Robert. *Domesticating Slavery: The Master Class in Georgia and South Carolina, 1670–1837.* Chapel Hill, NC: University of North Carolina Press, 1999.

THESES AND DISSERTATIONS

Butler, Clayton. "True Blue: White Unionists in the Deep South during the Civil War and Reconstruction, 1860–1880." PhD diss., University of Virginia, 2020.

Cain, Joshua Matthew. "Jacksonian Nationalist: Joel R. Poinsett's Role in the Nullification Crisis." MA thesis, Georgia Southern University, 2008.

Christopherson, Merrill G. "A Rhetorical Study of Hugh Swinton Legaré: South Carolina Unionist." PhD diss., University of Florida, 1954.

Dangerfield, David W. "Hard Rows to Hoe: Free Black Farmers in Antebellum South Carolina." PhD diss., University of South Carolina, 2014.

Furniss, Jack. "States of the Union: The Rise and Fall of the Political Center in the Civil War North." PhD diss., University of Virginia, 2018.

Gillikin, Margaret Wilson. "Saint Dominguan Refugees in Charleston, South Carolina, 1791–1822: Assimilation and Accommodation in a Slave Society." PhD diss., University of South Carolina, 2014.

Haumesser, Lauren N. "Party of Patriarchy: Democratic Gender Politics and the Coming of the Civil War." PhD diss., University of Virginia, 2018.

January, Alan F. "The First Nullification: The Negro Seamen Acts Controversy in South Carolina, 1822–1860." PhD diss., University of Iowa, 1976.

Killikelly, Timothy. "At the Crossroads: The Nullification Movement and the Crisis of Modernization." PhD diss., City University of New York, 1996.

Lurie, Shira. "Politics at the Poles: Liberty Poles and the Popular Struggle for the New Republic." PhD diss., University of Virginia, 2019.

Pack, Andrew Christopher. "Battle of the Press: The Nullification Crisis in South Carolina, 1828–1833." MA thesis, University of North Carolina at Charlotte, 2015.

Pribanic-Smith, Erika Jean. "Sowing the Seeds of Disunion: South Carolina's Partisan Newspapers and the Nullification Crisis, 1828–1833." PhD diss., University of Alabama, 2010.

Price, Thomas S. "Palmettos and Property: Historical Memory and Political Culture in Early National South Carolina." PhD diss., University of Chicago, 1994.

Ragonese, Sarah Rayser. "A Drayton Leads th'Embattled Line: Colonel William Drayton and the South Carolina Nullification Controversy." MA thesis, Temple University, 2000.

Schroeder, David. "Nullification in South Carolina: A Revisitation." PhD diss., University of Alabama, 1999.

Index

Abbeville District, 71, 78, 80, 102, 106, 123, 125, 163n31, 168n39; and Great Anti-Tariff Meeting, 9, 21; and slave panics, 51–52

abolition, 4, 17–18, 29, 33, 52, 84, 90, 114–128, 135, 138, 171n22, 172n30

Adams, Jasper, 88

Adams, John Quincy, 15, 18–19

African Americans, 5, 19, 74, 116, 121; and colonization, 15, 29; and Denmark Vesey conspiracy, 12–13, 146n8; executions of, 13, 52; restrictive laws, 13–14; slave panics, 12–13, 28–29, 51–52; white fears of, 4, 19–20, 35, 51–52, 67, 70, 84, 107, 115, 117, 122, 129, 135, 138–139

Alabama, 12, 75, 87, 146n7

allegiance, 32, 78; dual allegiance, 15, 64–65, 94, 100, 101, 105, 110, 111, 113; exclusive allegiance, 91, 93, 94, 99, 100, 105, 110

Allston, Benjamin, 125

American Anti-Slavery Society, 115, 116, 119–120, 121, 123, 125, 126, 135, 140, 171n30

American Colonization Society, 15–16, 29–30, 37, 151n30

American Revolution, 5, 7, 19, 26–27, 33, 34, 38, 43, 54, 56, 58, 74, 77, 107

Andrew, John, 137

Arkansas, 77

Barnwell District, 48, 71, 73, 85, 128

Bay, Elihu H., 104

Beardsley, Samuel, 125

Belcher, Susan, 97

Belgium, 8, 39, 60–61, 86, 131

Bennett, Thomas, 133

Berry, Micajah, 42

Blair, Francis P., 138

Blair, James, 40, 54–55, 95, 98, 106, 156n27

Blair, Montgomery, 138

Blanding, William, 91

Breathitt, George, 142

Brown, Julia, 58, 116, 117

Bryan, George, 141

Buchanan, James, 86, 137–138

Burt, Armistead, 55, 110

Butler, Pierce, 65, 118, 128

Bynum, Turner, 45, 58

Calhoun, John C., 11, 55, 111, 116, 135; as senator, 69, 89–90; as vice president, 15–16, 23, 30–32, 47

Calhounites, 11, 14, 19, 21, 24, 152n42

Camden Journal, 130

Cardozo, Jacob, 49, 131

Charleston, 5, 19, 20, 22, 26–28, 33, 35, 36–38, 57–58, 64, 69, 94, 95, 131–133; and American Anti-Slavery Society, 119–122; during Denmark Vesey conspiracy, 12–13; during election of 1830, 36–38, 41; during election of 1831, 52–53, 54; during election of 1832, 59–60, 63; during election of 1833, 97–98; during election of 1835, 114; during election of 1836, 131–133; and Elkison case, 14–15; and European revolutions, 39–40; during nullification winter, 1–3, 67, 69, 70, 73, 76–77, 79, 84–86, 88, 91, 92; and Nullifiers, 44, 47–49, 56, 73, 88, 91, 95; political violence in, 40–41, 46, 59–60, 107–108, 122; and Union Party, 5, 33, 35, 54, 57–58, 79, 91; during secession crisis, 136, 138, 139, 141, 142; during test oath controversy, 104, 105, 107–108

Index

CPSIA information can be obtained
at www.ICGtesting.com
Printed in the USA
LVHW101602010223
738413LV00003B/60